GERMAN CAMPAIGNS OF
WORLD WAR II

GERMAN CAMPAIGNS OF
WORLD WAR II

Edited by
Chris Bishop and Adam Warner

Grange
BOOKS

This edition first published in 2001 for Grange Books
An imprint of Grange Books plc
The Grange
Kingsnorth Industrial Estate
Hoo, nr Rochester
Kent ME3 9ND
www.grangebooks.co.uk

ISBN: 1-84013-420-8

Jacket design by
Amber Books Ltd
Bradley's Close
74–77 White Lion Street
London N1 9PF

This material was previously published as part of the reference set *Hitler's Third Reich*.

Contributors: Chris Bishop, Kurt Steiner, Adam Warner, William Wilson
Illustrators: Peter Harper, Chris Bishop
Picture credits: Aerospace, AKG, Bundesarchiv, John Weal, Popperfoto, Robert Hunt
Library, Topham, US Holocaust Memorial Museum

Printed in Italy

CONTENTS

In September 1939, Germany unleashed an entirely new kind of attack against Poland. Striking with unprecedented speed and precision, Hitler's armies launched the world's first Blitzkrieg, or Lightning War.

BLITZKRIEG

HITLER'S invasion of Poland in September 1939 marked the start of World War II in Europe. Many had foreseen the coming conflict, but when it came few could have predicted the astonishing successes of the Wehrmacht.

APRIL–AUGUST 1939
PLANNING AN INVASION

At the beginning of April, fresh from his almost unopposed annexation of Austria and Czechoslovakia, Hitler orders the German General Staff to commence planning the invasion of Poland. The attack is to be launched on 1st September or soon thereafter. The operation is to be known as *Fall Weiss* ('Case White')

The Army General Staff delivers its plan of action on 7 May. Poland is an ideal theatre for the new kind of 'lightning war' being developed by the Wehrmacht. In addition to being fairly flat (and at the time of the proposed invasion dry and hard-surfaced), her frontiers are much too long to be well defended. She is, moreover, flanked on three sides – East Prussia to the north, Germany to the west and the newly occupied Czechoslovakia to the south. Poland, in fact, protrudes like a tongue into hostile territory, with the most economically valuable areas of the country closest to the main threat.

The fatal weakness in Poland's defences lies in her lack of armour and mobile forces; the bulk of the army consists of 30 divisions of infantry supported by 11 brigades of horsed cavalry and two motorised brigades. The weakness is compounded by the fact that 17 of the best divisions are forward deployed to protect the valuable mining and industrial areas, rather than behind the much more strongly defensible lines of the Vistula and the San rivers.

Above: German troops were more than ready for the invasion of Poland. Well-trained and well-equipped, they were much more effectively led than their opponents, and time and again would outmanoeuvre and outfight the brave but tactically inferior Poles.

Providing the spearhead of the German invasion force will be six panzer divisions and eight motorised infantry divisions. These will be supported by 27 foot-slogging infantry divisions with largely horse-drawn logistics. The main role of the infantry will be to engage the attentions of the bulk of the Polish army while the German mobile forces race around the flanks, cutting through supply

POLAND

lines and striking at command and control centres to the rear.

All through the summer German troops train for action, and in August are moved to their start points. On 31 August, Hitler gives the go-ahead order which will launch *Fall Weiss*.

1 SEPTEMBER
SURPRISE ATTACK

At 4.45 on the morning of 1 September 1939, without the formality of a declaration of war, Germany's Luftwaffe crosses the Polish frontier. Nearly 1,400 bombers, dive-bombers and fighters begin the systematic destruction of Polish airfields and aircraft, of road and rail centres, of concentrations of troop reserves, and of anything which intelligence or observation has indicated as likely to house command headquarters of any

status. Although not entirely successful – surviving Polish aircraft will be able to put up a stiff resistance over the next week – the surprise attack removes most of the air threat against the advancing Wehrmacht.

One hour after the initial Luftwaffe strikes, Army Group South under General von Rundstedt smashes forward: Eighth Army on the left wing driving for Lodz, Fourteenth Army on the right aimed for Krakow and the line of the River Vistula and the bulk of the armour of Tenth Army under General von Reichenau in the centre piercing the gap between the Polish Lodz and Krakow armies, linking with Eighth Army mobile units and racing on for Warsaw.

Army Group North under von Bock attacks

simultaneously, Third Army under Kuechler driving south from East Prussia and von Kluge's Fourth Army, spearheaded by the panzers of Guderian's XIX Corps striking from the west, across the Polish Corridor.

2–3 SEPTEMBER
DECLARATIONS OF WAR

While tanks from Tenth Army cross the river Warta, capturing Czestochowa, Britain and France demand the instant withdrawal of all German forces. In the

Above: Stukas were fitted with wind-driven sirens, usually attached to the fixed undercarriage. When activated in the dive, this added a terrifying scream to the already great psychological effect of a near-vertical bombing attack.

THE POLISH CAMPAIGN
Speed and power in a double envelopment

THE INVASION of Poland gave the world its first taste of the power and swiftness of the Blitzkrieg-style of lightning war.

The campaign was envisaged as a massive double pincer movement, three armies being involved in the inner arms of the offensive while two more, spearheaded by strong armoured forces, provided the outer loop of the envelopment. The inner pincer was designed to close on the Vistula river, surrounding the bulk of the Polish field army, while the outer, faster-moving forces were targeted on the Bug, cutting off any possibility of escape.

It was a very effective plan, which achieved most of its objectives by the middle of September. Any hope the Poles may have had was shattered by the Soviet invasion from the east, launched on 17 September to take advantage of German success.

The inner loop had closed on Warsaw by 10 September, and the Panzers commanded by General Guderian reached Brest-Litovsk only four days later. Even though the Poles fought fiercely, they could manage only one serious counter-attack, on the river Bzura near Warsaw. Although it was enough to force the Germans to reinforce with troops from other parts of the front, the battle was a forlorn hope for the Poles, and after its failure they could offer only sporadic resistance to the Wehrmacht.

Above: German troops of von Kluge's IV Army destroy the border crossing at Sepolno, west of Bydgoszcz, on the first day of the war.

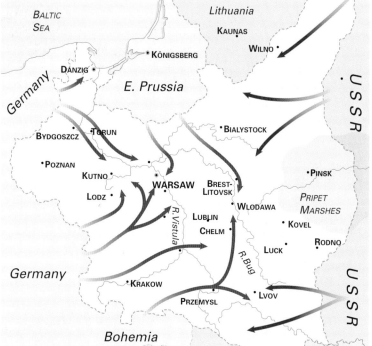

Below: The Panzer 2 with its 20-mm main gun was never envisaged as a true combat tank, but it made up a large part of the German tank force in Poland.

face of the contemptuous silence with which this is greeted in Berlin, the Allies consult on how best to implement their promises to Poland. That they must be implemented is agreed; but how, when and where are matters for lengthy discussion.

A final ultimatum is sent – and ignored. At 11 am on Sunday, 3 September 1939, British Prime Minister Neville Chamberlain broadcasts the news that Britain is now at war with Germany. The world will realise, he feels sure, what a bitter personal disappointment this is after Hitler had given his word not to attack.

4–6 SEPTEMBER
LIGHTNING WAR

By 4 September, Tenth Army spearheads are 80 kilometres into Poland, curving up towards the capital and isolating the Lodz Army from its supplies, while to the south Fourteenth Army panzers have reached the River San on each side of Przemysl.

Meanwhile Army Group North is driving down from Pomerania and East Prussia. Von Kluge's Fourth Army pushes east from Pomerania across the Polish corridor, cutting off Danzig and Gdynia and then following the line of the Vistula towards Warsaw. Third Army's route out of East Prussia will take it down the line of the Bug towards Brest-Litovsk, Lwow and eventual junction with Fourteenth Army coming up from the Carpathians. Thus two huge encirclements are planned, the outer intended to block any escapees from the inner.

On 5 September, Fourth Army takes Bydgoszcz, breaking through the forward Polish defence line and crossing the northern Vistula; Luftwaffe attacks devastate the town of Sulejow near Warsaw. The next day Southern Army Group's Eighth Army captures Tomaszow, outflanking the bulk of the Polish Pomorze army retreating from the north. The Polish government flees from Warsaw and at the end of the first week only the immediate confusion of battle masks the extraordinary success of the German attack.

7–10 SEPTEMBER
OBJECTIVE WARSAW

The ancient German pre-dreadnought *Schleswig-Holstein* shells Poland's main naval base at Hela near Gdynia. In spite of some successful counter attacks early in the campaign, the Polish

The Luftwaffe in Poland

Though the Luftwaffe had to keep much of its strength in the west to counter possible action by Britain and France, it was still able to field more than 1600 aircraft for the Polish campaign. The Polish air force was all but wiped out by 3 September, allowing the German pilots to concentrate on supporting the Wehrmacht.

Unlike most other airforces of the time who were developing long-range bombers, the Luftwaffe had little or no strategic responsibility. Its primary offensive function was to support the troops on the ground, acting as highly-mobile, hard-hitting artillery pieces.

Right: Junkers Ju 87B
300 Stukas drawn from six *Stukageschwader* provided the spearhead of the Wehrmacht's drive into Poland. This example was flown by the Group Staff Flight of IV *Gruppe*, *Lehrgeschwader* 1, commanded by Hauptmann von Brauchitsch.

Below: Dornier Do 17Z
The Dornier Do 17 was one of the most important elements of the Luftwaffe's *Kampfgruppen*. With an acceptable bombload of around one tonne and considered very fast for its day, the Do-17 was successful over Poland, but later campaigns were to show that it was too lightly armed and protected when faced with modern fighter opposition.

Right: Messerschmitt Bf 109E
By a wide margin the best fighter of the Polish campaign, the Bf 109 was more than 100-km/h faster than the PZL.11s of the Polish air force, and enabled the Luftwaffe to gain almost complete control of the air. This is a Bf 109E-3 of Jagdgeschwader 51, which entered service just after the final dismemberment of Poland.

air force has been all but wiped out and German Stukas are free to probe ahead of advancing Panzer columns without fear of interruption.

8 September sees the Wehrmacht continuing its drive for Warsaw while Poles entrench on the outskirts of the city. 4th Panzer Division has advanced 225 km since the start of war, an average of more than 30 km per day. To the North, Guderian's corps has continued eastwards and now turns south, spearheading the push towards Brest Litovsk.

The next day 4th Panzer Division reaches Warsaw and attempts to storm the city, but is

"The Stukas were lethal, especially as there was no real fighter opposition"

Lieutenant Baron Tassilo von Bogenhardt, 6th Rifle Regiment, German Army

held off. The Germans have surrounded the bulk of the Polish army, but the Poznan army makes a spirited counter attack down the line of the Bzura river, marking the start of the biggest battle of the campaign.

The inner pincers have certainly met successfully, but the chaos inside the trap is such that no one ccan be sure what is happening. Polish columns march and counter-march in frantic efforts to make contact either with the enemy or with their own support, and in doing so raise such clouds of dust that aerial observation can report nothing but general movement by unidentified forces of

unknown strength, engaged in unrecognisable activity in pursuit of incomprehensible aims.

On 10 September multiple Luftwaffe air raids target Warsaw; the Polish government orders a general military withdrawal to the south east.

11–12 SEPTEMBER
POLISH ARMY CRUMBLES

Units of the German 14th Army reach and cross the river San on the 11th, and begin driving north towards Brest Litovsk. Meanwhile, the battle for the Bzura pocket hots up. The general fog of war means that there is some doubt at German headquarters whether or not the bulk of the Polish forces have been trapped, and on the 12th tanks from the Tenth Army are wheeled north to form another block along the Bzura, west of Warsaw.

The battle is the most bitter of the campaign, but the imbalance of forces means that it can only end in defeat for the Poles. Despite their desperate gallantry, they are fighting in reverse against a strong, tactically superior enemy. After the first day the Poles are harried from behind by troops of the German Eighth Army from the south and of the Fourth Army from the north.

Only a very small number of Poles manage to break through the German armoured screen to join the garrison at Warsaw –

where they will very soon find themselves again cut off from escape by the outer encirclement.

On 13 September Southern Army Group infantry crosses the Vistula south of Warsaw, driving eastwards. The Luftwaffe launches heavy attacks on Warsaw itself. Increased irregular activity lead the German high command to threaten annihilation to towns supporting guerrillas.

A day later Gdynia, Poland's only port, is captured. To the east German mechanised forces reach and take Brest Litovsk, leaving only the citadel in Polish hands.

15–21 SEPTEMBER
RUSSIAN INVASION

Warsaw is surrounded and besieged. Southern Army group troops occupy the Galician oil fields on the Rumanian border.

Above: German divisions generally had two artillery regiments, one equipped with 12 heavy 150-mm howitzers and one with 24 or 36 light 105-mm guns. In infantry units the guns were horse drawn, while Panzer divisions used motorised transport. These 105-mm guns are being towed into action in Poland by a 3-tonne SdKfz 11 half-track.

Finding the weak spot
How Lightning War destroys the enemy's will to fight

On 16 September Polish air force bombers make their last effective attacks on the invaders before the few survivors flee to Rumania. Meanwhile, the Germans issue an ultimatum to Warsaw – surrender or be destroyed. The garrison, supported by as many as 100,000 civilians, fights on.

Army Groups North and South meet at Wlodawa on 17 September, completing the outer ring of the German double pincer. From this double encirclement only a small fraction of the Polish army can hope to escape, and on the same day even this hope is dashed. The contents of the secret clauses of the Russo-German Pact signed the previous month are cruelly revealed when the Soviet Union sends the Red Army in from the east to collect its share of the spoils.

While the Germans crush any

Below: Polish cavalry fought gallantly, but all too often found themselves pitted against a mechanised enemy whose armour shrugged aside the attack of lances.

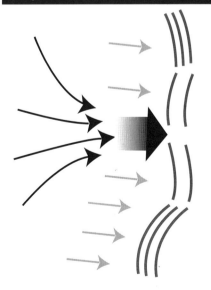

THE KEY to the success of Blitzkrieg was concentration of force to make an initial break-through, followed by extremely rapid, well-directed exploitation before the enemy could react.

Once a weak point in the enemy defences had been identified, the Panzers massed and then advanced under a rain of supporting fire supplied by artillery and dive bombers. The Panzers were also supported by mechanised infantry which could be used isolate enemy strongpoints by-passed in the headlong advance, and to counter any moves against the German lines of communication.

After the armour was clear of the immediate breakthrough point, the short-barrelled 75-mm guns of the new Panzer IV medium tanks could provide some fire support, but it was the innovatory use of dive bombers to crush any opposing strongpoints which was most characteristic of Blitz warfare.

The speed of the attack was designed to cut enemy lines of communication, spreading confusion through his rear echelons. With the enemy unable to respond or to make meaningful countermoves, the Panzers were then free to advance over hitherto impossible distances and towards distant objectives in days rather than the months of previous campaigns. As they moved the tanks retained the support of the mechanised

infantry, and the early absence of mobile artillery was overcome by the continued use of dive-bombers and other airborne support.

As the deep advances into the enemy rear continued, marching infantry following behind assumed the roles of guarding the flanks and preventing counterthrusts on the lines of communication.

The theory of Blitzkrieg may have been simple, but in practice it required an immense amount of skill. It called for good communications and a very high level of cooperation,

not only between the constituent arms but also between the army and the Luftwaffe.

By 1939 the Germans had been able to train and practice such tactics to the point where they were almost routine, with dress rehearsals in the bloodless annexation of the Sudetenland in 1938, followed by the occupation of the rest of Czechoslovakia early in 1939. These operations revealed many shortcomings in German organisation and equipment, but these had mostly been ironed out by the time Blitzkrieg became a reality in September 1939.

STAGE 1 CONCENTRATION OF FORCE

Above: The Wehrmacht formed a powerful offensive spearhead where the enemy was weakest. Known as the *schwerpunkt*, this critical point was chosen using all possible information about enemy deployments.

STAGE 2 PENETRATION OF DEFENCE

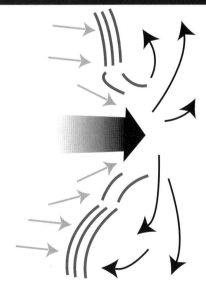

Above: Once through the front line the armoured formations thrust deep into enemy territory and then fanned out. The mobility and firepower of the tanks enabled them to range far and wide in the enemy's rear areas.

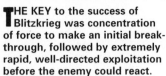

remaining resistance in Brest-Litovsk, the Red Army advances on two fronts north and south of the impassable Pripet marshes, meeting negligible opposition. The Polish government, which has already changed its location five times, flees from the town of Kuty into Rumania.

On 19 September the Polish army in the Bzura pocket is finally defeated: more than 100,000 men are taken prisoner. Further south the Germans surround Lvov.

21–28 SEPTEMBER
THE FALL OF WARSAW

On 21 September the Germans launch a massive artillery bombardment of Warsaw. The next day, the Soviets occupy Lvov, and with the Germans mount a joint victory parade in Brest-Litovsk.

A further ultimatum is issued on 25 September to the citizens and defenders of Warsaw, emphasised by attacks by more

Weapons of the Blitzkrieg

Although the word 'Blitzkrieg' conjures up images of hordes of massive tanks, smashing through an enemy's strongest defences, the truth was very different. For a start, the first stunning victories were achieved with light tanks of limited fighting power – in many respects, German armour and artillery was less capable than those of their opponents. It was the way that the vehicles were used which was to prove decisive.

Right: PzKpfw II light tank
Designed as a training machine to prepare German armoured troops for the larger Panzer III and IV tanks then entering service, the Panzer II with its light 20-mm cannon nevertheless provided the bulk of the Wehrmacht's tank strength in 1939 and 1940, with more than 1,000 in use in Poland.

Above: The tiny PzKpfw I was of limited combat value, but was used in some numbers in Poland. This is a command version, with an extended superstructure to house communications gear. The white cross was a recognition symbol used only during the Polish campaign.

Left: SdKfz 231 armoured car
The first German armoured vehicles built after World War I were armoured cars, based on truck chassis and developed abroad to avoid the constraints of the Treaty of Versailles. The SdKfz (*Sonderkraftfahrzeug*, or special purpose vehicle) 231 was classed as a *schwere Panzerspähwagen*, or heavy armoured reconnaissance vehicle. It was used extensively in Poland and later in the invasion of France, even though its commercial chassis meant that it was not really suitable for prolonged cross-country use.

than 400 bombers. Polish resistance starts to weaken, and on 26 September the Wehrmacht launches an infantry assault on the city after another heavy artillery bombardment.

Within a day the Germans are in control of the outer parts of the city, and the Polish commander, recognising a lost cause, offers to surrender. A ceasefire comes into effect the next day, 28 September.

29 SEPTEMBER– 6 OCTOBER
POLAND DISMEMBERED

The Soviet-German partition of Poland comes into force with the signing of a 'treaty of frontier regulation and friendship' on the 29th.

Poland as a nation ceases to exist, and a new international frontier runs from East Prussia past Bialystok, Brest-Litovsk and Lwow as far as the Carpathians.

Already, SS and SD parties are moving in behind the victorious troops, tasked with

rounding up and segregating Jews, the intelligencia, political and military leaders.

German troops occupy Warsaw on 1 October and begin disarming defenders. Mopping up operations against the remainder of Polish troops still under arms to the east of Warsaw continues until 3 October.

To seal his triumph, Hitler flies into Warsaw on 5 October and takes the salute at a victory parade. Organised Polish resistance ceases the next day with the surrender of 8,000 troops southeast of Warsaw.

Hitler is now free to think about further campaigns in the west. For the moment, Germany and Stalin's Soviet Union are on the same side. But historically, common frontiers between the two countries have rarely provided anything but friction and animosity, and many wonder how long such essentially antagonistic neighbours can exist side by side.

Above: A Russian officer fraternises with a German tank commander after the two invading armies meet at Brest-Litovsk. The friendship over the dismembered remains of Poland is more apparent than real: within 20 months the two dictatorships will begin to fight the bloodiest war in history.

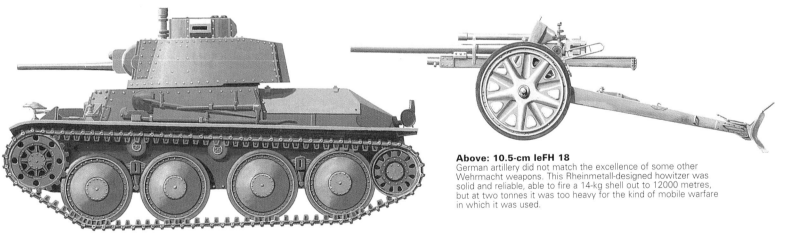

Above: 10.5-cm leFH 18
German artillery did not match the excellence of some other Wehrmacht weapons. This Rheinmetall-designed howitzer was solid and reliable, able to fire a 14-kg shell out to 12000 metres, but at two tonnes it was too heavy for the kind of mobile warfare in which it was used.

Above: PzKpfw.38(t) light tank
The German annexation of Czechoslovakia gave the Wehrmacht access to the noted Skoda armaments works. The PzKpfw 38(t) was roughly equivalent to the Panzer II, though with a more powerful 37.2-mm gun. Originally designed for the Czech army, it became an important Wehrmacht tank in 1939 and 1940.

Right: SdKfz 7 medium half track
Standard prime mover of the Wehrmacht in the early years of the war, the SdKfz 7 was used mainly as an artillery tractor. It could carry 12 men and their equipment along with ammunition and supplies, at the same time as it towed loads of up to eight tonnes. More than 6,100 were produced in the ten years from 1934.

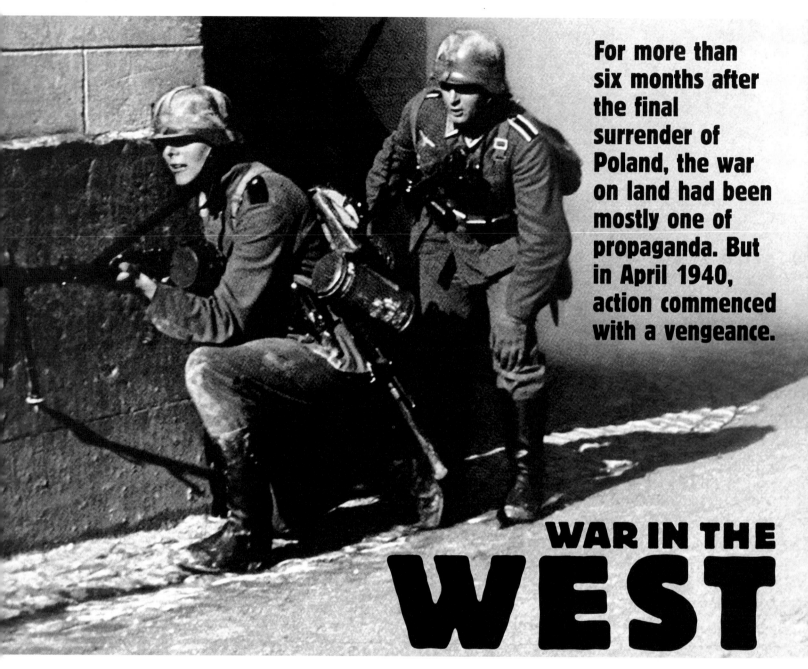

For more than six months after the final surrender of Poland, the war on land had been mostly one of propaganda. But in April 1940, action commenced with a vengeance.

WAR IN THE WEST

HITLER became aware of the importance of Norway during the Russo-Finnish war of 1939. The British and French planned to send aid to Finland across the northern tip of Scandinavia, which would have cut off the Swedish iron supply to the Reich.

Sweden was Germany's primary source of high grade iron ore, the vital raw material being exported via the Norwegian port of Narvik. Hitler's naval advisors had also been pointing out the value of Norway's ports since the first weeks of the war – possession by Germany would mean that the Kriegsmarine would have a much easier task of getting out into the North Atlantic shipping lanes.

On December 14 1939, Hitler issued OKW – *Oberkommando Der Wehrmacht* or High Command of the Armed Forces – with orders to begin planning a Norwegian campaign. Hitler's determination to invade was heightened in February, when the British destroyer *Cossack* seized the German supply ship *Altmark* in Norwegian waters. The *Altmark* had been supporting the *Graf Spee's* raid, and the action liberated nearly 300 British merchant seamen who were being held prisoner.

On March 1, Hitler issued the formal directive for *Weserubung* or Operation 'Spring Awakening'. But German naval preparations and troop movements could not be hidden, and the Allies reacted.

On 8 April, at Churchill's urging, the Royal Navy began laying mines in the waters off

The invasion of Norway was mounted primarily to protect Germany's main source of iron ore. The plan was to take key Norwegian cities with only a limited number of troops.

Norway to disrupt the movement of shipping. British and French troops were being moved to the north of Scotland, ready for intervention if necessary. But it was too late.

On the night of April 8-9, the Kriegsmarine deployed two battlecruisers, one pocket battleship, six cruisers and 14 destroyers in the assault on Norway. One force struck directly for Oslo, while further landings were made up the coast – at Kristiansand, Stavanger, Bergen, Trondheim and Narvik. They were supported by airborne landings.

The destroyer HMS *Glowworm*, commanded by Lieutenant-Commander Gerard Roope, encountered the heavy cruiser *Admiral Hipper*. Knowing that British troopships in the area would be severely handled if the *Hipper* were to locate them, Roope launched torpedoes and then, even though battered to ruin by the cruiser's heavy eight-inch main armament, brought his little ship round to ram the German warship. Roope was awarded a posthumous Victoria Cross.

NAVAL LOSSES

At Oskarsborg in Oslo Fjord, the Norwegian coastal defences sank the cruiser *Blücher* and damaged the pocket battleship *Lützow*, before airborne forces captured the capital. King Haakon VII had rejected a German ultimatum delivered at 0530 and, profiting from the confusion following the sinking of the *Blücher,* escaped inland and eventually reached the United Kingdom on June 7. Meanwhile, an attempt at a coup d'etat by the far right pro-Nazi Norwegian politician Vidkun Quisling actually

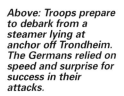

Above: Troops prepare to debark from a steamer lying at anchor off Trondheim. The Germans relied on speed and surprise for success in their attacks.

Right: Hit by shore batteries and torpedoes, the heavy cruiser Blücher *lies wrecked in Oslo Fiord. More than 1,500 sailors and troops were killed.*

Danish Walkover
Seizing a base for the attack on Norway

The attack on Denmark was the logical military precursor of the assault on Norway. Luftwaffe planners working on the attack, code named Operation Weserubung, (Spring Awakening) needed airfields in Denmark to support air attacks and operations in southern Norway.

The swift occupation of Denmark which began at 0415 on April 9 is notable for the first use of airborne forces in war. At 0500 paratroops were used to seize the unarmed fortress of Madnes and soon afterwards the important airfield at Aalborg in north Jutland. Danish forces in North Schleswig did resist for a few hours, but the navy, which had not been alerted, allowed a German troopship to enter Copenhagen harbour unmolested.

Right: The Danish army was unprepared for a major conflict, and its equipment was no match for the full might of the Wehrmacht which it had to face.

Below: German troops arrived in Copenhagen almost unopposed, arriving by troopship in the harbour. The Danish navy had no advance warning of the attack, and could offer little to stop the enemy.

The Battles of Narvik
German naval defeat in northern Norwegian waters

In the north, the Royal Navy 2nd Destroyer Flotilla under Captain B.A.W. Warburton-Lee entered Narvik Fjord on the night of the 9-10 April. At dawn they caught the German invasion forces. The flotilla sank the German destroyers *Wilhelm Heidkamp* and *Anton Schmidt* and six transports, damaging three more destroyers in the process. British losses were HMS *Hunter* sunk, HMS *Hardy* driven ashore and HMS *Hotspur* damaged. As they withdrew the British engaged the German transport *Rauenfels* which was carrying the bulk of the invasion force's ammunition. The ship blew up and sank. Warburton-Lee, mortally wounded, was awarded a posthumous Victoria Cross.

The British returned to Narvik at dawn on April 13, with a more powerful force under Vice-Admiral W.J. Whitworth which included the battleship HMS *Warspite*, and the destroyers *Bedouin, Cossack,* Eskimo, Punjabi, Hero, Icarus, Kimberley, Forester and Foxhound. The *Warspite*'s floatplane located the German destroyer *Erich Koellner* which was waiting in ambush at the mouth of the fjord and she was torpedoed and left a blazing wreck. The floatplane also located the submarine *U-64*, which the aircraft bombed and sank.

Six German destroyers now emerged to fight a fast-moving battle in which three, *Dieter von Roeder, Hermann Kunne* and *Erich Giese* were sunk. The survivors were pursued into Rombaksfjord where *Georg Thiele* was driven ashore, but not before damaging HMS *Cossack* with a torpedo. The three remaining German destroyers, the *Bernd von Arnim, Hans Ludemann* and *Wolfgang Zenker* were found abandoned at the head of the fjord – one having been scuttled as a result of damage from the April 10 battle.

Having wrecked these ships, Whitworth's force withdrew and were able to pick up *Hardy*'s surviving crew from a Norwegian vessel at the mouth of Ofot Fjord. The two battles of Narvik reduced the Kriegsmarine destroyer force by half – a loss which was to have great significance later in the year.

Left: The port of Narvik burns as a Royal Navy destroyer noses in to the pier. Although the British had the better of the sea battles, on land the Allies were much less successful, and withdrew.

---

helped to stiffen Norwegian resistance.

At sea, the submarine HMS *Truant* sank the cruiser *Karlsruhe* and the battlecruiser *Gneisenau* was damaged in an action with the battlecruiser HMS *Renown*.

On April 10 the cruiser *Konigsberg* was sunk by air attack at Bergen, and the following day the *Lutzow* sustained further damage when she was hit by a torpedo fired by the submarine HMS *Spearfish*.

NARVIK BATTLES

The German forces in Norway which came under the toughest pressure were those in Narvik. British and French troops, including the Foreign Legion, had been readied to assist the Finns who had been attacked by the Soviet Union in the winter of 1939-40. They were deployed to counter the Germans in the north of Norway. Narvik was invested by the British 24th Guards Brigade, French *Chasseurs Alpins*, a demibrigade of the Foreign Legion and a brigade of

Right: The campaigns in Norway and Denmark were the first in history in which airborne troops played a part, Luftwaffe paratroopers making attacks on numerous targets.

the Polish *Chasseurs du Nord*. The Allied expeditionary force landed at Narvik on 15 April, at Namsos on the 16/17th and at Andalsnes on the 18th.

The German forces under Lieutenant-General Eduard Dietl consisted of mountain infantry, paratroop reinforcements and German sailors from the wrecked destroyers who were armed and equipped from captured Norwegian stocks.

Allied progress under Major General Macksey was slow and he was replaced by General Bethouart, who pressed on to capture Narvik on May 28 and link up with Norwegian forces. However, by now events in France had made Norway a side show. Moreover, free of commitments elsewhere in Norway the Germans could direct more men and resources to the recapture of Narvik.

In a chaotic campaign much of the German naval strength in the area was destroyed, and Allied ground forces slowed down the German attacks, but the British and French lacked air cover. From their base in Oslo the Germans pushed northwards up the valleys of the Gudbrandsdalen and Osterdalen towards Andalsnes and Trondheim. Allied troops were withdrawn from Andalsnes on 1 May, Namsos on May 2-3 and Narvik on 8 June.

LOSSES IN NORWAY

German losses in the Norwegian campaign were 5,500 men and more than 200 aircraft on top of the significant naval losses. The British lost 4,500 men, of whom 1,500 were drowned when the old aircraft carrier HMS

Above: British 'Tribal' class fleet destroyers prowl the waters of Rombaksfjord. Having disposed of half the entire German destroyer inventory, the Kriegsmarine's strength is severely depleted.

Below: The veteran battleship HMS Warspite may have been slow by modern standards, but her powerful guns could and did overwhelm anything the Kriegsmarine had at Narvik.

Above: Any German destroyers which escaped being sunk by the British forces were driven into nearby Rombaksfjord, where their crews either scuttled or abandoned them.

Below: HMS Warspite leaves the drifting destroyer Erich Koellner. The German vessel had been battered into ruin by the battleship and her escorts on their way in.

Glorious and her two escorting destroyers were sunk by the battle cruiser Scharnhorst. About 1,800 Norwegians were killed and French and Polish losses were about 500.

There is a case for saying that the Norwegian campaign marked the first Allied land victory of the war. The joint Polish, British, Norwegian and French force fought the Germans to a standstill in Narvik, though ultimately in vain. Whether or not Narvik was a victory,

the sea battles between the Royal Navy and the Kriegsmarine severely weakened the German navy, and this was a factor in the delay and later cancellation of Operation Sealion – the planned invasion of the United Kingdom.

THE LOW COUNTRIES
As the campaign in Norway drew to a close an operation far bigger and more momentous was under way in the Netherlands, Belgium and France.

In the Netherlands the

Below: German troops quickly established a dominant position in Norway.

THE NORWEGIAN CAMPAIGN

8 June 1940
HMS Glorious sunk by battlecruisers Scharnhorst and Gneisenau.

10 April
Battlecruisers HMS Renown and Gneisenau engage and damage each other

8 April
Admiral Hipper sinks HMS Glowworm

10 April
Königsberg sunk by Royal Navy dive-bombers

16 February
Cossack takes Altmark

10 April
Karlsrühe torpedoed

11 April
Lützow torpedoed

Narvik

Bodo

Trondheim

NORTH SEA

SWEDEN

Bergen

Oslo

NORWAY

Kristiansand

DENMARK

Copenhagen

BALTIC SEA

government of prime minister D.J. de Geer urged a defensive posture. They were convinced that flooding the canal system would prove an effective obstacle. A series of four defensive lines anchored on the Ijssel Meer to the north and the river Maas and Belgian border to the south protected 'Fortress Holland', the group of major cities in the Netherlands, including the capital at The Hague. This strategy, however, made no allowance for the speed of German mechanised attacks and vertical envelopment by paratroopers and air landing troops.

A strong pacifist movement in Holland had ensured that the army was ill-equipped for modern war. Though its total strength was 400,000 men, they had only 26 armoured cars, 656 outdated artillery pieces and no tanks. Pre-war pacifism and parsimony would cost the Netherlands dearly – the cost

including 2,100 dead and 2,700 wounded before the end of hostilities in May 1940.

The German force assigned to attack Holland was Field Marshal Fedor von Bock's Army Group B. Under his command were the 18th Army under General Kuechler and General Reichenau's 6th Army, who also had the XVI Panzer Corps attached. Reichenau – a favourite of Hitler's and one of the most committed Nazis in the higher echelons of the army – was tasked with pushing through the southern border of Holland into northern Belgium. Kuechler's mission was to link up with the airborne forces who were to capture key bridges across the water obstacles.

THE TRAP IS SPRUNG

With an almost suicidal alacrity, the allied armies in the north of France – five divisions of the British Expeditionary Force, together with eight divisions of

Above: German infantrymen wait on the Belgian border as the Wehrmacht launches its diversionary attack in the Low Countries.

Below: The Wehrmacht deployed three experimental multi-turreted NbFz VI tanks to Norway in a propaganda exercise to convince the Allies that Germany had heavy tanks in production. There were no others in operation.

No more Phoney War

French and British forces lured into a trap

The German attack in the west was known as Fall Gelb – 'Plan Yellow'. During World War I the Imperial German Armies, using a scheme devised by General Schlieffen, had invaded neutral Belgium in an attempt to work round the left flank of the French and British armies. The Netherlands had remained neutral. It was assumed by the Allies that the Germans would try the Schlieffen Plan again.

In 1939-40 the Netherlands and Belgium were again neutral, though they were aware that they were in the firing line if the German armies attempted a repeat manoeuvre. Neither would allow Allied troops on their soil, but the French and British governments signed an agreement with the Belgians that in the event of an attack they would come to the assistance of Belgium, advancing northwards to hold a line along the river Dyle.

Unfortunately for the Allies, the Germans were planning something very different. The attacks on Holland and Belgium were diversions, a 'matador's cape' designed to draw French and British troops out of northern France. This would leave the Ardennes border near the Meuse at Sedan only weakly protected. The Germans would then launch a reverse Schlieffen plan through the Ardennes, which the Allies considered impossible terrain for modern armoured forces.

Devised by General Erich von Manstein, the plan envisaged a powerful armoured thrust through the Ardennes, with the panzers quickly forcing their way across the Meuse. They would then swing north and west at speed, cutting lines of communication and trapping the British and French in a pocket against the Channel.

THE LOW COUNTRIES

The bulk of the German forces employed in Holland and Belgium was infantry, though parachute assaults ahead of the advancing armies were used to capture and hold key defences and river crossings.

NORTH SEA

HOLLAND

The Hague

Rotterdam

British and French armies swept forward into Belgium

Ostende

Dunkirk

Bruges

Antwerp

BELGIUM

GERMANY

Cologne

The main German attack outflanked the Allies by attacking at Sedan

Brussels

As the Allies advanced, they left their rear lines unguarded

German panzers raced forward, reaching the Channel coast ten days after bursting through the Ardennes.

Sedan

FRANCE

Paris

Left: Lightweight PzKpfw IIs race through the forests of southern Belgium. Although small and lightly armed, such tanks were very mobile, and mobility was the key to the success of Germany's Blitzkrieg tactics.

Below left: The Dutch army was seriously outmatched, without a tank to its name and with only 656 artillery pieces. Most of the guns were small and obsolescent, and many were mounted in fortresses which the Germans bypassed.

Below: German infantry fight through a small Dutch town. The German high command deployed a total of 77 divisions for the campaign in the West. Of these, 30 were assigned to Army Group B, under the command of General von Bock. Flooding forward across Belgium and Holland, they faced 11 Dutch divisions and 22 Belgian divisions, with a further 20 Allied divisions moving north out of France. However, these would soon be distracted by the 44 German divisions to the south.

Airborne Pioneers

The first paratroopers go into battle

On May 10 German forces quickly overran the Ijssel Line, the first Dutch line of defence. Paratroops and airborne forces from the 7th Air Division and the 22nd Airlanding Infantry Division made landings at bridges at Moerdijk across the river Maas, Dordrecht across the Waal, Rotterdam across the Lek and Valkenburg near Leyden.

The Dutch fought bravely and attempted to eliminate the airborne bridgeheads, particularly those at Moerdijk. The attack on The Hague went awry, with paratroops scattered and unable initially to secure the airfields. As men drawn from the 22nd Infantry Division began to fly in aboard Ju 52 trimotor transports they realised they were to land under fire.

The plan had been to attack Den Hague with the intention of capturing Queen Wilhelmina and her government, but the delays in landing allowed the Royal Family to escape aboard two Royal Navy destroyers. They had initially hoped to fight on from the islands of Zeeland, but the situation deteriorated so rapidly that they sailed to Britain.

The Dutch troops holding the bridges at Moerdijk fought for three days until dislodged by the 9th Panzer Division. Then the advance pressed on towards Rotterdam. To the south the Seventh French Army was too weak to intervene, and withdrew. Dutch marines who were holding the approaches to bridges in Rotterdam were still offering stout resistance, and on the evening of May 13 the Luftwaffe received orders to 'break resistance in Rotterdam by all possible means'.

Below: German infantrymen link up with Fallschirmjäger or paratroopers who had seized the crossings over the Lek, leaving the route to Rotterdam open to the invaders.

Above: Although the Wehrmacht got many of its parachute techniques from Soviet experiments of the 1930s, the Germans in 1940 were the first to show that unexpected assaults from the air could reap massive tactical dividends – just as long as the lightly-armed paratroopers were quickly relieved by conventional troops.

Below: German paratroopers used shaped explosive charges – another combat first – to penetrate the thick concrete of Belgian and Dutch fortifications at key river crossings.

Left: Dutch soldiers are herded into captivity. The Dutch lost around 3,000 soldiers killed during the campaign, along with at least 2,500 civilians.

the French First Army and seven of the French Seventh Army moved into Belgium. They left the defensive positions that they had spent the bitterly cold winter so arduously preparing and moved forwards to join the Belgian army in a defensive line along the Dyle and Meuse rivers.

In spite of many Luftwaffe raids, in which untried Allied soldiers experienced the attacks of the Stuka dive bomber for the first time, the Allied armies reached their allotted positions by the 14th. Some battalion and brigade commanders were dismayed by the sketchy nature of the defences they now occupied, especially compared to those they had left behind. More senior commanders were getting worried about news of German movements to the south.

As yet, none of them had

realised that von Bock's slowly advancing Army Group was a feint – a huge feint to be sure, but it was not the main axis of the German attack. Even as the British and French advanced, German panzers were thrusting through the Ardennes towards Sedan, and the Allied forces were in danger of being cut off.

The 'matador's cape' had worked to perfection. By tempting the bulk of the Allies' best troops into the open, they were leaving the way clear for von Kleist's Panzer group, even now pouring across the Meuse at Sedan, to outflank them.

RAID ON ROTTERDAM

Meanwhile, on the morning of the 14th, German ground forces requested that the Luftwaffe raid on Rotterdam be cancelled because they had entered surrender negotiations. The message did not reach the bombers and 57 out of 100 dropped their payloads before a signal flare was seen. The attack

had been aimed at Dutch defences and used only high explosives, but 2.8 square kilometres (1.1 sq mile) of the city centre was destroyed, and between 800 and 980 civilians were killed. Within a few hours the Dutch government surrendered, even though its army was still largely intact.

The Rotterdam raid was seen as an act of airborne terrorism

and ended the British policy of not bombing Germany. On May 15 the first RAF raid hit the Ruhr, heralding the beginning of the strategic bombing offensive against Germany which would grow in ferocity and intensity over the next five years.

Above: Stubborn resistance to the German attack on Rotterdam brought a brutal response: 100 Heinkel He 111 bombers were sent to attack the city. Around 1,000 civilians were killed, and more than 70,000 made homeless.

Below: The next stage of the war was to see the tanks of Germany's panzer divisions come to the fore, as they smashed through France.

BATTLE OF

Germany's attack on Scandinavia was followed by an even more devastating campaign. In less than a month, the Wehrmacht's fast-moving Panzers smashed the armies of Britain and France.

"W AR," declared Adolf Hitler, "is for man what childbirth is for woman". It was not only natural, an integral part of the human experience – it was a duty. "As a boy," he wrote in Mein Kampf, "I longed for the chance to prove that my patriotism was not mere talk".

But for all his devotion to duty and the unquestionable bravery under fire that won him an Iron Cross First Class in 1917, Adolf Hitler was never promoted beyond corporal. He treasured the medal to the end of his life; it was often the only decoration on his tunic. He also kept a front-line soldier's cynical regard for the generals, the bewhiskered, monocled

aristocrats who had presided over four years of carnage on the Western Front.

The former corporal became head of state with the passive endorsement of the German army high command, generals whose contempt for the Weimar regime exceeded their distaste for Hitler and his vulgar, lower-class Nazi movement. He stamped his authority on the

generals by engineering dismissal of the minister of defence, Field Marshal von Blomberg, whose second wife's past career as a pornographic actress was exposed by Goering's agents. The army's favoured successor, von Fritsch was then arrested on false accusations of homosexuality. But until the invasion of France and the breakthrough at Sedan,

FRANCE

Above: German light tanks pound through a French village, relying on speed rather than gun power to disrupt French defences.

Above right: A beaten French poilu graphically shows the low state of morale in the French Army.

Hitler shrank from telling the generals their job.

In September 1939, Hitler unleashed his forces against Poland, leaving no more than a covering force in the west to face a French army of 70 divisions, supported by 3,000 tanks and with complete air supremacy – but only if the *Armee de l'air* had been ordered to fight. Hitler's intuition that the

French would do nothing paid off. The huge French army sat still, while a small British Expeditionary Force was shipped to northern France.

THE SHOOTING STARTS

The 'Phoney War' lasted through the winter and into the spring, until German forces invaded Denmark and Norway, forestalling an Allied landing by a matter of days. It was not until 10 May, eight months after the outbreak of war, that Hitler sent his armies west.

The last time German soldiers had poured into France, in 1914, their initial drive had taken them

close to Paris. But they were driven back, and had to endure four bloody years of trench warfare. This time they would break the back of enemy resistance in a single week.

Within a fortnight, the British would be evacuating their soldiers, and France would be at Hitler's mercy. The humiliation of 1918 would be avenged – and it would be the Führer's master strategy that did it, not the General Staff.

The original army plan for the invasion of western Europe was based on Germany's opening attack in World War I, but was actually less ambitious than the

Schlieffen Plan of 1914. The generals intended to occupy Belgium and France's northern industrial regions but no further. They had no intention of repeating the ill-fated march on Paris they tried in 1914. The army high command believed that the ratio of forces and the power of modern defence admitted no other strategy; new objectives would require a further campaign in 1941.

The German generals were not alone in thinking that this was how it would be: the French and British generals agreed too, drawing up plans to push their main mobile forces into Belgium the moment hostilities began.

Had the attack been delivered when first ordered in autumn 1939, the generals would have had the war they planned. But Hitler had other ideas. He had fought in Belgium, among the shattered villages around Ypres where a million British and German soldiers were killed in 1917. He knew the ground, how artillery bornbardments reduced the ground to a quagmire. Countless small rivers and streams offered endless obstruction to an invader. Surely it would be better to attack further south, perhaps through the forested hills of the Ardennes? The generals looked down their noses at the idea.

CHANGE OF PLAN

By the time the postponed offensive was ready to roll in the spring, Hitler discovered that at least some officers shared his vision. General Erich von Manstein was chief of staff to General von Rundstedt, commander in chief of Army Group A in the West. Manstein had studied the Ardennes region

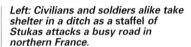

Right: The Ju-87 Stuka added the devastating psychological effect of screaming sirens to the pinpoint accuracy with which they could deliver bombs. The Stukas worked closely with the Wehrmacht, taking the place of artillery support for the fast-moving German panzers.

Left: Civilians and soldiers alike take shelter in a ditch as a staffel of Stukas attacks a busy road in northern France.

Below: Although the panzers provided the sharp spearhead of the German attack on France, the bulk of the troops involved – 37 out of 44 divisions in von Runstedt's Army Group A – were infantry.

and come to the same conclusion as the Führer. He discussed the idea with the Germany's most influential tank expert, General Heinz Guderian. They argued for a radical strategy: to rush German panzer divisions along the narrow forest tracks and out onto the gently rolling hills of

northern France. Bursting into open country they would punch through the enemy before the defences were ready for them.

It would be difficult to bring enough artillery with these fast moving formations, and other German commanders envisaged a pause while the guns were

Around the Maginot Line
The ultimate fortification proves to be a waste of time and money

brought forward; a World War I-style battle would then take place along the river Meuse. Guderian and his tank men were far more sanguine, confident they could storm the French defences. The Luftwaffe's bombers, especially its fearsome Ju-87 'Stuka' dive-bombers, would provide close support in place of artillery.

Hitler adopted the Manstein plan and changed the orders to his commanders in the west. Manstein would receive due credit in time, but the orthodox generals resented having a relatively junior officer's plan thrust upon them, and posted von Manstein to command an infantry corps in the rear.

One thing Hitler could not change was the odds. Although Germany enjoyed superiority in the air, with 4,000 aircraft against 3,000 Allied, the Wehrmacht had only 141 divisions with which to attack 144 Allied divisions. The Allies had some 3,383 tanks compared to the German total of 2,335 – many of these being light tanks of limited fighting capacity.

OFFENSIVE BEGINS
When the German offensive began on 10 May, the Allies followed their agreed strategy, pushing their best troops across the border to take up defensive positions along the river Dyle between Antwerp and Namur. However, the Ardennes front was not left unguarded: the French 9th army assembled along the Meuse river around Sedan.

Here, in 1870, the French Emperor Napoleon III had been decisively beaten by the Germans, going into captivity with his surviving soldiers while revolution broke out in Paris. The French commander-in-chief, 68-year old General Maurice Gamelin, expected German units to emerge from the Ardennes at

The Allies did not just outnumber the Germans. The majority of the French frontier was protected by an elaborate network of fortifications – the Maginot Line. Behind great fields of barbed wire and concrete anti-tank obstacles (known as dragon's teeth) lay an immensely strong chain of underground forts with heavy guns in retractable armoured turrets. Machine guns swept every approach, and the gunners were safe behind steel and reinforced concrete walls.

The Maginot Line seemed impregnable, but there was one major problem. The imposing fortifications stopped at the Belgian border. It had never been possible to get Belgian agreement to extend the fortifications into Belgium, yet it was politically unacceptable to continue them up to the coast, leaving Belgium outside the defences.

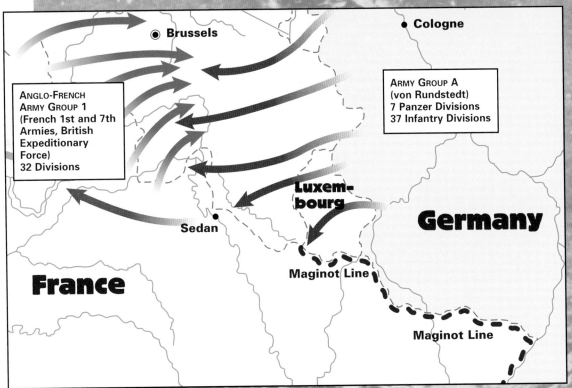

ANGLO-FRENCH ARMY GROUP 1 (French 1st and 7th Armies, British Expeditionary Force) 32 Divisions

ARMY GROUP A (von Rundstedt) 7 Panzer Divisions 37 Infantry Divisions

Left: The Maginot Line was the strongest defensive fortification ever built, a mass of steel and concrete with whole towns underground, manned by hundreds of thousands of French troops.

Right: The Germans proved that they were capable of dealing with modern concrete fortifications when they had to: this is one of the Belgian forts guarding the Albert canal. However, they simply by-passed the Maginot line, leaving a large part of the French army unharmed but completely impotent.

Left: The key point in the whole German attack came with the crossing of the River Meuse at Sedan. First across the river were assault pioneers, who immediately began setting up a ferry service.

Right above: Wehrmacht signals specialists string wire across a partially demolished bridge. The German's made extensive use of wireless in the front line, but as the infantry toiled in the wake of the fast-moving panzers they laid land lines for more reliable and more secure telephone communication.

Right: A motorbike reconnaissance unit is ferried across the Meuse. Soon the engineers will complete a pontoon bridge, and the panzers will start moving across.

some stage in the battle. But since he did not anticipate anything more than a light, probing force, the 9th Army was stretched more thinly than other French armies.

Once the attack was launched, German forces stormed across Holland and Belgium as the Allies expected, the imposing concrete and steel fortress at Eban Emael falling to a crack unit of paratroops who landed by glider right on the roof.

However, the forces under General von Bock – 30 infantry divisions of Army Group B – were actually a feint, designed to convince the Allies that the Germans were following the same old plan. The real punch came through the Ardennes, with the 44 divisions of von Runstedt's Army Group A, including 7 Panzer divisions under von Kleist.

Encountering little resistance from Belgian troops in the Ardennes, the panzer divisions headed down the dirt roads in alarmingly dense columns. Military traffic police have seldom had a more decisive impact on a campaign: thousands of vehicles kept to schedule and by the evening of 12 May, German spearheads had reached the river Meuse.

The French infantry divisions around Sedan were mostly reserve formations, with only a handful of regular officers or NCOs and the ordinary soldiers had received very little training. There were some five French cavalry divisions – reconnaissance units that included light tanks and motorised infantry as well as mounted troops – in the way, but they could not stop the German assault. Hammered by professional armoured forces, mostly combat veterans of the Polish campaign, the French formations disintegrated.

On 13 May, Guderian's infantry paddled across the Meuse in rubber dinghies while the French defences were pulverized by 300 twin-engine bombers and 200 Stukas. The dive-bombers attacked with particular accuracy, knocking out key French gun positions. The foot soldiers were across by 3.00 pm. Combat engineers had

Left: Smaller and less heavily armoured than the heaviest Allied tanks, the German Panzer IV could still pack quite a punch with its short-barrelled 75-mm cannon. However, its main advantage was that it was more mobile than British and French heavy tanks.

The Fighter War
Control of the skies

The Luftwaffe fought over Poland with very little opposition, and their confidence was sky high. The pilots knew that they flew the best planes in the world, and no other nation had such finely trained aircrew. Yet although they knew that attacking France would be a very different proposition, their confidence remained high. Success in the air war depends upon winning control of the air, and the Messerchmitt Bf 109 was just the aircraft to give the Luftwaffe that control.

Messerschmitt Bf 109E-3

The standard German fighter at the outbreak of war, the Bf 109 had been combat tested in Spain and Poland before being unleashed in the skies over France. The 'E' model was faster than any Allied fighter with the possible exception of the British Spitfire, but there were no Spitfires in France.

Messerschmitt Bf 109E-3

The Bf 109 served with 7. Staffel, part of II Gruppe, Jagdgeschwader 2 'Richthofen'. Armament was heavy for the time: two or three 20-mm cannon and two fast-firing 7.92-mm machine guns

Messerschmitt Bf 110C

Fast and very powerfully armed, the Bf 110C was designed as a Zerstörer or long-range heavy fighter. It proved reasonably effective during the French campaign: It was not until the Battle of Britain that its crews learned that it was no match for a high-performance single-engined fighter like the Spitfire or the Hurricane.

Gloster Gladiator

Last of Britain's front-line biplane fighters, the Gladiator was obsolete by the start of World War II. It saw considerable combat where its agility and toughness were evident, though it was no match for the Bf 109. Gladiators served with a number of air forces. This example was flown by 1ere Escadrille 'La Comète', 2e Regiment, Aeronautique Militaire in Belgium, and was based at Diest-Schaffen during the German invasion.

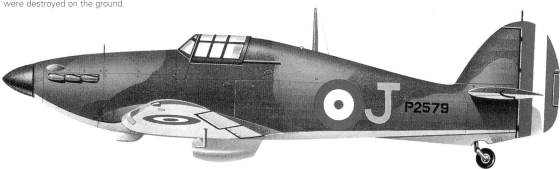

Morane Saulnier MS.406

The backbone of French fighter strength with around 300 aircraft serviceable in May 1940, the MS.406 was considerably less capable than the Bf 109. A good pilot could still achieve success, but its true worth can best be assessed by the fact that during the Battle of France 150 were lost in combat and another 100 were destroyed on the ground.

Hawker Hurricane Mark I

Flown by two RAF squadrons supporting the British Expeditionary Force, the Hawker Hurricane was slower than the Bf 109, but could turn more quickly. Its eight .303-in calibre machine-guns poured out a lot of ammunition, but they lacked the ultimate punch of the cannon-armed French and German fighters.

Above: Major General Erwin Rommell, former military aide to Hitler, commanded the 7th Panzer Division. A hero of World War I, Rommell proved to be a master of mobile tactics, and could improvise when necessary to get the job done.

Left: General Gamelin, the French commander in Chief, was an old man. Poorly served by his subordinates, and with little of the energy needed to keep a grip on modern warfare, he could not deal with the fast-moving German panzers.

Below: General Guderian's panzers reached the Channel coast on 20 May, 10 days after the start of the offensive. The BEF and many of the best French troops were now trapped in a pocket around Dunkirk.

a ferry operational in an hour, and by 4.30 a bridge was in place and the tanks could cross to the far bank.

LITTLE RESISTANCE

French counter-attacks came too little and too late. All the first-line troops had been committed to the northern flank. The Allies' strategy unravelled as the panzer divisions fanned out, racing ahead of their infantry and threatening to cut off the British and French armies in Belgium.

The Germans were vulnerable to a determined counter-attack, but the only one which threatened the speeding Panzers was by British tanks at Arras on 21 May. Five British brigades managed to inflict a stinging reverse on the SS *Totenkopf* division, but they were forced back after the commander of the 7th Panzer Division – Major-General Erwin Rommell – used his 88-mm anti-tank guns to engage the otherwise invulnerable British infantry tanks.

Gamelin ordered a retreat – without telling the British. The scale of the catastrophe suddenly became apparent and the French government prepared to evacuate Paris. With political will equally paralysed in London – Winston Churchill had only just replaced Neville Chamberlain as Prime Minister – it was left to Lord Gort VC, commander of the British Expeditionary Force, to choose between abandoning the French or hazarding most of Britain's tiny regular army in a last attempt to salvage the situation.

BRITISH CUT OFF

Meanwhile, Guderian's Panzers had reached the coast, and Gort chose to withdraw the BEF to Dunkirk. Trapped in an ever-decreasing pocket, it seemed only a matter of time before the British were annihilated. But then fate stepped in. The Führer ordered his panzers to stop, allowing the British a breathing space in which a fleet of civilian boats helped the Royal Navy

evacuate over 338,000 soldiers, including 100,000 Frenchmen, in nine days. The 'Stop Order' may have been to allow Hermann Goering to make good on his boast that the Luftwaffe could finish the job. In the event, the Germans met with stiff resistance from the Spitfires and Hurricanes of the RAF, and in spite of some successes were never able to seriously impede the evacuation.

FRANCE FALLS

The miracle of Dunkirk kept Britain in the war. However, there was no hope for France, who had replaced the ageing Gamelin with the even older General Weygand. In spite of stiffening resistance in places, the Panzers turned west, moving with incredible speed to secure the Atlantic coast. Others sped south, completely bypassing the Maginot line, leaving more than 400,000 French troops bewildered and demoralised in their suddenly useless fortifications.

On 16 June, prime minister Reynaud resigned, and was succeeded by Marshal Philippe Pétain. Almost the first act of the ancient hero of Verdun was to ask the Germans for armistice terms. By 20 June, Italy had declared war on France (though Mussolini's troops seemed reluctant to push too far into the south of France) while German troops had reached the Swiss border in the east, Lyon and Grenoble in the South and controlled the Biscay coast as far south as Royan.

To complete the humiliation of France, Hitler insisted on signing the one-sided armistice in the same railway carriage at Compiègne which had seen Germany's surrender in 1918.

In a few short weeks, Norway, Denmark, Holland, Belgium and France had surrendered to Germany. Only Britain remained to oppose Hitler as master of Europe, and it was towards the British Isles that Hitler was to turn his attention next.

Left: Adolf Hitler steps out of the railway carriage at Compiègne where France has been forced to sign a humiliating armistice. Only Britain was left for him to conquer.

Above: The French collapse was due to the paralysis and fear caused by German panzer tactics. Many of the poorly-trained French conscripts surrendered without a fight.

Below: Panzer crews add insult to injury by riding captured French Somua medium tanks – better than most German tanks – in the Wehrmacht's victory parade down the Champs Elysees.

Battle of Britain

It was the world's first purely aerial conflict, and the Luftwaffe's inability to destroy the Royal Air Force would ultimately cost Germany the war.

RANCE, to most Germans, was the most vindictive of the victorious powers of 1918, and the French collapse in June 1940 gave Hitler and his Wehrmacht the victory they most desired. However Britain, now led by Winston Churchill, adamantly refused to accept that she too had lost the war.

Hitler and the German high command knew that it was essential to keep the UK under pressure, initially from the air and then by the threat of a seaborne invasion. On July 16, the Führer issued Directive 16, ordering that plans for 'Operation Sealion' be prepared. Directive 16 stated that "a landing against

England (is) to be prepared and, if necessary carried out". Landings were to be made along the south coast and work began converting large river barges into landing craft.

There was a problem, however. Any invasion forces trying to cross the channel would be at the mercy of the Royal Navy. The first step in dealing with British sea power would be to win air superiority, so the Luftwaffe was tasked with neutralising the RAF. If the RAF could be eliminated, the Luftwaffe could, along with the Kriegsmarine, hold back the Royal Navy long enough for the German ground forces to be ferried across the Channel.

The German air attacks which Churchill was to call the Battle

of Britain did not begin officially for the Luftwaffe until *Adlertag* – Eagle Day – on August 13, 1940. However as early as June 30, Goering issued 'General Directions for the Operation of the Luftwaffe against England'. It defined the primary targets as the Royal Air Force, its airfields and the industries that supported it. On July 11 the *Reichmarschall* announced that convoys in the Channel were a legitimate target, and the Luftwaffe went into action.

STUKAS SLAUGHTERED

However, as the German bombers tried to interdict British shipping, the RAF attacked the bombers, with the previously all-conquering Stuka especially proving vulnerable. A BBC

reporter on the south coast witnessed one of the daylight actions and broadcast a breathless account which was afterwards described as "sounding too much like a cricket commentary".

In June and July, the Luftwaffe launched small-scale raids from bases in the occupied territories of northern France, Belgium and Holland and Scandinavia. These reduced the distance over which the Luftwaffe was to attack, but at the same time the raids allowed the RAF to test their defences before the bigger raids which would inevitably come. What emerged, and was to be confirmed later, was that although the Luftwaffe had the advantage in numbers, the RAF

Height of the Battle
August 15, 1940

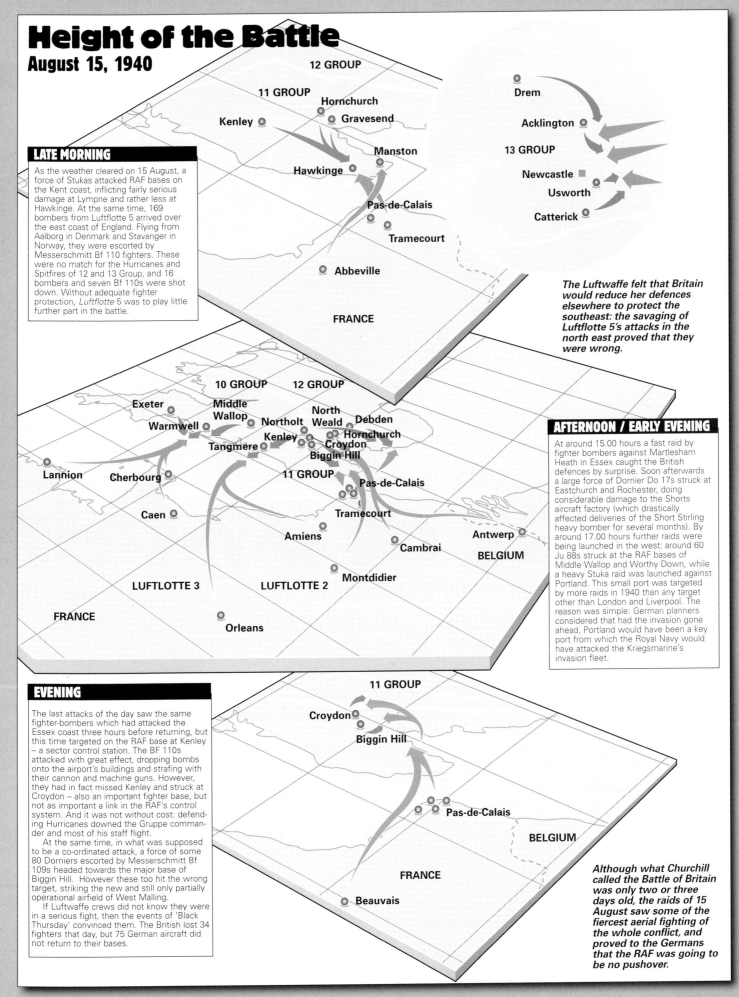

12 GROUP

11 GROUP

Hornchurch
Kenley ·   · Gravesend

Manston

Hawkinge

Pas-de-Calais

Tramecourt

Abbeville

FRANCE

Drem

Acklington ·

13 GROUP

Newcastle ▪

Usworth

Catterick ·

LATE MORNING

As the weather cleared on 15 August, a force of Stukas attacked RAF bases on the Kent coast, inflicting fairly serious damage at Lympne and rather less at Hawkinge. At the same time, 169 bombers from Luftflotte 5 arrived over the east coast of England. Flying from Aalborg in Denmark and Stavanger in Norway, they were escorted by Messerschmitt Bf 110 fighters. These were no match for the Hurricanes and Spitfires of 12 and 13 Group, and 16 bombers and seven Bf 110s were shot down. Without adequate fighter protection, *Luftflotte* 5 was to play little further part in the battle.

The Luftwaffe felt that Britain would reduce her defences elsewhere to protect the southeast: the savaging of Luftflotte 5's attacks in the north east proved that they were wrong.

10 GROUP   **12 GROUP**

Exeter
Middle Wallop
Warmwell   Northolt   North Weald   Debden
Kenley   Hornchurch
Croydon
Tangmere   Biggin Hill

11 GROUP

Lannion   Cherbourg

Pas-de-Calais

Caen

Tramecourt

Amiens   Antwerp

Cambrai   **BELGIUM**

Montdidier

LUFTLOTTE 3   **LUFTLOTTE 2**

FRANCE

Orleans

AFTERNOON / EARLY EVENING

At around 15.00 hours a fast raid by fighter bombers against Martlesham Heath in Essex caught the British defences by surprise. Soon afterwards a large force of Dornier Do 17s struck at Eastchurch and Rochester, doing considerable damage to the Shorts aircraft factory (which drastically affected deliveries of the Short Stirling heavy bomber for several months). By around 17.00 hours further raids were being launched in the west: around 60 Ju 88s struck at the RAF bases of Middle Wallop and Worthy Down, while a heavy Stuka raid was launched against Portland. This small port was targeted by more raids in 1940 than any target other than London and Liverpool. The reason was simple: German planners considered that had the invasion gone ahead, Portland would have been a key port from which the Royal Navy would have attacked the Kriegsmarine's invasion fleet.

11 GROUP

Croydon

Biggin Hill

Pas-de-Calais

BELGIUM

FRANCE

Beauvais

EVENING

The last attacks of the day saw the same fighter-bombers which had attacked the Essex coast three hours before returning, but this time targeted on the RAF base at Kenley – a sector control station. The BF 110s attacked with great effect, dropping bombs onto the airport's buildings and strafing with their cannon and machine guns. However, they had in fact missed Kenley and struck at Croydon – also an important fighter base, but not as important a link in the RAF's control system. And it was not without cost: defending Hurricanes downed the Gruppe commander and most of his staff flight.

At the same time, in what was supposed to be a co-ordinated attack, a force of some 80 Dorniers escorted by Messerschmitt Bf 109s headed towards the major base of Biggin Hill. However these too hit the wrong target, striking the new and still only partially operational airfield of West Malling.

If Luftwaffe crews did not know they were in a serious fight, then the events of 'Black Thursday' convinced them. The British lost 34 fighters that day, but 75 German aircraft did not return to their bases.

Although what Churchill called the Battle of Britain was only two or three days old, the raids of 15 August saw some of the fiercest aerial fighting of the whole conflict, and proved to the Germans that the RAF was going to be no pushover.

Above: A flight of Messerschmitt Bf 109s heads across the English Channel. The relatively short range of the 109 was a serious handicap to the Luftwaffe, limiting the numer of targets which escorted bombers could attack.

had some advantages as well.

On July 19 Hitler directed a speech in the Reichstag at Britain. Dubbed 'The Last Appeal to Reason', he said, "If we do pursue the struggle, it will end with the complete destruction of one of the two combatants. Mr Churchill may believe that it will be Germany. I know it will be England". The speech was translated and dropped as leaflets over Britain

Since there was no positive political response from the British government, the orders were given to launch Eagle Day on 13 August, though the first heavy attacks began the day before, on 12 August. Among the targets was the important radar station at Ventnor on the Isle of

Wight, which was put out of action. On the 13th the weather was poor and, though some squadrons took off, it was not the planned mass assault.

It was not until the 15th that the three *Luftflotten* attacked in concert, putting 2,000 aircraft over Britain, with raids of between 100 and 150 aircraft crossing the Channel all through the afternoon.

During the air operations both the RAF and the Luftwaffe overestimated their victories –

understandable in the confusion of a dogfight, when two pilots attacking from different sides might both claim the same aircraft as a 'kill.' The huge figures of enemy losses were undoubtedly good for morale, but were not the basis for sound planning. Similarly, bomb damage to airfields, which could look spectacular in aerial photographs, was often relatively superficial. Luftwaffe planners took such intelligence at face value, however, and thought that

the RAF had been hurt more than in fact it was. Luftwaffe commanders now believed that the RAF had only 300 front line aircraft, and they decided to go all-out to destroy Fighter Command once and for all.

Small groups of bombers flew to Britain as bait to draw up the RAF fighters. As Spitfires, Hurricanes and Bf 109s tangled across the summer skies, more bombers slipped through, hitting key targets including airfields at Biggin Hill, Hornchurch, North Weald and West Malling. RAF losses started to climb and were now close to matching those of the Luftwaffe.

RAF REPRIEVED

However, just as they were close to achieving their operational goal, the Germans switched their attacks to the cities of Britain, notably London. Why the Luftwaffe high command took the pressure off the RAF is still disputed. They might have been convinced that they had broken the back of the Brtish fighter force. An alternative explanation is that a night raid on Berlin by the RAF on August 25 may have enraged Hitler and prompted retaliation. The RAF raid was itself a retaliation for the actions of a Luftwaffe bomber crew which jettisoned its payload over the East End of London.

German air attacks against British cities began on September 7 with daylight raids on London. Carried out by 300 bombers with 600 escorting fighters, these initially enjoyed considerable success – mass incendiary raids caused huge fires around the London docks. On 15 September, the Luftwaffe abandoned its usual practice of sending diversionary attacks to confuse radar and ground controllers – possibly believing that the RAF was a spent force. But the British were waiting.

The respite from attacks had

Left: A Bf 109E-3 flown by Adolf Galland, one of Germany's greatest fighter aces who commanded a Gruppe of JG 26 during the Battle of Britain.

The Dogfighters
Low-wing monoplanes struggle for air superiority

Messerschmitt Bf 109E-3
9 Staffel JG 26, Caffiers,
August 1940

In the Messerschmitt Bf 109 the Germans had an excellent single seat fighter. Very fast, with decent agility and a good climb and dive performance, its only major drawback was its range, which limited it to escort missions over southeast England. Going as far as London meant that its pilots had only a few minutes of combat time before having to turn for home.

Supermarine Spitfire Mark 1
No.74 Squadron, Manston, June 1940

The Spitfire was the best British fighter of its time. A good match for the Bf 109, it was a little more manoeuvrable, but could not accelerate in a dive as quickly. Its eight machine guns could put out a lot of rounds, but they lacked the sheer stopping power of the Bf 109's 20-mm cannon. This Spitfire Mark I was flown by Flight Lieutenant Adolph 'Sailor' Malan during the early part of the Battle of Britain. The South African-born Malan, a former merchant seaman, was promoted Squadron Leader in August, and was to prove one of the most inspiring RAF leaders of the war.

Hawker Hurricane Mark 1
501 (County of Gloucester) Squadron, Gravesend, August 1940

The Hurricane provided 60 per cent of the RAF's fighter strength in the Battle of Britain. Much slower than the Bf 109, it was nevertheless very agile, and its thick wing made it a very steady gun platform. It was also very tough and could take a considerable amount of combat damage. No. 501 Squadron had been the first Auxiliary unit to be equipped with the Hurricane, and as part of 11 Group in the southeast was intensely involved in the battle against the Luftwaffe.

Luftwaffe strength

Luftwaffe forces were divided into three air fleets: *Generalfeldmarschall* Albert Kesselring's Luftflotte 2 in eastern France and the Low Countries, *Generalfeldmarschall* Hugo Sperrle's Luftflotte 3 in western France, and *Generaloberst* Hans-Jurgen Stumpff's Luftflotte 5 operating across the North Sea from bases in Scandinavia. The combined force totalled 1,260 long-range medium bombers, about 320 dive-bombers, 800 single-engined and 280 twin-engined fighters and some reconnaissance aircraft. Luftflottes 2 and 3 alone could call on 750 long range bombers, 250 dive bombers, 600 single-engined and 150 twin-engined fighters. However, operating at a greater distance, Luftflotte 5 in Scandinavia was obliged to operate without single-seaters.

Royal Air Force strength

Ranged against the Luftwaffe was RAF Fighter Command, led by Air Chief Marshal Sir Hugh Dowding. Each of the major areas of the country was covered by a fighter Group – 10 Group covered the south-west, 11 Group under Air Vice Marshal Park closest to the enemy in the south-east, 12 Group commanded by Air Vice Marshal Leigh-Mallory was based in East Anglia and the Midlands and 13 Group operated from the north and Scotland. Fighter Command had 900 fighters in the main operational area in 11 and 12 Groups, of which Dowding could commit 600 to action. The RAF were supported by the Chain Home belt of radar stations. Radar was a new invention which had only successfully been demonstrated in 1935. It could detect high-flying aircraft deep into northern France, though at low level (500 feet or 150 metres) it could only range across the width of the Straits of Dover – about 20 miles (35 kilometres). Information from radar intercepts allowed RAF fighters to be scrambled to attack the Luftwaffe before it had reached its targets. ULTRA intercepts of coded German radio signals decrypted at Bletchley Park also gave Dowding a strategic view of German plans and operations, which meant that he was able to conserve pilots and aircraft. Though some of the radio traffic contained routine items like the strength of Luftwaffe squadrons, this helped to build up a picture of the enemy and his losses.

Above: One of the keys to British survival was the sector control centre, which together with good communications allowed fighter controllers to make the most effective use of limited resources.

allowed the Fighter Command to replenish its fighter strength in the south, and the attacks on London gave 11 Group in particular more time to get fighters aloft. Air-Vice Marshal Park was able to get paired squadrons airborne, and Air-Vice Marshal Leigh-Mallory's 12 Group formed even larger formations in what were known as 'Big Wing' attacks. The Luftwaffe was met by massed fighters, and by the close of the day had lost 60 aircraft. Total Luftwaffe losses since September 7 had reached 175 aircraft, all caused by a force they had been told was beaten.

Two days later, as Hitler turned his attention towards the Soviet Union, he postponed Operation Sealion indefinitely. But for RAF fighter pilots and Royal Artillery anti-aircraft gun crews the pressure did not end, as the Luftwaffe switched to

night raids against British cities, especially London. Up to 400 bombers attacked each night until mid-November, weather permitting. Contrary to pre-war theories, the raids, known to the citizens of the UK as the Blitz, did not cause panic, or break the national will.

There was a lull in mid-winter, but the raids restarted in the new year. Luftwaffe bombers also attacked Liverpool, Birmingham, Plymouth and Bristol by night.

Between 19 February and 12 May 1941, the Luftwaffe intensified attacks against London and the Channel ports. Some raids were flown by single fighter-bombers, flying low across the Channel to keep under the British radar cover. Larger raids employed as many as 700

bombers; the intensification of the bombing was to some extent a cover for the German military redeployment eastwards. By 21 May the Luftwaffe had shifted 90 per cent of its forces to eastern Germany, occupied Poland and East Prussia, ready for operations against the USSR.

FACTS AND FIGURES

During their attacks on Britain in 1940 and 1941, the Luftwaffe dropped 54,420 tons of bombs and incendiaries. Though the attacks could hardly be called precision strikes, being primarily aimed at area targets, they killed 40,000 people and injured 86,000. Two million homes were destroyed, of which 60 per cent were in London.

Air losses were grossly exaggerated at the time, but the best postwar estimates are that the Luftwaffe lost 1,294 aircraft between 10 July and 31 October

1940, while the British lost 788. During the night Blitz, the Luftwaffe lost a further 600 bombers, though many of these were due to flying accidents in bad weather. However, by 1941 RAF had become a formidable enemy even at night, with twin-engined radar-equipped night fighters supplemented by radar-controlled searchlights and anti-aircraft guns on the ground.

The Battle of Britain was the first major setback for Germany's armed forces. Even though the British were gravely weakened, they remained implacably opposed to Hitler and the Nazis, and would provide one of the springboards by which Germany would ultimately be defeated. For now, the Luftwaffe's attentions were turned eastwards, while the battle against Britain would shift to the Atlantic and the U-Boats of the Kriegsmarine.

Above: A Bf 109 attacks a Spitfire. Shot-down RAF pilots who survived could be flying within 24 hours or less. Shot-down Germans went straight to the POW camps.

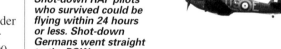

Below: Hawker Hurricanes of No.56 Squadron scramble from North Weald during the Battle of Britain. Although German pilots feared the Spitfire, more Luftwaffe aircraft were destroyed by Hurricanes in the summer of 1940.

Bombers over England
Germany's airborne spearhead in action.

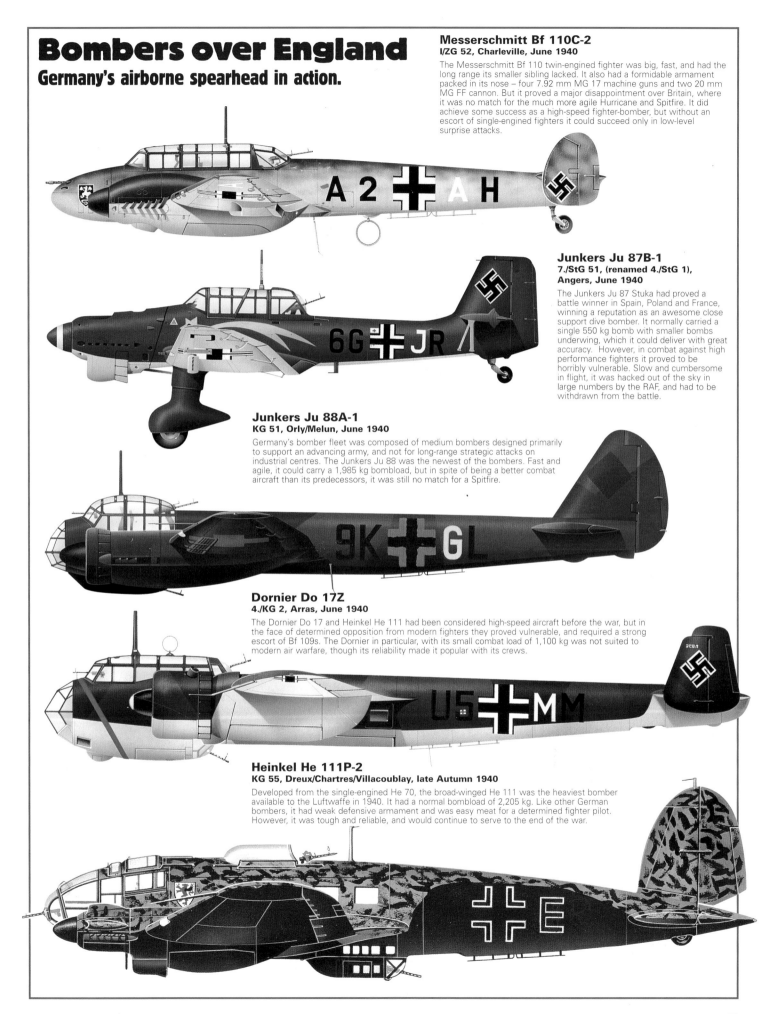

Messerschmitt Bf 110C-2
I/ZG 52, Charleville, June 1940

The Messerschmitt Bf 110 twin-engined fighter was big, fast, and had the long range its smaller sibling lacked. It also had a formidable armament packed in its nose – four 7.92 mm MG 17 machine guns and two 20 mm MG FF cannon. But it proved a major disappointment over Britain, where it was no match for the much more agile Hurricane and Spitfire. It did achieve some success as a high-speed fighter-bomber, but without an escort of single-engined fighters it could succeed only in low-level surprise attacks.

Junkers Ju 87B-1
7./StG 51, (renamed 4./StG 1), Angers, June 1940

The Junkers Ju 87 Stuka had proved a battle winner in Spain, Poland and France, winning a reputation as an awesome close support dive bomber. It normally carried a single 550 kg bomb with smaller bombs underwing, which it could deliver with great accuracy. However, in combat against high performance fighters it proved to be horribly vulnerable. Slow and cumbersome in flight, it was hacked out of the sky in large numbers by the RAF, and had to be withdrawn from the battle.

Junkers Ju 88A-1
KG 51, Orly/Melun, June 1940

Germany's bomber fleet was composed of medium bombers designed primarily to support an advancing army, and not for long-range strategic attacks on industrial centres. The Junkers Ju 88 was the newest of the bombers. Fast and agile, it could carry a 1,985 kg bombload, but in spite of being a better combat aircraft than its predecessors, it was still no match for a Spitfire.

Dornier Do 17Z
4./KG 2, Arras, June 1940

The Dornier Do 17 and Heinkel He 111 had been considered high-speed aircraft before the war, but in the face of determined opposition from modern fighters they proved vulnerable, and required a strong escort of Bf 109s. The Dornier in particular, with its small combat load of 1,100 kg was not suited to modern air warfare, though its reliability made it popular with its crews.

Heinkel He 111P-2
KG 55, Dreux/Chartres/Villacoublay, late Autumn 1940

Developed from the single-engined He 70, the broad-winged He 111 was the heaviest bomber available to the Luftwaffe in 1940. It had a normal bombload of 2,205 kg. Like other German bombers, it had weak defensive armament and was easy meat for a determined fighter pilot. However, it was tough and reliable, and would continue to serve to the end of the war.

Air assault on Crete

The British had been kicked out of Greece, but the German Navy did not have the amphibious capability to get the Wehrmacht onto Crete. So how could the island be attacked and taken?

I T IS HARD now to realise just what a shock it was. To the British forces who were on the receiving end, the airborne attack on Crete in May 1941 was almost like an attack by forces from a science fiction film.

It was a world where fighting men wore buttoned woollen battle dress, leather-soled steel-studded boots and puttees or canvas gaiters, and were armed with bolt action rifles or water cooled machine guns. The Germans, in their zippered jump smocks, high-laced rubber-soled boots, sub-machine guns and automatic rifles, could almost have come from another planet.

Their arrival on the Greek island by glider and parachute was the final, futuristic feature of the battle.

The decision to attack Crete followed from the successful German campaign through Yugoslavia into Greece in the spring of 1941, which had forced the British off the mainland of Europe in a humiliating seaborne evacuation.

THREAT FROM CRETE

For Hitler and his planners, Crete presented a potential problem. Should the RAF base bombers on Cretan airfields, they would be within range of the Romanian oil fields at Ploesti. And Romanian oil was going to be vital to the success of Operation Barbarossa, the massive attack about to be launched against the Soviet Union. Crete would have to be neutralised.

But that was easier said than done. The problem was that though the Axis powers enjoyed

local air superiority, they did not command the sea. The Italian fleet had been severely mauled by the Royal Navy and was in no position to support a major amphibious operation.

However, British warships would not be a factor if the attack came from above, and it was decided to mount a major airborne assault. This was not without its risks. German *Fallschirmjager* had achieved great success in small-unit actions on the Western Front in 1940. But an airborne invasion was a vastly greater challenge.

Unlike most of the major combatants in World War II, whose airborne forces were usually army troops, the elite German airborne units were part of the Luftwaffe. Though this had some operational disadvantages when fighting alongside the Wehrmacht, it

Luftwaffe Fallschirmjäger drop from a Junkers Ju 52 transport. The new plan called for a surprise assault from the air to capture key airfields, after which reinforcements could be flown in.

Above: The original German plan called for a seaborne assault on Crete, which would be supported by paratroopers. But transport would have had to rely on fishing boats and other small craft available in the small Greek ports. In any case, the Kriegsmarine did not have the strength in the Mediterranean to push the Royal Navy aside, and losses among the seaborne invasion force were high.

AIRBORNE PIONEER

In many ways, Kurt Student was the creator of modern airborne forces. Born in in Birkhonz in 1890, he was an infantryman turned pilot during World War I. Between the wars he advised the Reichswehr on aviation, and was sent as an observer to watch Soviet air exercises, during which he saw paratroopers in action for the first time. Transferring to the newly-formed Luftwaffe in 1934, he became chief of parachute and glider forces. In 1938, he formed a parachute battalion, and by the outbreak of war he was in command of the world's first airborne division. The 7th *Fliegerdivision* was not used en masse until Crete, but detachments of his *Fallschirmjäger* performed highly successful special operations in Norway, Belgium, Holland, France and in the Balkans.

provided a unique bond between the transport pilots and ground-attack aircrew who supported the paratroopers in combat.

German intelligence about the island and garrison was patchy. They knew that there were about 6,000 British and Greek troops stationed on Crete, but did not know that numbers had been swelled with 27,000 men who had been evacuated from Greece – though most had had to leave their arms and equipment on the mainland.

The men, aircraft and equipment necessary for the assault were scattered all over France, Germany and Greece. There was a lot of message traffic as the force was gathered, and as coded signals passed back and forth, they were intercepted by British ULTRA codebreakers. As a result, Major General Freyberg, the New

> "At dawn on the morning of 20 May, my men heard a new tone in the regular Luftwaffe morning visit: like a swarm of bees, which got louder. They saw a huge fleet of aircraft coming across the sea, and the sky blossomed with parachutes"
>
> **Major-General Bernard Freyburg VC**

Zealander commanding Commonwealth forces on the island, knew the enemy plans in almost the same level of detail as the paratroopers who were about to land. He was able to anticipate them – but only up to a point, since the British intelligence services feared that too much pre-planning might compromise ULTRA. For years after the battle, the Allied explanation of their initial effective reaction to the airborne assault was to say that tactics had been based on a Luftwaffe manual captured during fighting in Holland in 1940.

The assault opened just after dawn on the morning of 20 May, with intensive air raids against Maleme and Canea. The first assault troops to arrive, the spearhead of Group West, were 500 glider troops delivered to the airfield at

Maleme, followed by more than 1,800 paratroopers.

The garrison reacted very aggressively. Many Germans were killed as they floated down on their parachutes; others died struggling out of their harness. Some of the ten-man gliders crashed, killing their passengers. The Germans did manage to achieve a toehold around Canea, and in the dry river bed of the Tavronitis west of Maleme, but they were hard-pressed.

In the afternoon the second wave of 1,500 men from *Fallschirmjagerregiment* 2 (FJR 2) in Group Centre attacking Retimo were effectively neutralised as a fighting force, and 2,000 men of FJR 1 in Group East landing at Heraklion suffered heavy casualties. The survivors of the Retimo drop were reduced to two groups, besieged in a chapel and an olive oil factory.

At the Hotel Grand Bretagne, the Luftwaffe's operational headquarters in Athens, General Student learned that a Ju 52 transport flown by Captain Kleye had managed to land at Maleme, albeit under small arms fire. He decided that reinforcement was a viable risk, but should only be committed to Group West.

FATAL MISTAKE

Two understrength New Zealand battalions, the 22nd and 23rd, covered Maleme and Point 107, the high ground which dominated the airfield. In the confusion of the battle they were convinced that they were being outflanked, and on the night of the 20th-21st pulled back. It was a move that would prove critical to the campaign, since their

withdrawal left Point 107 unoccupied, and fire from that high ground would have prevented the use of the airfield for reinforcement.

During the nights of 21 and 22 May the Royal Navy, directed by ULTRA intelligence, intercepted and sank most of the seaborne elements of the German army mountain division commanded by *Generalleutnant* Ringel. Three cruisers and a number of destroyers made short work of the fishing boats, and the glare of the searchlights and flashes of gunfire could be seen by the soldiers in Canea and Maleme less than 30 kilometres away.

German patrols discovered that Point 107 was undefended at dawn on the 21st and occupied it. With Maleme almost secure, the Germans piled on the pressure. Student

Above: **Fallschirmjäger** *land on Crete. The RZ-16 parachute used by the Germans had no quick-release mechanism, and in windy weather paratroopers were often dragged for long distances.*

Below: Luftwaffe bombers strike at a British-held village as the German paratroopers try to retain their precarious foothold on Crete.

Bottom: **Fallschirmjäger** *move casually through the streets of Heraklion after the withdrawal of Commonwealth forces to the south coast.*

Hit by anti-aircraft fire, a Junkers Ju 52 crashes to the ground. Operation Merkur cost the Luftwaffe more than 220 aircraft destroyed and 158 damaged – most were Ju 52s.

Plan of Attack

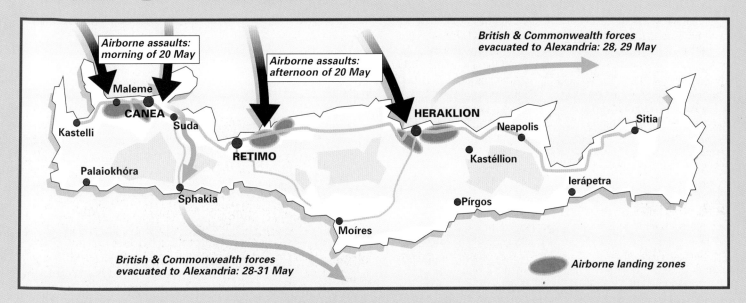

Airborne assaults: morning of 20 May

Airborne assaults: afternoon of 20 May

British & Commonwealth forces evacuated to Alexandria: 28, 29 May

Maleme

CANEA

Suda

Kastelli

Palaiokhóra

Sphakia

Moíres

RETIMO

HERAKLION

Neapolis

Kastéllion

Pírgos

Ierápetra

Sitia

British & Commonwealth forces evacuated to Alexandria: 28-31 May

Airborne landing zones

The German plan of attack involving the paratroops of Fliegerkorps XI was the result of a compromise. *Generaloberst* Alexander Lohr of *Luftflotte* 4, in overall command of the operation, favoured landings around Canea and Maleme in the west and a thrust eastward along the island.

Commanding the paratroopers was *Generalleutnant* Kurt Student, the founding father of German airborne forces. He wanted landings at three points – Canea/Maleme, Retimo in the west of the island and Heraklion in the centre.

The compromise was a two-phase attack, phase one consisting of a drop on Maleme/Canea on the morning of 20 May, with further drops on Retimo and Heraklion in the afternoon.

Balance of forces

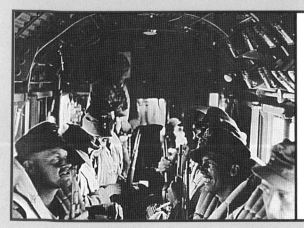

THE ATTACKERS

General Student's *Fliegerkorps* XI comprised *Fliegerdivision* 7 – three parachute regiments each of three battalions with divisional artillery, engineers and signals – and an Airborne Assault Regiment with three parachute battalions and a gliderborne battalion. These could muster a strength of around 8,100 men. *Generalmajor* Conrad commanded the transport element of the corps – nearly 500 Ju 52 transports and 72 DFS 230 gliders.

Air support came from 180 single- and twin-engined fighters, 205 dive-bombers and 228 medium bombers of *Fliegerkorps* VIII, commanded by *Generalleutnant* von Richthofen.

Although mainly a Luftwaffe operation, the invasion relied on the army for follow-up troops. These consisted of the 5th *Gebirgsjager* division under *Generalleutnant* Julius Ringel, whose three mountain rifle regiments and single motor-cycle battalion were to be flown into action once the paratroopers had secured an airfield. Two further battalions of mountain troops would come by sea, with vehicles, AA guns, field artillery and engineers being transported in two lifts aboard 25 and 38 Greek fishing boats respectively, escorted by Italian motor torpedo boats.

THE DEFENDERS

Commonwealth forces on Crete were commanded by the formidable Major-General Bernard Freyberg VC. Troops under the New Zealander's command included the British 14th Infantry Brigade at Heraklion, reinforced with one Greek and two Australian battalions; the 19th Australian Brigade at Retimo, reinforced with two Greek battalions; two Australian battalions as mobile reserve at Suda Bay and Canea, alongside a mixed force of army, Navy and Royal Marine personnel.

The decisive sector proved to be in the west at Galatas, Maleme and Maleme airfield. Here the 2nd New Zealand Division was positioned, with its 10th Brigade around Galatas and two Greek battalions to the south. Astride the so called 'Prison Valley' were the 5th New Zealand Brigade, the 28th Maori Battalion, the divisional engineers acting as infantry and the 21st, 22nd and 23rd New Zealand Infantry Battalions. The understrength 22nd NZ Battalion covered Maleme airfield.

There was limited transport, little anti-aircraft and artillery support and almost no radios for the garrison: even basic defence stores such as barbed wire, sand bags and picks and shovels were in very short supply.

Luftwaffe attacks wreaked havoc during the evacuation. British naval losses were so high – three cruisers and six destroyers sunk and 17 warships damaged – that the evacuation was abandoned on the 30th leaving 5,000 men to be taken prisoner. At Heraklion the Royal Navy was able to evacuate the garrison, but at Retimo, which had put up the most effective defence, they were all taken prisoner. Some of the men who had not been evacuated evaded capture. A few even managed to find craft to cross the 300 km of water to North Africa. Others were evacuated by submarine.

When the fighting was over, unfounded rumours circulated that German paratroopers had been murdered by Cretan civilians. The Cretans suffered a harsh occupation, which began with the execution of 698 men whom the Germans regarded as *francs-tireurs* – civilian snipers. In four months, the occupation forces executed 1,135 Cretans and destroyed four villages.

committed his last reserve of 1,880 parachute troops into Maleme. Nearly 2,000 mountain troops were landed on the 22nd, and by the 23rd the total had reached 3,650.

On the 22nd, the paratroops and men of the Mountain Division started to push eastwards to link up with their comrades at Canea. Under constant air attack, the British and Commonwealth garrison began to pull back.

BRITISH EVACUATION

With victory snatched from his grasp, General Freyberg realised reluctantly that he would have to order the evacuation of Crete. The only viable port for the Royal Navy to evacuate troops from around Canea and Maleme was the tiny fishing village of Sphakia

on the south coast. But by now the Germans held the village of Galatas on the road south.

On the 25th Colonel H. K. Kippenberger tasked two companies from the New Zealand 23rd Battalion with the mission of clearing the village. The two companies found their numbers swelled by individuals and groups who were eager for revenge against the Germans. New Zealand, Australian and British troops who only a few days earlier had had the enemy on the run were determined to prove they could do it again. Yelling a Maori haka, or war song, and supported by two light tanks, the men charged into the village and drove the Germans out, clearing the road south. Men began the long climb over the Cretan mountain spine to Sphakia.

The town of Heraklion burns after a heavy attack by German Stukas and medium bombers.

The cost of Crete

Although large numbers of British and Commonwealth troops were rescued from Crete, several thousand could not reach the evacuation points. Most were taken prisoner.

British and Commonwealth losses were 1,742 killed and missing, 2,225 wounded, with 11,370 captured. The Royal navy lost 2,000 men killed and 183 wounded.

However Crete was a Pyrrhic victory for the Germans. They lost more than 4,000 killed or missing and over 2,500 wounded. The bulk of the casualties were paratroopers, who suffered near 50 percent losses. Of the 500 Ju 52 transport aircraft employed over half were destroyed.

Faced by these casualties Hitler announced to Student that "the day of the parachutist is over. The parachute arm is a surprise weapon and without the element of surprise there can be no future for airborne forces".

Left: Mountain troops patrol on Crete after its capture. The Germans did not have an easy time on the island: resistance was fierce, and the people were treated with great brutality.

German air supremacy cost the Royal Navy many ships. Wrecked British ships litter the anchorage at Suda Bay, with the heavy cruiser HMS York in the background.

Desert

In many ways, the North African campaign was a sideshow for the Germans. But it was in the desert sands that the first missteps in Germany's march to triumph were to be made.

HITLER'S MOST implacable enemy, Winston Churchill, recognized the Nazis for what they were long before other British political leaders. He sensed the evil at the heart of Nazism; that it was not just another right-wing regime, but a deadly threat to the civilized world. All the more remarkable then, that Churchill, speaking in the Commons, once described one of Hitler's favourite commanders as 'a very daring and skilful opponent... and, may I say across the havoc of war, a great general'. The officer he praised then is probably the only one of Hitler's officers whose name is still remembered in Britain today. He was Erwin Rommel, the 'Desert Fox', whose Afrika Korps fought British and Commonwealth forces in North Africa from February 1941 to May 1943: over two years of cut and thrust battles, mostly in the Libyan desert, an area aptly described as a tactician's paradise and a quartermaster's nightmare.

ITALIAN DISASTER

The war in North Africa began in earnest on 9 December 1940. Italy had shipped some 200,000 men to its colony of Libya, seized from the Turks in 1912. The Italian 10th Army, under General Graziani, assembled near the frontier of Eygpt, then defended by just 40,000 British and Commonwealth troops. To the south-east were another 250,000 Italian troops in Abyssinia (Ethiopia) and Eritrea. At stake was the Suez canal, strategically vital to the British. The 10th Army invaded Egypt in September, but stopped after only 100 km and dug itself into a series of entrenched camps. The canal lay another 500 km to the east.

The British commander-in-chief, General Wavell, retaliated with two divisions, christened the 'Western Desert Force'. Led by Lieutenant-General Richard O'Connor, the 4th Indian division and 7th Armoured division (the 'Desert Rats') launched a five-day raid to put the enemy off balance. It did rather more than that. The Italians collapsed, some 20,000 surrendering in the first 24 hours. They were driven back

War

The German expeditionary force to North Africa was not large, but under the command of Erwin Rommel it was to have an effect out of all proportion to its size.

Right: The German troops in North Africa were veterans, proven in battle. To the British, who had swept far larger Italian units aside with almost contemptuous ease, the fast-moving, hard-hitting Afrika Korps would come as a severe shock.

"In view of the tenseness of the situation, and the sluggishness of the Italian command, I decided to ignore my orders and to take command at the front with my own hands as soon as possible – at the very latest after the arrival of the first German units."

**Generalleutnant
Erwin Rommel
The Rommel Papers**

into Cyrenaica (eastern Libya) and back along the coast road. The British kept going, leap-frogging around the retreating Italians and compelling more to lay down their arms. The port of Tobruk fell on 22 January. By early February the British had reached El Agheila, over 800 km from their startline. Men were exhausted, vehicles run into the ground by the pace of the operation. But for less than 2,000 casualties, the Western Desert Force had taken 130,000 prisoners-of-war, wiping eight divisions from the Italian order of battle.

The fruits of this stunning victory were thrown away. General Wavell decided against a further attack on the Italians, one that might have seen the

surrender of all Libya. British reinforcements were diverted to the doomed intervention in Greece. The 7th Armoured division was withdrawn to refit in Egypt, its place taken by the inexperienced 2nd Armoured division, which had one of its tank brigades sent to Greece. It was at this point that Rommel entered the stage.

ROMMEL ARRIVES

On 14 February 1941 he landed in North Africa to lead a German expeditionary force, rushed across the sea to prevent the total loss of Libya. His orders were to stabilize the situation. But within days, Rommel was planning nothing less than a full-scale counter-attack.

Rommel flew back to Berlin

on 19 March to request permission to attack. It was denied. He attacked anyway, sending the 5th Light division to assault Mersa Brega, just east of El Agheila, The British occupied a 12 km front with one flank resting on a marsh, the other on the Mediterranean coast. What followed set the pattern for the next year. The aggressive and skilful German attack was halted by a very bloody-minded defence, the situation still in the balance by late afternoon. The British infantry and artillery holding the position were exhausted, their opponents equally disorganized. The moment was ripe for an armoured counter-attack, but the British tank commander decided there was too little daylight left and refused to intervene. The British withdrew during the night, enabling the equally battered Germans to pass through the defile and into the open desert. Free to manoeuvre there, Rommel pushed his reinforcements forward. With numerical, and, more importantly, psychological advantage, the Germans surged east. A helter-skelter retreat ensued, British and German units frequently intermingled. With dreadful luck, Lt.-General O'Connor was captured when his staff car ran into a German patrol. This removed the only British general in Africa who had shown a flair for armoured warfare. One who had not, the CO of 2nd Armoured, was captured too when the garrison of Mechili surrendered. Only the commander of the 9th Australian division escaped the prison cage.

Rommel's headlong advance recovered all the territory lost by the Italians. He was soon talking to his staff about Egypt and the Suez canal. However, before we examine his first attack in that direction, the so-called 'dash to the wire', it is worth noting that the Axis forces in North Africa remained under Italian command until early 1943. Rommel was a corps and latterly army commander, but the superior officer in Africa was Italian. The majority of Rommel's troops were Italian. Most of their supplies came from Italy in Italian ships. And there was the problem. The Royal Navy attacked the Italian convoys with merciless professionalism, cruiser and destroyer squadrons sortieing from Egypt, submarines from the island of Malta which lay conveniently astride the convoy routes. By the end of

Above: A German 10.5-cm light field howitzer fires on Australian positions around Tobruk during Rommel's first offensive. The capture of the strategically-located port became something of an obsession with the German commander.

Below: Italian infantrymen advance, covered by an Autoblinda 41 armoured car. Although the Italian army had been smashed by the British at the beginning of the campaign, its best units were to prove effective under Rommel's capable direction.

Italian disaster 13 Sept 40 - 7 Feb 41

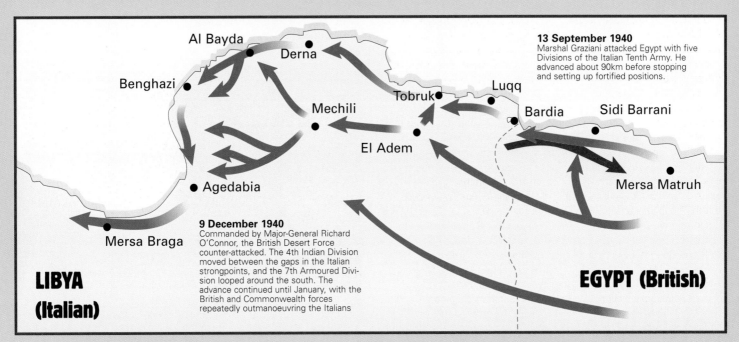

13 September 1940
Marshal Graziani attacked Egypt with five Divisions of the Italian Tenth Army. He advanced about 90km before stopping and setting up fortified positions.

9 December 1940
Commanded by Major-General Richard O'Connor, the British Desert Force counter-attacked. The 4th Indian Division moved between the gaps in the Italian strongpoints, and the 7th Armoured Division looped around the south. The advance continued until January, with the British and Commonwealth forces repeatedly outmanoeuvring the Italians

LIBYA (Italian)

EGYPT (British)

Map labels: Al Bayda, Derna, Benghazi, Mechili, Tobruk, Luqq, Bardia, Sidi Barrani, El Adem, Mersa Matruh, Agedabia, Mersa Braga

ITALY INVADED EGYPT on 13 September, 1941, but without any great verve. By December they had penetrated a few miles over the border, but were not ready for the British counterattack which came on 9 December. Outnumbered three to one, the British smashed the Italians in just four days: for just 600 casualties they had captured almost 40,000 soldiers, 240 guns and 70 tanks. Keeping up the momentum, they swept through Cyrenaica. In a ten week campaign, 31,000 British troops inflicted 38,000 casualties on the Italians, and captured 130,000. If Mussolini's army was to survive, it would need help from Germany.

Rommel's riposte 31 Mar 41 - 15 May 41

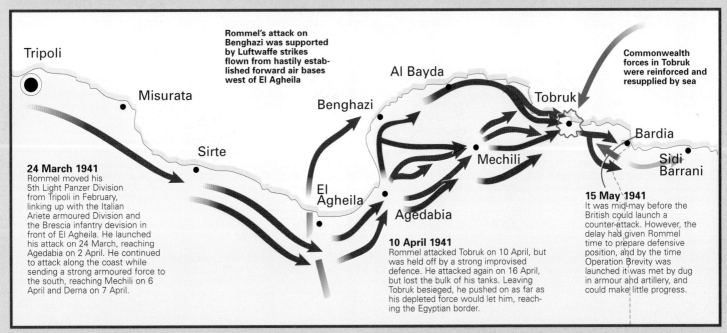

Rommel's attack on Benghazi was supported by Luftwaffe strikes flown from hastily established forward air bases west of El Agheila

Commonwealth forces in Tobruk were reinforced and resupplied by sea

24 March 1941
Rommel moved his 5th Light Panzer Division from Tripoli in February, linking up with the Italian Ariete armoured Division and the Brescia infantry division in front of El Agheila. He launched his attack on 24 March, reaching Agedabia on 2 April. He continued to attack along the coast while sending a strong armoured force to the south, reaching Mechili on 6 April and Derna on 7 April.

10 April 1941
Rommel attacked Tobruk on 10 April, but was held off by a strong improvised defence. He attacked again on 16 April, but lost the bulk of his tanks. Leaving Tobruk besieged, he pushed on as far as his depleted force would let him, reaching the Egyptian border.

15 May 1941
It was mid-may before the British could launch a counter-attack. However, the delay had given Rommel time to prepare defensive position, and by the time Operation Brevity was launched it was met by dug in armour and artillery, and could make little progress.

Map labels: Tripoli, Misurata, Sirte, El Agheila, Benghazi, Al Bayda, Agedabia, Mechili, Tobruk, Bardia, Sidi Barrani

COMMONWEALTH FORCES in North Africa were sadly depleted, in part by men and equipment worn-out in the headlong advance against the Italians, but also by the calls for reinforcements to be sent to Greece and Crete. Since Rommel had only one of his two Panzer divisions ashore, British General Wavell did not expect an immediate attack. However, he did not know Rommel. Seeing the British weakness, Rommel decided to attack. His aim was to recover Cyrenaica and to drive on Egypt. Launching his attack on 23 March, he recovered most of the British gains in a lightning month-long campaign.

Above: A British Vickers light tank speeds across the desert. North Africa placed unique demands on weapons and machinery, and both the British and the Germans struggled to keep armour serviceable.

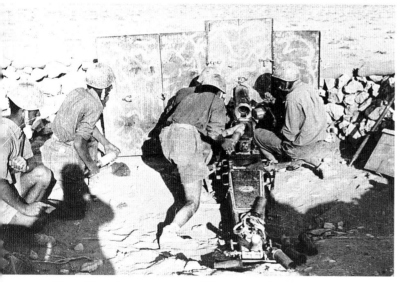

Above: The wide open spaces of the desert offered almost perfect tank warfare terrain, but they also gave anti-tank gunners like these Italians the chance to engage the enemy at maximum range.

Below: British prisoners taken in North Africa. The desert war was generally fought in a chivalrous manner, with both sides respecting their opponents and treating their captives honourably.

1942 Italy had hardly a merchant ship left in service; the rest were on the bottom of the Mediterranean.

Much as they would like to, German commanders could not simply override their Italian allies. Under Rommel's leadership several Italian divisions, notably the Ariete armoured division and Trieste motorized division fought extremely well. (Ironically, as he joked to their officers on more than one occasion, Rommel won his *Pour le mérite* against the Italians at Longarone in 1917). But there was no doubting a general lack of enthusiasm for the war among Italian conscripts.

The desert war was unusual in many respects. There were few cities, few obstacles to the rapid movement of mechanized forces. Armies required vast quantities of petrol and water. Supplies of fresh vegetables and fruit were scarce for both sides. Rommel insisted on eating the same rations as his men and his health steadily deteriorated as a result. His officers fell by the wayside too. The future General-major von Mellethin served on the staff of *Panzergruppe Afrika* until evacuated with amoebic dysentery late in 1942.

HOT DAYS, COLD NIGHTS

Daytime temperatures were often more than 110°F. Nights were always bitterly cold and winter days often far from the popular image of the desert war: O'Connor's men fought their final battles in January 1941 wearing thick army greatcoats. The great British counter-offensive that ended 1941 began in a rainstorm that caused extensive flooding along the battlefront. Yet if the climate was unforgiving, the conventions of the desert war harked back to more civilized days. Rommel was a star in the Nazi propaganda machine, yet had no time for the ideology of the *ubermensch*. There were no SS units in Africa, no murdering *einsatzgruppen,* and the civilian population, such as it was,

consisted of Arab nomads, often well disposed to the Germans.

Rommel's forces reached Tobruk on 10 April, but a hastily-organized assault was beaten off by the largely Australian garrison. The commander of the newly-arrived 15th panzer division was ambushed and killed when he drove into what was thought to be an abandoned enemy position. Rommel's offensive attracted the interest of the General Staff, which despatched *Generaloberst* Friederich Paulus to investigate. He was not impressed, describing Rommel as 'headstrong' and highlighting the danger that what had begun as a sideshow could become a major drain on resources just as the invasion of Russia was about to begin.

BRITISH ATTACKS

Arguments about German offensive aims in Africa were rendered academic by a succession of British attacks. In May, General Wavell launched 'Operation Brevity' which was defeated. In June they tried again, this time reinforced with nearly 300 new tanks shipped from England. 'Operation Battleaxe' showed Rommel and the Afrika Korps at their best. British armoured units tried to seek out and engage Rommel's armour in a tank v. tank battle. But the Germans made masterful use of their towed anti-tank guns, firing from well concealed positions and inflicting terrible losses before the panzers wheeled in from a flank to finish the business.

TANK DESTROYERS

The Luftwaffe's 8.8-cm anti-aircraft guns were pressed into service in the ground role since the army's standard 3.7-cm weapon could not penetrate British 'infantry' tanks, the Matilda and Valentine. It speaks volumes that the British had a similar weapon available, the equally high velocity 3.7-in (93-mm) anti-aircraft gun; but lack of imagination and inter-service squabbling prevented them from

The Desert Fox

Rommel, like other German Panzer commanders, was not content to sit in his headquarters far to the rear. He preferred being well forward, relying on radio communications to keep up with the big picture. While undoubtedly good for the morale of the men that he led, most military historians now consider that for all of his brilliance that command style was a weakness which hindered control of his widely dispersed forces.

ERWIN ROMMEL was young for his rank, and had never served on the General Staff. As a result, he was not really trusted by the staff officers who ran the German army. He had originally trained as an infantryman, with little armoured experience before commanding the 7th Panzer Division in the French campaign. But from his earliest days he had been an apostle of the doctrine of speed and manoeuvrability, and his mastery of small unit infantry tactics quickly became a mastery of mobile warfare on a larger scale.

It was obvious to the new German commander that mobility was even more vital in the desert than it had been in France. Leading from the front, he launched his first offensive little more than a month after first setting foot in Tripoli, and he caught General Wavell and the overextended British and Commonwealth forces completely by surprise. It would not be the last time he would do that.

Below: Rommel confers with senior Italian officers at the British strongpoint of Tobruk. Rommel decided to bypass and isolate the port in his first offensive – a mistake which he would take more than a year to rectify.

using it the way the Germans employed their '88'.

In three days' fighting, designated the battle of Sollum by the Germans, the Afrika Korps demonstrated its superior leadership and vastly better staffwork. Wavell was sacked and replaced by General Auchinleck, who was pressed by London to renew the attack and relieve Tobruk, still besieged by the Axis forces. Both sides sent reinforcements, but Germany had little to spare as the invasion of the USSR was now in full swing. Rommel developed jaundice in August, but soldiered on, his forces now designated *Panzergruppe Afrika*.

TARGET: TOBRUK

Under his command were two panzer divisions, the 15th and 21st (formerly the 5th Light division) and the Afrika division (later, the 90th Light division) assembled from various other units. The Italian XX Armoured Corps (Ariete and Trieste divisions) and XXI Corps (four non-motorized infantry divisions) plus the Savona division gave Rommel a total of ten divisions at his command. Tobruk was the key: by capturing the port, Rommel would get his supplies landed just behind the front, instead of having them driven

hundreds of kilometres of coast road from Benghazi.

Thanks to the ULTRA code-breakers Britain knew all about Rommel's plans for Tobruk. Auchinleck staged his own offensive days before of Rommel's planned assault. On 17 November Rommel's signals staff reported 'complete English radio silence'. He ignored them, and ignored the first reports of a major British attack.

The British Eighth Army under Lt-General Cunningham advanced to relieve Tobruk, its powerful tank force surging across the desert to find and destroy the German armour. On 19 November, the key airfield at Sidi Rezegh was overrun by British tanks. Rommel was

reluctant to abandon his own attack on Tobruk, but when he reacted, he did so with his usual vigour. Fighting raged around Sid Rezegh until 23 November, both sides manoeuvering aggressively in the open terrain. There was no real frontline. Both sides had headquarters units and supply columns taken by surprise by enemy tanks. Both sides suffered heavily, but had only a hazy idea of enemy losses. In such a battle, psychological strength is a priceless asset.

On 24 November Rommel struck out behind the British, heading for the Egyptian frontier rather than beat back the British assault along the coast road that was poised to relieve Tobruk. Cunningham, who had only

narrowly avoided capture in the chaotic battle, was sacked by Auchinleck who placed his own chief-of-staff, Lt-General Ritchie in command of the Eighth Army. Rommel's 'dash to the wire' failed to relieve the small garrisons left in the wake of the British advance; his own staff regarded it as premature, and it was ended by *Oberstleutnant* Westphal at Rommel's HQ who ordered the 21st panzer division back to Tobruk on his own initiative. Rommel remained out of touch for several days, as he raced around the battlefield micro-managing the operation.

SETBACK FOR ROMMEL

Rommel admitted defeat and fell back towards Gazala. Tobruk was relieved and by the end of the year the Germans had abandoned Benghazi again. The situation seemed a repeat of nine months earlier: the victorious British scattered and disorganized after a long advance, the enemy pushed back deep into his own territory. But, it would soon be shown, the Afrika Korps had recoiled like a spring.

By January 1942 it was ready to be unleashed. The 'Benghazi handicap', as some wags had dubbed it, was not over yet.

Heavily armoured British Valentine tanks burn after being engaged by German 'Eighty-Eight' flak guns.

Vehicles of the Afrika Korps

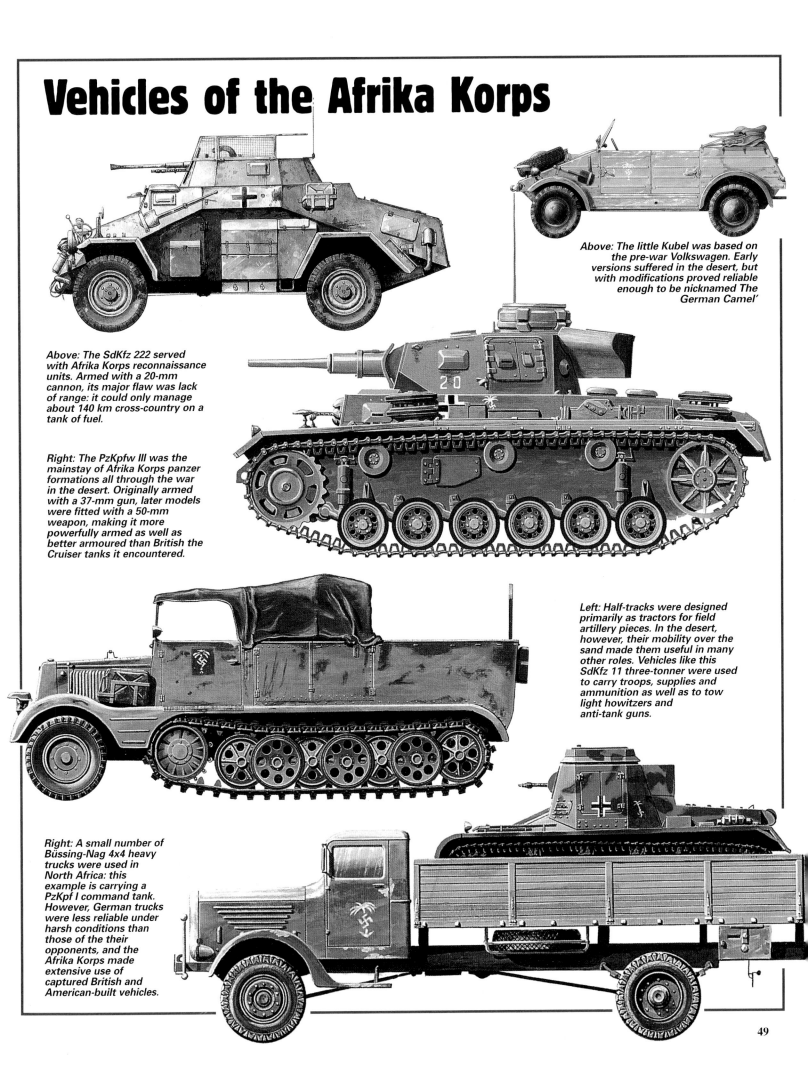

Above: The little Kubel was based on the pre-war Volkswagen. Early versions suffered in the desert, but with modifications proved reliable enough to be nicknamed The German Camel'

Above: The SdKfz 222 served with Afrika Korps reconnaissance units. Armed with a 20-mm cannon, its major flaw was lack of range: it could only manage about 140 km cross-country on a tank of fuel.

Right: The PzKpfw III was the mainstay of Afrika Korps panzer formations all through the war in the desert. Originally armed with a 37-mm gun, later models were fitted with a 50-mm weapon, making it more powerfully armed as well as better armoured than British the Cruiser tanks it encountered.

Left: Half-tracks were designed primarily as tractors for field artillery pieces. In the desert, however, their mobility over the sand made them useful in many other roles. Vehicles like this SdKfz 11 three-tonner were used to carry troops, supplies and ammunition as well as to tow light howitzers and anti-tank guns.

Right: A small number of Büssing-Nag 4x4 heavy trucks were used in North Africa: this example is carrying a PzKpf I command tank. However, German trucks were less reliable under harsh conditions than those of the their opponents, and the Afrika Korps made extensive use of captured British and American-built vehicles.

Battle of the

The most critical battle of the war took place not on the European mainland but across thousands of miles of ocean, as Germany tried to strangle the supply lines to Britain.

HITLER'S 'Z-PLAN', the Nazis' insanely ambitious naval construction programme, called for a fleet of 250 submarines by 1943. But this was not the main striking force: the Kriegsmarine was to have two squadrons of giant battleships, armoured behemoths capable of destroying any other warship in the world. Kapitän z.S. Karl Dönitz, Führer der Uboote, despaired. The High Command's obsession with battleships delayed his submarines and was, in his view, irrelevant. Dönitz believed that the new submarines developed in the 1920s offered a realistic prospect of blockading Britain. He had served in submarines

during World War I, ending his war in command of UB-68 which was sunk in action with an Allied convoy off Sicily. Dönitz was given command of Germany's first post-war submarine flotilla in 1935 and set about training a new U-boat fleet that could succeed where his generation had – by a narrow margin – failed.

BUILDING PROGRAMME

Hitler was still lying to his naval commanders as late as the summer of 1939, telling Admiral Raeder that there was little danger of war. The Kriegsmarine's building schedule was based on the assumption that peace would continue until the mid-1940s. When Britain and France declared war in

September 1939 the great surface fleet had yet to be built. And Dönitz, promoted to Konteradmiral (Rear-Admiral) and BdU (Befehlshabers der Uboote – Commander-in-Chief submarines) had only 46 operational submarines of which more than half were the coastal 'ducks' (Type IIs) primarily used for training.

Most Allied merchantships sunk by U-boats during World War I were sent to the bottom almost in sight of land. The submarines congregated around focal points – traditional landmarks and the approaches to major ports. Many of their victims were sunk by gunfire on the surface, until the use of 'Q-ships' – merchantmen with hidden guns – led them to rely on

Atlantic

their limited supply of torpedoes. After the war Dönitz thought deeply about how to improve U-boat tactics. Once in control of Hitler's U-boats, he tested the concept of 'wolf pack' attacks: co-ordinated strikes by groups of submarines. Initially he tried 'command U-boats' that would control an operation like the flagship of a battleship squadron; but this proved impractical. Instead, he managed the submarines by radio from his shore-based headquarters. It worked in the Baltic. And in 1939 it worked on exercise in the Atlantic.

While the Royal Navy put its faith in ASDIC (sonar) to locate submerged submarines, Dönitz publicly advocated the technique he had learned in World War I:

a night attack on the surface. In 1939 he published a book, describing these methods, how the small silhouette of a submarine would be hard to see at night, and how the surfaced submarine of the 1930s enjoyed a considerably higher speed than the average merchant ship. No-one in Britain appears to have noticed.

U-BOAT TACTICS

At the outbreak of war, some 3,000 ocean-going merchant ships flew the British flag and another 1,000 coasters plied the waters around the UK: a combined total of 17.5 million tonnes of shipping. The ships were organised into convoys, typically protected by four to six escorts armed with depth-charges.

Britain could not even feed its population, let alone manufacture weapons and fight a war if the flow of imports stopped. If Dönitz's U-boats could win the Battle of the Atlantic, Hitler would win the war.

It was soon apparent that Germany's small surface fleet could not inflict serious damage on the convoys. The heavy cruiser *Hipper* and the battlecruisers *Scharnhorst* and *Gneisenau* snapped up a number of ships on forays into the North Atlantic, but only the 'pocket battleships' were purpose-built for such missions. Scheer's five-month raid sank 16 ships for 100,000 tonnes and like her short-lived sistership *Graf Spee* kept a large number of otherwise unemployed Allied cruisers very busy. The prospect

of a German battleship (or two) getting amongst a convoy kept British naval staff awake at night; but although there were some close shaves, Hitler's big ships failed to land a significant blow. When massacres did occur, it was Dönitz's U-boats putting his pre-war theory into deadly practice. For instance, in October 1940 the convoy SC7 was attacked by a 'wolf pack' including 'aces' Kretschmer, Schepke, Endrass and Frauenheim. Twenty ships went to the bottom in a single night.

The 'aces' were the new heroes of the Nazi pantheon: young, aggressive skippers prepared to attack on the surface and close to point-blank range before firing their torpedoes. The top three, Kretschmer, Luth and Topp sank 121 ships (687,000

Above: Grand Admiral Karl Dönitz had absolute faith in the supremacy of the U-boat. Hitler and the Naval High Command did not listen to him until it was too late.

grt) between them. As with fighter pilots, it was the small number of 'aces' who inflicted most of the damage: the U-boat top-scorers accounted for 70 per cent of sinkings in 1939-41. 'Ace' status required a 'score' of 50,000 tonnes (later increased to 100,000) and was recognised by the award of the Ritterkreuz (Knight's Cross). And as triumphant captains returned to port in triumph, white caps perched at a jaunty angle, their crews were awarded medals too – on the dockside by Dönitz in person. He would continue to greet his men as they made port, through the 'happy time' and into the grim months of 1943 when losses soared to unsustainable levels. Dönitz was an inspiration to the U-boat men, his praise desired, his anger dreaded.

HUNGRY FOR SUCCESS

There was a downside to the 'ace' system of course: it led to the 'sore throat' phenomenon in which skippers took grave risks to get the extra tonnage needed to grace their necks with a Ritterkreuz. Scores were inflated. All eyes were focused on tonnage, the sole measure of success. This was as detrimental to the High Command as to the individual captains. When monthly tonnage 'scores' fell off in the critical mid-Atlantic area, Dönitz dispatched submarines to less well-defended areas, inflicting sudden bursts of damage in the South Atlantic,

Indian Ocean or Caribbean. His tonnage totals revived, but he had failed to address the real issue: the increasing effectiveness of the Allied escorts. The fall of France ushered in what U-boat crews would look back on as the 'happy time'. Based on the Atlantic coast, the submarines no longer had to make the long passage across the North Sea and around Scotland: the number of operational U-boats in mid-Atlantic was increased by about 25 per cent. This compensated for the tantalisingly slow pace of submarine construction. U-boat losses exceeded new production throughout 1940 and by January 1941 there were just 22 boats operational: fewer than the number available in September 1939. From July 1940 until the worsening winter weather – and more numerous escort vessels – began to have effect, the U-boats had a clear run. U-boats sank 520 ships (2.4 million tonnes) by December 1940. They would have sunk considerably more, but German torpedoes were unreliable and the problem not traced until late 1941.

THREAT FROM THE AIR

Airbases in Canada, Iceland and the British west coast enabled RAF Coastal Command to maintain anti-submarine patrols at either end of the convoys' journey. But not in the middle. Once a convoy reached the 'Atlantic gap' it was on its own. Without the threat of aerial attack during the day, the U-boats could assemble in lines up to 12 nautical miles apart; positioned across likely convoy routes, they assembled into informal groups

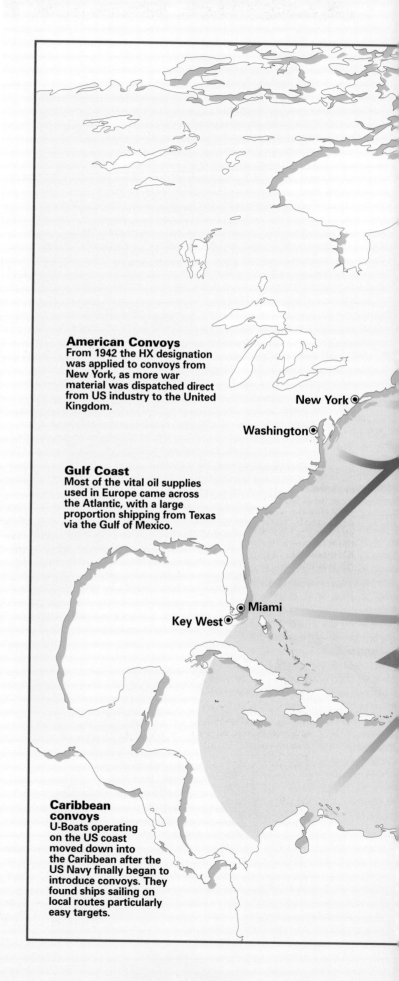

American Convoys
From 1942 the HX designation was applied to convoys from New York, as more war material was dispatched direct from US industry to the United Kingdom.

New York

Washington

Gulf Coast
Most of the vital oil supplies used in Europe came across the Atlantic, with a large proportion shipping from Texas via the Gulf of Mexico.

Miami

Key West

Caribbean convoys
U-Boats operating on the US coast moved down into the Caribbean after the US Navy finally began to introduce convoys. They found ships sailing on local routes particularly easy targets.

Atlantic Battle Zone

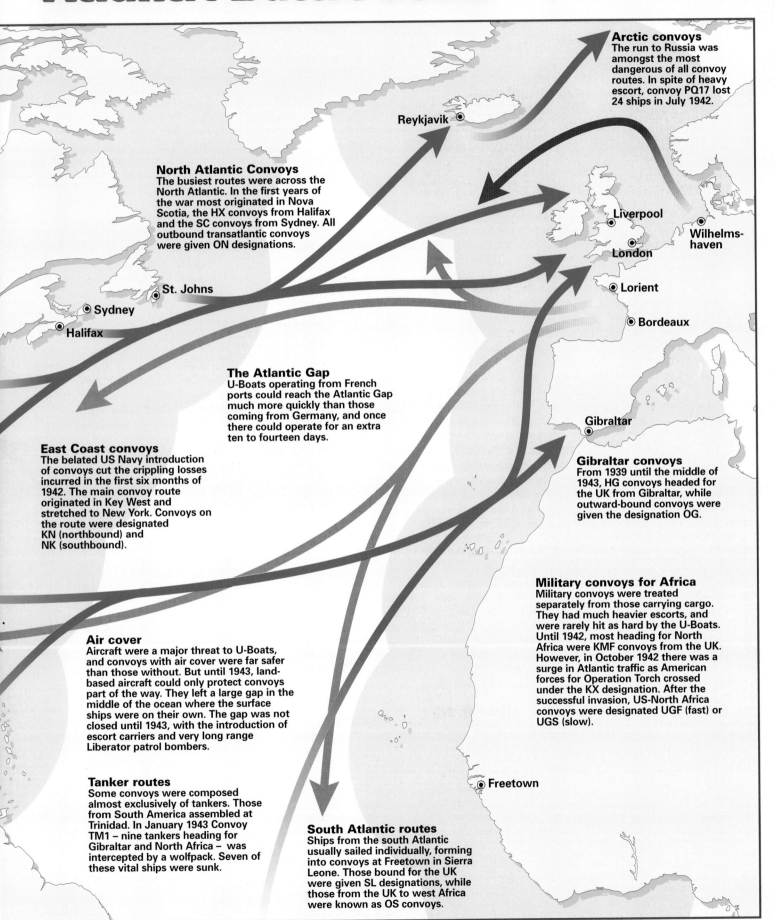

Arctic convoys
The run to Russia was amongst the most dangerous of all convoy routes. In spite of heavy escort, convoy PQ17 lost 24 ships in July 1942.

Reykjavik

Liverpool

Wilhelms-haven

London

Lorient

Bordeaux

North Atlantic Convoys
The busiest routes were across the North Atlantic. In the first years of the war most originated in Nova Scotia, the HX convoys from Halifax and the SC convoys from Sydney. All outbound transatlantic convoys were given ON designations.

St. Johns

Sydney

Halifax

The Atlantic Gap
U-Boats operating from French ports could reach the Atlantic Gap much more quickly than those coming from Germany, and once there could operate for an extra ten to fourteen days.

Gibraltar

East Coast convoys
The belated US Navy introduction of convoys cut the crippling losses incurred in the first six months of 1942. The main convoy route originated in Key West and stretched to New York. Convoys on the route were designated KN (northbound) and NK (southbound).

Gibraltar convoys
From 1939 until the middle of 1943, HG convoys headed for the UK from Gibraltar, while outward-bound convoys were given the designation OG.

Military convoys for Africa
Military convoys were treated separately from those carrying cargo. They had much heavier escorts, and were rarely hit as hard by the U-Boats. Until 1942, most heading for North Africa were KMF convoys from the UK. However, in October 1942 there was a surge in Atlantic traffic as American forces for Operation Torch crossed under the KX designation. After the successful invasion, US-North Africa convoys were designated UGF (fast) or UGS (slow).

Air cover
Aircraft were a major threat to U-Boats, and convoys with air cover were far safer than those without. But until 1943, land-based aircraft could only protect convoys part of the way. They left a large gap in the middle of the ocean where the surface ships were on their own. The gap was not closed until 1943, with the introduction of escort carriers and very long range Liberator patrol bombers.

Freetown

Tanker routes
Some convoys were composed almost exclusively of tankers. Those from South America assembled at Trinidad. In January 1943 Convoy TM1 – nine tankers heading for Gibraltar and North Africa – was intercepted by a wolfpack. Seven of these vital ships were sunk.

South Atlantic routes
Ships from the south Atlantic usually sailed individually, forming into convoys at Freetown in Sierra Leone. Those bound for the UK were given SL designations, while those from the UK to west Africa were known as OS convoys.

Above: Air power was vital in the Battle of the Atlantic. German Focke Wulf Fw 200 Condors enjoyed considerable success early in the war, in spite of the fact that there were rarely more than 12 available for operations. This was because the airframe, designed as an airliner, often suffered catastrophic failure in the stress of combat flying.

Below: The defeat of France gave the Kriegsmarine access to the French Atlantic ports. U-Boats now had a much shorter journey out into the Atlantic, and could stay on patrol 10 days longer. However, the ports were vulnerable to British air attack, and massive concrete bunkers were built to house and protect the U-Boat flotillas.

named after pirates or characters from Norse mythology. One or two U-boats would be nominated as shadowers, reporting to Dönitz's headquarters from where the BdU would co-ordinate the battle. It generated a lot of radio traffic, which would eventually contribute to the submarines' defeat, but until the codes were broken and direction-finding equipment perfected, Dönitz's system worked well.

The Battle of the Atlantic was dramatically changed after December 1941 when Hitler declared war on the United States. Dönitz anticipated his chief's decision, sending five long-range boats to the US coast 48 hours before the declaration.

In some respects this merely formalised an existing state of war in the north Atlantic: US warships had attacked German submarines, provided escorts for convoys, shadowed U-boats with aircraft and surface ships, broadcasting their location to the British, and repaired both merchantships and warships in US harbours. However, Hitler's fatal gesture added the world's greatest industrial power to his enemies. Now Dönitz's men would have to sink merchant ships faster than the whole world could build them.

WAR WITH AMERICA

By the end of 1941 some 153 U-boats had seen action. Forty-nine of them (32 per cent) had been lost, taking 1,322 U-boat men with them; 828 submariners were rescued by the Allies and sent to POW camps. They sank 1,124 merchant ships for a total of 5.3 million tonnes and killed nearly 10,000 Allied merchant sailors. However, the very success of German forces ashore increased the opposition afloat: much of the Norwegian, Dutch and Danish merchant fleets escaped to continue the fight. This added some four million tonnes of shipping, which, together with another two million tonnes of new construction, meant that the Allied merchant fleet grew to over 20 million

tonnes over the same period!

Nevertheless, Britain suffered severe shortages and stringent rationing was required. Imports were approximately 60 million tonnes in 1939, falling to 45 million tonnes in 1940 and just 31 million tonnes in 1941. Priority went to oil and strategic materials: vegetable gardens were dug in the most unlikely places to maximise food production.

CONVOY MASSACRE

After the war, Churchill claimed that the only thing that had really worried him was the Battle of the Atlantic. The genuine fears of the government and the Royal Navy, the universal impact of rationing and horror stories like the destruction of convoy SC-7 created an enduring impression. But impressions can be deceptive. For every convoy massacre, many others reached Britain without serious loss. By December 1941 the British had sailed some 900 convoys: and of 12,000 inbound ships, the U-boats had sunk less than 300. Dönitz's obsession with tonnage painted a misleading picture.

And by this time, the best of the pre-war trained U-boat men were at the bottom of the Atlantic in the shattered hulls of their 'iron coffins'. Few 'aces' enjoyed their glory for long. Endrass was lost in the same month as the attack on SC-7 attacking the Gibraltar convoy HG76. That battle earned Gerhard Bigalk the *Ritterkreuz* for sinking the British escort carrier *Audacity* and Klaus Scholtz received the same for reaching 61,760 tonnes. But it had been a bloody defeat: apart from the carrier, the U-boats claimed only three small freighters from the convoy. Dönitz had lost five U-boats including the much-fêted Endrass in U-567. (One, U-127 had in fact been caught by the destroyer escorts of a Royal Navy task force in the same area.) But whether it was four or five, the U-boats could not afford to lose one of their number for every merchantmen sunk. Germany was losing the Battle of the Atlantic.

DEATH OF THE BISMARCK

Above: At the time of her launch, Germany claimed Bismarck *was a 35,000-tonne ship. In fact, at full load both* Bismarck *and her sister* Tirpitz *displaced more than 50,000 tonnes.*

Below: The Bismarck *and the* Prinz Eugen *refuelled at Bergen fiord before setting off into the Atlantic via the Denmark straight. Despite the stormy, foggy weather the German squadron was picked up on radar by two British heavy cruisers, and the chase was on.*

KMS *BISMARCK* was launched by the Iron Chancellor's great grand-daughter on 14 February 1939. From completion to destruction the huge battleship lasted only nine months, eight of which were spent on training. When she slipped out of the Baltic on 20 May 1941, escorted by the heavy cruiser *Prinz Eugen*, her task was to disrupt the British supply line in the Atlantic.

The Royal Navy was very conscious of the threat, and detailed considerable resources to neutralise her. Initially shadowed by the cruisers *Suffolk* and *Norfolk*, the German squadron was intercepted by the powerful battlecruiser HMS *Hood* and the new battleship HMS *Prince of Wales*.

Hood sunk

The meeting was a disaster for the Royal Navy. The *Hood* was sunk with virtually all hands and *Prince of Wales* was damaged and had to withdraw. No more serious blow was made by German warships to the British navy in the whole of WWII. But *Bismarck* had been hit below the water line, and had lost fuel. Admiral Lütjens, the German commander, ordered *Bismarck* and *Prinz Eugen* to proceed independently to Brest.

In retrospect Lütjens should have returned to Norwegian waters, perhaps polishing off the *Prince of Wales* on the way. He could then have waited until the *Bismarck*'s sister-ship *Tirpitz* was completed. The two massive battleships could then have tried to break out into the Atlantic again.

Although Lütjens succeeded in shaking off the shadowing British cruisers, she was sighted again by a Catalina flying boat on the morning of 26 May. By then she was so far from the British Home Fleet that only a carrier strike could touch her before she reached friendly air cover. Launched from HMS *Ark Royal*, a strike by 15 Swordfish disabled the *Bismarck*'s steering gear.

Unable to steer, the *Bismarck* was attacked mid-morning on the 27 May by the Home Fleet battleships HMS *Rodney* and HMS *King George V*. Within half an hour the German ship had been battered into a ruin by 14-inch and 16-inch shells. The heavy cruiser *Devonshire* was then called in to administer the *coup de grace*.

After taking three torpedoes the *Bismarck* sank by the stern, taking Admiral Lütjens and virtually the whole of her complement of 2,192 men to the bottom.

Right: Bismarck *was armed with eight 38-cm (15-inch) guns. The battleship's broad beam made her a very steady gun platform even in rough seas, and her fire-control equipment was excellent.*

Below: Bismarck *unleashes a broadside against the* Hood. *The old British battlecruiser had thinly-armoured decks, and the plunging German fire soon penetrated her magazines. Within five minutes, the* Hood *had blown up. Three of her 1,400 crew survived.*

Below: HMS Dorsetshire's *torpedoes administered the* Bismarck's *coup de grace. However, British efforts to rescue survivors were aborted after a U-Boat report, and only about 100 of the battleship's crew were picked up.*

U-Boat Aces – The Doomed Heroes

As with fighter pilots, a relatively small number of 'ace' commanders sank a high proportion of Allied shipping. Thirty-two had scores above 100,000 tonnes, the most successful being Otto Kretschmer who sank 44 ships of 266,000 tonnes. A further 53 commanders topped 50,000 tonnes. Between them, these 87 skippers sank more than 1,500 Allied ships totalling eight and a half million tonnes.

There was no one typical kind of U-Boat commander. Some – especially those with pre-war training – were highly professional killers. Others were former merchant seamen who were often equally skilful seamen, but who lacked the Prussian stiffness of the regular navy men. Towards the end of the war, numbers were filled out with young, highly committed Nazis, who in the words of one British officer "were perfectly bloody". Whatever their type, however, few who commanded the 'Iron Coffins' were to survive the war unscathed.

Guenther Prien
Dönitz's favourite commander Prien was a committed Nazi. He sank the battleship *Royal Oak* and his U-47 went on to sink 30 ships of 165,000 tonnes. Prien's boat disappeared on 7/8 March 1941 while attacking Convoy OB 293. It may have been sunk by the British destroyer HMS *Wolverine*.

Joachim Schepke
Trained alongside Prien, Schepke was a more buccaneering type of skipper. After commanding two small Type II boats, he took command of U-100 in May 1940 and sank 37 ships of 156,000 tonnes. Schepke was killed ten days after Prien when U-100 was rammed by HMS *Vanoc*.

Erich Topp
Third highest scoring 'ace', Topp served from the beginning of the war to the end. Most of his 33 kills came while in command of U-552. In 1945 he made the only operational patrol with the advanced new Type XXI boat. He rejoined the Bundesmarine in 1958, retiring in 1969 as a Rear Admiral.

Otto von Bülow
A middle-ranking 'ace', von Bülow transferred to the U-Boat arm in 1940. He commanded U-404 on six patrols in 1942 and 1943, sinking 14 ships of 70,500 tonnes. In 1945 he led a naval assault battalion. After the war von Bülow joined the Bundesmarine, and commanded a destroyer squadron in 1963.

Left: By the end of 1941 effective submarine counter-measures were beginning to take effect, although results would not become obvious until 1943. Aircraft and airborne radar forced the U-boats to submerge, where their performance was limited. By the end of 1942 Dönitz was arming his boats with a large number of anti-aircraft guns, and skippers would often stay on the surface to fight it out.

Below: An American tanker blazes off the mouth of the Chesapeake Bay. It took the US Navy a long time and considerable bitter experience to apply the anti-submarine tactics learned by the British and Canadians in the North Atlantic. Until they did, the U-Boats revelled in a second 'Happy Time'. In the first six months after Pearl Harbor, they sank over 360 ships of 2,250,000 tonnes off the US coast and in the Caribbean.

Surface Raiders

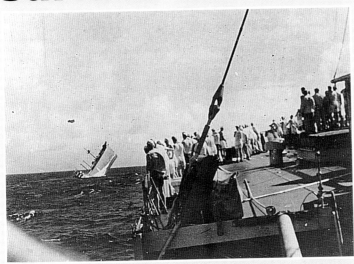

As the war opened the woefully unprepared Kriegsmarine had to fall back on stealth for what it lacked in firepower.

The pocket battleships *Graf Spee* and *Admiral Scheer*, and the heavy cruiser *Admiral Hipper* enjoyed some early successes.

At the same time the Kriegsmarine utilised armed merchant cruisers to even greater effect. These vessels were designed to look like ordinary merchantmen. But their sheep's clothing concealed very heavy weaponry. Their task was to attack merchant vessels sailing individually. In terms of numbers of vessels sunk, their effect was not large and they never threatened Allied command of the seas. But their activities did spread alarm, and forced the Royal Navy to devote considerable resources to tracking them down. They achieved most of their successes in distant waters before the end of 1941.

Whilst the activities of the Kriegsmarine's surface raiders made good copy for the propaganda machine, the German navy was never able to concentrate its capital ships to make a decisive difference, and the piecemeal operations of those raiders had little more than nuisance value.

Above: Convoys were generally used on the North Atlantic, but in more distant waters ships often sailed independently. In the first two years of the war many fell victim to German auxiliary raiders – disguised merchantmen fitted with hidden armament.

Right: The Kriegsmarine's heavy surface units were not ideal for surface raiding, though a few made successful cruises. The heavy cruiser Admiral Hipper, seen here sinking the British destroyer HMS Glowworm during the invasion of Norway, made one fruitless cruise at the end of 1940. In a more successful operation in February 1941, she intercepted a convoy off West Africa, sinking seven ships of 30,000 tonnes.

Right: The 'Deutschland'-class pocket battleships were Nazi Germany's first major warships. Purpose-designed for commerce raiding, the Admiral Scheer and the Graf Spee achieved some success, though the latter's cruise came to a violent end at the Battle of the River Plate.

Below: Too lightly armed to take on a real battleship, the battlecruisers Scharnhorst and Gneisenau had an indifferent war, largely failing in their attempts to harry the Atlantic and Arctic convoys. They had their place in German propaganda, but the Battle of the Atlantic was to be won or lost by the submarine.

Barbarossa
The Invasion of Russia

Panzers and panzergrenadiers of von Kleist's 1st Panzergruppe fight through Zhitomir, in the Ukraine.

Operation Barbarossa, the German attack on the Soviet Union, was the biggest invasion in history. It was designed to give Hitler what he wanted most: *Lebensraum* for the 'Aryan' race.

HITLER'S MOST senior generals were invited to the Berghof at the end of August 1939, on the eve of the invasion of Poland. There, in the tranquil surroundings of the Führer's alpine getaway, they realised the true extent of their master's war aims. "In the East I have put my Death's Head formations in place with the command… to send into death many women and children of Polish origin," Hitler proclaimed, "…Poland will be depopulated and settled with Germans… the fate of Russia will be exactly the same." Some of the generals were shocked by what they heard, but most would later deny any knowledge of Hitler's intentions. Hermann Goering was in no doubt though:

witnesses recorded how he literally danced with glee.

It was to be nearly two years before Hitler could realise his ambition. In 18 months his forces had over-run western Europe, smashing every army that stood in their way. Only Britain held out, for reasons Hitler was still unable to comprehend. But there was nothing to stop Germany now. Defeat Russia, and the European land mass would become the new German Empire; Britain would have to make peace.

Invasion

On 22 June 1941 Hitler launched the greatest invasion in military history: three million German and Axis troops attacked the Russian border from the Baltic coast to the Romanian frontier.

His forces included over 150 divisions, including 19 panzer divisions, 1,945 German aircraft and another 1,000 Axis planes. They faced some three million men of the Red Army, which had another million soldiers deployed across southern republics of the USSR and in the Far East where they had recently beaten the Japanese in a series of border clashes. This obscure battle in Manchuria, won by an unknown commander called Georgi Zhukov was little noticed at the time. It was the Red Army's recent dire performance in Finland that attracted comment: the 1939-40 'winter war' had been an unmitigated disaster that cost the lives of some 200,000 Russian soldiers. Against the hopelessly outnumbered Finnish army, the Red Army appeared to

be no better than the Tsar's hapless army of 1916 – brave soldiers sent to their deaths by incompetent, politically-appointed generals.

The Russians were taken by surprise. Stalin was determined to do nothing that could provoke a German invasion before he had reorganised his forces to meet it. Apparently unable to believe that Hitler would break their cynical alliance so soon, he saw to it that the USSR continued to deliver strategic materials right up to the very night of the attack. A German soldier who deserted on 21 June with news of the attack was interrogated by the NKVD. His story was reported to Stalin who paused, then whispered his familiar instruction into the telephone. The unfortunate corporal was taken outside and

shot.

The Luftwaffe had been overflying Russian airbases for months before the invasion – at least one Russian officer was shot for firing on German photo-reconnaissance planes that blamed 'navigational errors' for their intrusion. Now it scored the greatest victory in its history, wiping out the VVS (Russian air force) in a matter of days. VVS bases were in the process of expansion, so many air regiments were doubled up on the airstrips, aircraft packed together where a single bomb could destroy a whole squadron. If they got into the air, the Russians had neither the skill nor the aircraft to challenge the Messerschmitt Bf 109 and many German fighter pilots began to run up incredible numbers of

victories. German bombers met little opposition, and attacked the endless columns of Russian ground troops that moved here and there with little sign of strategic direction. Indeed, the bombers attacked so successfully that by late summer, Germany was running short of bombs!

The invasion force was

Above: A BA-32 armoured car of the Red Army blazes as the Wehrmacht punches through and destroys Soviet opposition. The Red Army was woefully unprepared for the German invasion, partly because Stalin refused to believe that Hitler would invade, and partly because the purges of the previous three years had slaughtered many of the army's most intelligent and flexible commanders.

Above: A Czech-built Panzer 38(t) speeds through a burning oil facility at Mariepol on the Sea of Azov. This was reached by spearheads of Army Group South in October, cutting off large Soviet forces in the Crimea and in southern Ukraine.

Left: A Panzer IV passes marching German infantrymen in the summer of 1941. Although German equipment was no better than (and in some cases worse than) that used by the Russians, superior German tactics gave them the advantage.

Below: A mortar team engages a Soviet infantry force. At first, the Russians seemed to be easy prey for the Wehrmacht, but ordinary Russian soldiers often proved capable of extraordinary resistance, and by-passed units had to be attacked and nullified.

divided into three army groups. Army Group North started in East Prussia and advanced rapidly through the Baltic States. Its ultimate objective was Leningrad, the former Russian capital, birthplace of the Communist revolution, and a key industrial centre. Army Group Centre was aimed at Moscow, via Minsk and Smolensk, the same route taken by Napoleon in 1812. Army Group South, deployed on a giant arc from southern Poland to Romania, was tasked with occupying the great plains of the Ukraine and southern Russia.

"Before three months have passed, we shall witness a collapse in Russia, the like of which has never been seen in history," Hitler announced on the day of the invasion. "Kick in the door, and the whole rotten edifice will collapse," he told his generals. And he seemed to be right. The German tank forces, organised into four *panzergruppen* broke clean through the frontline and headed unchecked deep into Russia. Whole Russian armies were trapped, as hard-marching German infantry divisions swept on to link up with the tanks, German aircraft pounding anything that looked like a Russian counter-attack.

Red Army ruin

Cut off, with little ammunition or fuel, and often no instructions from Moscow, the Red Army forces along the frontier disintegrated. Army Group Centre's tanks advanced 200 miles in five days, captured Minsk and left the Russian 3rd, 10th and 13th armies surrounded. Some 350,000 Russians surrendered.

The advance of Army Group Centre and an equally rapid sweep into the southern Ukraine by Army Group South created a deep salient around Kiev. The *panzergruppen* peeled off to seal nearly 50 Russian divisions in what became known as the Kiev Pocket. Denied permission to retreat until it was too late, the trapped Russian forces made desperate attempts to break out, their commander dying on a German minefield in the process. Between 500,000 and 650,000 Russian soldiers were captured.

It seemed Russia was finished. In America, President Roosevelt's advisors predicted a German victory in the eight weeks that Hitler had promised. British Prime Minister Churchill received an equally gloomy prognosis from his generals.

OKH, the German army high command was so confident that it reduced its requirement for winter clothing and equipment. It was decided that only enough winter equipment would be needed for a 60-division garrison to keep order in the conquered land.

On 6 September, Hitler decreed that Moscow would be the next objective. Army Group North's breakneck advance had come to a sudden stop as it entered the swampy forests that surrounded Leningrad. Its *panzergruppe* was assigned to Army Group Centre, which now had three-quarters of Germany's tank forces at its disposal. In another giant battle of encirclement, two *panzergruppen* were to bypass Moscow to the north while General Heinz Guderian's *Panzergruppe 2*

The biggest invasion in history

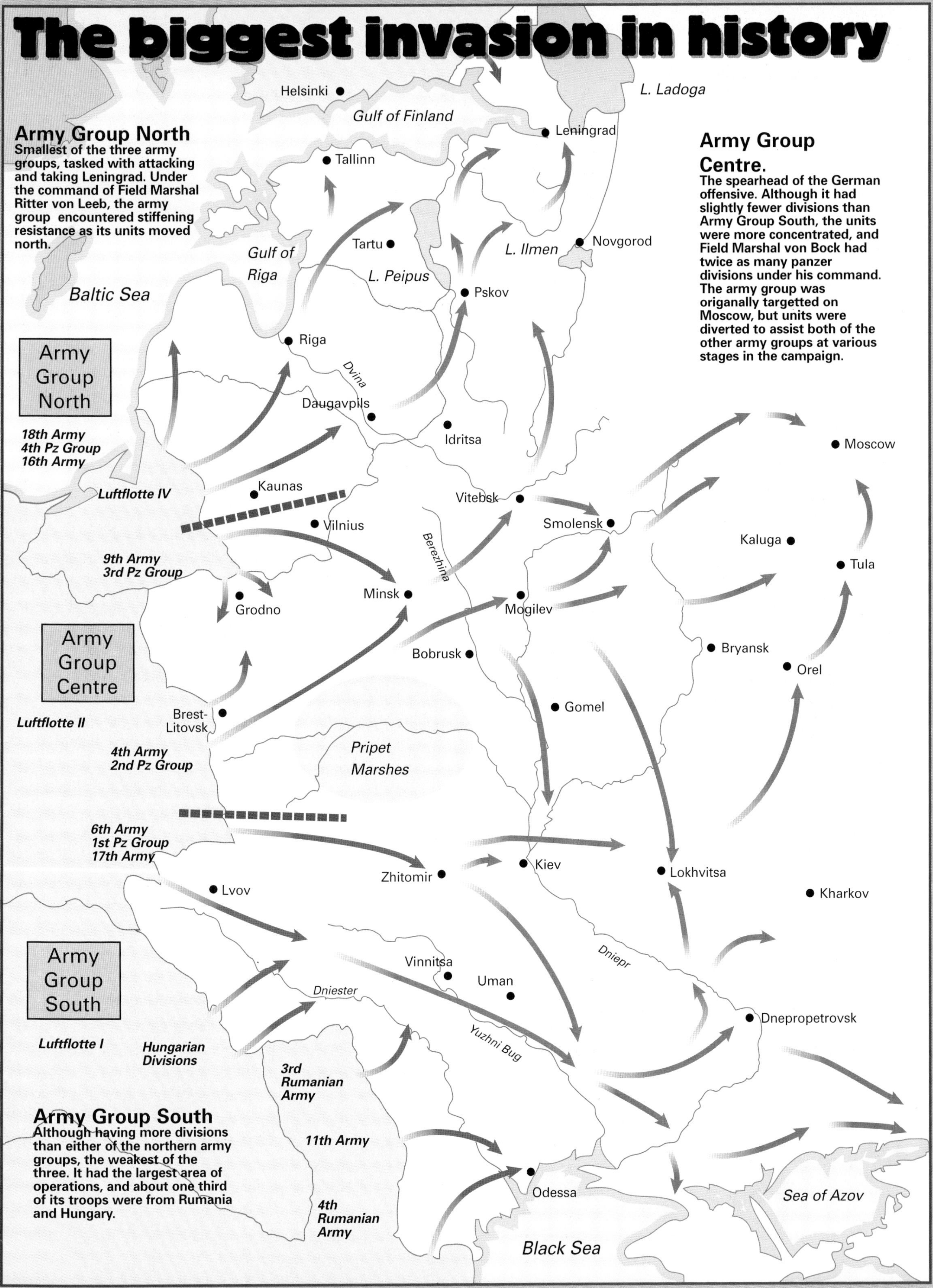

Army Group North
Smallest of the three army groups, tasked with attacking and taking Leningrad. Under the command of Field Marshal Ritter von Leeb, the army group encountered stiffening resistance as its units moved north.

Army Group North

18th Army
4th Pz Group
16th Army

Luftflotte IV

9th Army
3rd Pz Group

Army Group Centre

Luftflotte II

4th Army
2nd Pz Group

6th Army
1st Pz Group
17th Army

Army Group South

Luftflotte I

Hungarian Divisions

3rd Rumanian Army

11th Army

4th Rumanian Army

Army Group Centre.
The spearhead of the German offensive. Although it had slightly fewer divisions than Army Group South, the units were more concentrated, and Field Marshal von Bock had twice as many panzer divisions under his command. The army group was originally targetted on Moscow, but units were diverted to assist both of the other army groups at various stages in the campaign.

Army Group South
Although having more divisions than either of the northern army groups, the weakest of the three. It had the largest area of operations, and about one third of its troops were from Rumania and Hungary.

Helsinki

L. Ladoga

Gulf of Finland

Leningrad

Tallinn

Army Group North

Tartu

L. Ilmen

Novgorod

L. Peipus

Pskov

Gulf of Riga

Baltic Sea

Riga

Dvina

Daugavpils

Idritsa

Moscow

Kaunas

Vitebsk

Vilnius

Smolensk

Kaluga

Berezhina

Tula

Minsk

Mogilev

Grodno

Bobrusk

Bryansk

Orel

Brest-Litovsk

Gomel

Pripet Marshes

Zhitomir

Kiev

Lokhvitsa

Kharkov

Lvov

Dniepr

Vinnitsa

Uman

Dniester

Dnepropetrovsk

Yuzhni Bug

Odessa

Sea of Azov

Black Sea

passed to the south of the city. The tanks would link up east of Moscow, cutting the Soviet capital off from reinforcements and supplies.

Assigned the codename Taifun (typhoon) the German drive on Moscow began on 2 October. The Russians had concentrated huge forces to bar the road to their capital, but these were smashed yet again. In two more great battles of encirclement another 650,000 Russians were captured. The citizens of Moscow sensed which way the wind was blowing: party officials started burning documents and whole government departments were transferred east. BBC correspondent Alexander Werth reported a palpable sense of panic. Then Stalin announced that he would be staying.

There were three reasons why the wily Soviet leader refused to abandon the Kremlin. On 6 October German forces on the Moscow front awoke to find their tanks dusted with snow. Autumnal rains alternated with freezing nights, a seasonal phenomenon known to Russians as the *rasputitza* (lit. 'time without roads'). There were few metalled roads in the USSR, most were wide dirt strips that now dissolved into a sticky quagmire that even tanks were unable to cross. Germans on foot sank past the top of their jackboots. Airfields became unusable and the advance ground to a halt. Stalin's second source of confidence came from his spy ring in Japan where, it was reported, Tojo's cabinet had definitely ruled out an attack on the USSR. Japan would attack America instead. The 750,000 Russian soldiers in the Far East were available to reinforce the depleted Russian forces fighting the Germans. Thirdly, the Red Army was replacing its staggering losses with unbelievable speed: 143 new divisions were mobilised between July and December, and 84 of the divisions destroyed in battle were reconstituted.

Winter arrives

The *rasputitza* lasted for four weeks. Then, on 7 November, the temperature plunged and the liquid mud turned rock hard. The German advance began again with breakthroughs in the south as well as towards Moscow; General von Manstein's 11th Army broke into the Crimea, the great factories of Kharkov were taken, and the Donbass region, heart of Russia's coal and steel industries, was finally over-run. At the end of the month, the 7th panzer division established a bridge-head over the Volga canal. Its advance elements were soon within 12 miles of the city and in the cold, clear winter air the spires of the Kremlin were visible through binoculars.

Daytime temperatures around Moscow varied from -5 to -12°C and the Germans found it increasingly difficult to keep fighting in the same uniforms they had worn through the baking heat of summer. Supplies of every kind were simply failing to arrive at the front, where battalions were reduced to a fraction of their authorised strength, panzer divisions counted themselves lucky to have 50 tanks still running.

Supply logjam

The Russian railways used a wider track than the German rail system, and it took longer than anticipated to convert them. In fact, the German supply network had begun to falter during the great advances of the summer. It proved impossible to sustain the frontline units using the primitive Russian rail and road network. It did not help that the German forces had been filled out with vehicles from all over Europe. There were 2,000 different types in service, with few interchangeable parts; Army Group Centre's spare parts inventory ran to over one million items. By early autumn the Luftwaffe had been forced to ferry its own supplies forward in bombers. Its fuel and other essential supplies were all held up in bottlenecks from Poland to the Smolensk-Moscow highway.

The logistical disaster had actually been predicted by the quartermaster general, Generalmajor Friederich Paulus. In a 1940 wargame he had demonstrated that even if the Germans defeated the Russian army hands-down, it would be unable to supply its forward units properly and the advance would stop of its own accord. Russia could not be defeated in a single campaign like Poland or France.

And now they were facing a new Soviet commander. General Zhukov had risen fast after his success against Japan. One of the

Above: As the Wehrmacht advanced, the number of cut-off pockets of Soviet resistance increased. Although millions of Red Army men had surrendered, those that continued to fight did so to the last bullet.

Below: The Germans received a shock when a new Soviet tank began to appear. The T-34 was more powerful than anything in the Wehrmacht's inventory, and once available in numbers it would be a major threat.

Below: As the Germans pressed closer to Moscow, its citizens began to improvise barricades and tank traps. Had the Wehrmacht managed to get to Moscow, it would have faced a vicious street fight.

SLAUGHTER IN THE UKRAINE

THE LARGEST concentration of Red Army troops lay at Kiev and in the area immediately to the north. On 24 August Hitler ordered Guderian to lead his Panzergruppe down to assist in the occupation of the Ukraine.

By 10 September Stalin was receiving direct appeals from the Soviet commanders, Marshal Budenny and his political commissar Nikita Khrushchev, for permission for their still large forces to be allowed to escape through the rapidly narrowing gap between Guderian and Kleist. Stalin insisted that all armies, all divisions should stand fast where they were.

Guderian's panzers met Kleist's at Lokhvitsa on 15 September and by the evening of the 17th, the biggest encirclement of the campaign – perhaps the biggest in history – had been formed. It was tight, and few caught within could have escaped. Budenny and Khrushchev were flown out, Major-General Bagramyan brought out about 50 men; but most of the senior officers of the South-West Front were killed as they tried to escape, or were rounded up and captured. And with them into graves or prison camps of the most appalling nature went nearly 500,000 Russian soldiers.

Guderian and Kleist were jubilant, Rundstedt modestly gratified that the greatest single success of German arms had been won by the army group under his command. In that atmosphere of heady euphoria, few remarked that for all their triumphs and all the ground won, something had been lost: time.

Above: A Stuka's-eye view of a Soviet column in the Ukraine. With the Red air force all but wiped from the skies, the vulnerable dive-bombers could go about their business in safety, and they wreaked havoc.

Below: German troops were welcomed by Ukrainians, who had suffered under Stalin in the previous decade. But the SS, SD and Einsatzgruppen soon moved in, and potential allies were turned into enemies.

Above: The massive German pincer movement around Kiev trapped four Soviet armies with all of their equipment. Much of it was to be salvaged and used by the Wehrmacht.

Below: At least half a million Russian Soldiers went into captivity at Kiev: most were to die over the next two years after being kept under barbaric conditions with minimal food or medical care.

Hitler's top commanders

Hitler's senior commanders in Russia shared a number of characteristics: most had been in the army since the 1890s and were vastly experienced General Staff officers. They all had hands-on experience in directing large numbers of troops, both before the war and in the Wehrmacht's successful campaigns in Poland and France. They could also call on the abilities of battle-tested subordinates, who had invented and had already proven themselves masters of the new style of warfare known as Blitzkrieg.

Gerd von Rundstedt
Commander of Army Group South, von Runstedt was the senior serving officer in the German Army. Called out of retirement for the Polish campaign, he would command army groups in France and on the Eastern and Western fronts in the war before finally being dismissed in 1945.

Wilhelm Ritter von Leeb
The Bavarian von Leeb commanded the troops in the occupation of the Sudetenland in 1938 and led Army Group C against the Maginot Line in 1940. He led Army Group North in the Russian campaign, before being dismissed in January 1942 for making an unauthorised retreat.

Fedor Von Bock
Bock commanded the troops involved in the Anschluss with Austria and went on to command Army Groups in Poland, France and on the Eastern Front. He was dismissed in 1942 for disagreeing with Hitler's plans to mount simultaneous attacks on Stalingrad and in the Caucasus.

Heinz Guderian
Guderian did not hold an Army Group command, but as Germany's leading armoured expert he had immense influence. His Panzergruppe headed the Wehrmacht's drive on Moscow, but he was dismissed in December 1941 after pulling his units back from an impossible position.

Above: A KV-1 heavy tank rolls through Moscow on its way to the front line in December 1941. By now the Red Army had learned how to use its tanks effectively.

Below: A T-34 crew prepares for action. The Soviet counterattack in front of their capital gave the all-conquering Wehrmacht its first setback of the war.

masterminds behind the Soviet reserve system, he had been posted to the front in September after an argument with Stalin. He administered a sharp defeat to German forces outside Smolensk before his recall to command a full-scale counter-attack outside Moscow.

It came on 5 December. The temperature plummeted to -15°C and snow lay more than a metre thick in places. Unable to dig in properly, the under-manned German units were torn apart; the few serviceable German tanks were unable to manoeuvre in these conditions and the fuel was stuck hundreds of miles behind the front. The Luftwaffe was unable to help: its aircraft took an average of five hours to get airborne even if the ground crews maintained fires under the engines to keep them from freezing. Russia's latest tanks, the T-34 and KV-1 had wide tracks and engines designed to keep running even in Arctic weather; Russian guns and small arms were similarly robust, built to function in snow or mud, and their soldiers wore thickly insulated uniforms.

The Germans had to retreat – in spite of Hitler's demand that they give up no ground. All three Army Group commanders were sacked, along with previous favourites like panzer generals Guderian and Hoepner. Hitler fired army chief-of-staff von Brauchitsch and appointed himself commander-in-chief. The former corporal would take personal charge of the war in the East.

Widening war

As his soldiers fought for their lives in the snow, Hitler re-doubled the stakes. On 7 December he learned of the Japanese attack on Pearl Harbor and his ambassador in Washington reported (quite wrongly) that President Roosevelt was likely to declare war on all the Axis powers. Determined to show the world who held the initiative, Hitler now declared war on the USA.

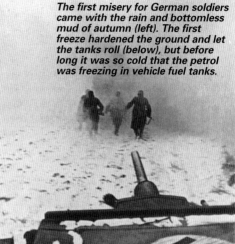

The first misery for German soldiers came with the rain and bottomless mud of autumn (left). The first freeze hardened the ground and let the tanks roll (below), but before long it was so cold that the petrol was freezing in vehicle fuel tanks.

General Winter

Anyone fighting in Russia has to remember one thing: the major adversary for a third of the year is not the Russian army. It is the Russian winter, and failure to deal with it effectively means death.

After the triumphs of the heady summer of 1941, the war had settled down into a vicious battle of attrition – in conditions for which the Soviets were prepared better than the Germans.

In 1812, Napoleon's huge army had been driven from Moscow by 'General Winter' and 130 years later the Wehrmacht encountered the same foe. Hitler had expected the battle to be a walkover, but once the first snow fell early in October, any thought of an easy victory disappeared.

The onset of the Russian winter found the invading armies woefully unprepared. The misery generated by sustained sub-zero temperatures was compounded by the mud that, each autumn and spring, turned the steppe into a bottomless mire.

The German army fell apart. It had already suffered some 750,000 casualties, but losses soared once the full fury of winter descended. The army reported over 100,000 frostbite cases in December alone. The generals tried to pull back, but Hitler countermanded their orders. "Where would they retreat to?" he asked, "was it warmer 100 km to the west?" There would be no retreat. The German army would stand fast, just as it had in World War I.

Right: On the fringes of Moscow, the overstrained German supply system broke down. Units were short of food, fuel, ammunition and medical supplies. And frostbite was striking down thousands.

Below Right: By contrast, the fresh Siberian divisions thrown into the battle by the Soviets were well-equipped and thoroughly used to the cold. Now it was the turn of the Germans to be outclassed.

New T-34 tanks roll direct from the factory to the front line. The Russians had weathered the Nazi storm and now the war settled down to a fierce battle of attrition.

"Remember thou art mortal". A triumphant Rommel is interviewed for a German newsreel. The capture of Tobruk on 21 June 1942 was Rommel's greatest victory – but it was also his last against the British.

The Race to Suez
Gazala to El Alamein

In January 1942, against orders, Rommel opened a brilliant campaigning season taking him agonisingly close to the ultimate prize of Suez. But he was fated never to see the promised land.

JANUARY 1942 SAW German forces pushed onto the defensive. In Russia, the Red Army had stopped the Germans on the outskirts of Moscow, then launched offensives all along the front, prematurely anticipating total victory. In North Africa, the siege of Tobruk had been lifted by the British 'Operation Crusader', and Rommel was back where he started in March 1941. British Commonwealth forces were re-organising, ready to resume the invasion of Libya, confidence boosted by America's entry to the war. Yet their rosy view of the situation was to prove as false as Stalin's.

General Cunningham had been replaced as the British 8th Army's commander during the last stage of the battle. The fighting was confused, swirling around the desert, a situation in which both sides lost senior officers, headquarters and logistic units in unexpected encounters. It tested the nerves of all commanders, but Rommel held his nerve longer than Cunningham. The British theatre commander, General Sir Claude Auchinleck – the inscrutable 'Auk' – replaced him with one of his own staff officers, Major-General Neil Ritchie. But responsibility was blurred. Ritchie, not the most assertive of generals, was cursed with some very independent-minded, some might say, insubordinate divisional commanders. The Auk showered him with a daily

stream of signals and written memoranda and his occasionally uncanny appreciations, the fruit of ULTRA intelligence, lent even greater weight to his authority.

GERMAN INTELLIGENCE
Rommel enjoyed good intelligence too. The Italians had broken the US diplomatic code and both Axis armies had been reading the voluminous and rather pessimistic reports of Colonel Bonner F Fellers, US military attaché in Cairo since summer 1941. As the representative of a once friendly neutral, now allied nation, he received comprehensive briefings from the British, which he passed back to the US war department. In January 1942 Rommel knew he had a window of opportunity to counter-attack.

The summer of 1942 was a happy time for the Luftwaffe and Afrika Korps units. A year later the smiles for the propaganda ministry would be more forced.

The British were preparing their own offensive, but judged the Axis forces too weakened by their recent defeat and withdrawal to be capable of immediate action.

In contrast to the divided counsels of the British Eighth Army, Rommel was very much his own man. Theoretically subordinate to OKH south-west and the Italian high command, he would ignore his German superiors, and his Italian superiors only learned of his plans once their own formations were discovered to be on the move.

ARMS AND THE MAN

The veteran British 7th Armoured division had been replaced by the inexperienced 1st Armoured division, itself divided into brigades for training. Both sides knew the Germans had landed over a hundred new tanks in North Africa, but only the Germans understood how quickly they could get them into action. British tanks tended to require a complete overhaul on arrival; occasional failures like the omission to refill water pumps, emptied prior to shipment, could cause more vehicle losses than enemy action.

On 21 January, the Axis forces caught the British by surprise. Brief resistance collapsed into chaotic retreat until the British established themselves between Gazala and Bir Hacheim. There they dug in on a 70 km front, re-organised and, prodded by impatient memos from Churchill, prepared to attack.

Both sides were engaged in a logistic race, to assemble as powerful a force as possible for the next battle. The Germans were hampered by Malta, from which the RAF and Royal Navy inflicted unsustainable losses to the Italian convoys on which Rommel's army depended. German and Italian airborne forces were assembled to take the island and began training for 'Operation Hercules'.

Malta could support no submarines or bomber aircraft under the ferocious aerial bombardment that ensued; Italian merchant ships enjoyed a welcome respite and Rommel's forces were replenished. On the other hand, the first American supplies reached Egypt, including numbers of M3 medium tanks, known to the British as Lee/Grants (depending on the model). These featured a 37 mm gun in a turret plus a 75 mm gun in a sponson; the vehicle could not fight 'hull down', but it compared well to the thin-skinned cruiser tanks still in widespread service and, being American, did not break down with the depressing regularity of so many British-built tanks.

BRITISH BOXES

By mid-May Rommel's excellent battlefield reconnaissance and SIGINT teams detected signs of an imminent British offensive. He was still outnumbered, but persuaded Kesselring to release squadrons from the proposed Malta operation, including dive bombers and Messerschmitt Bf 109F fighters.

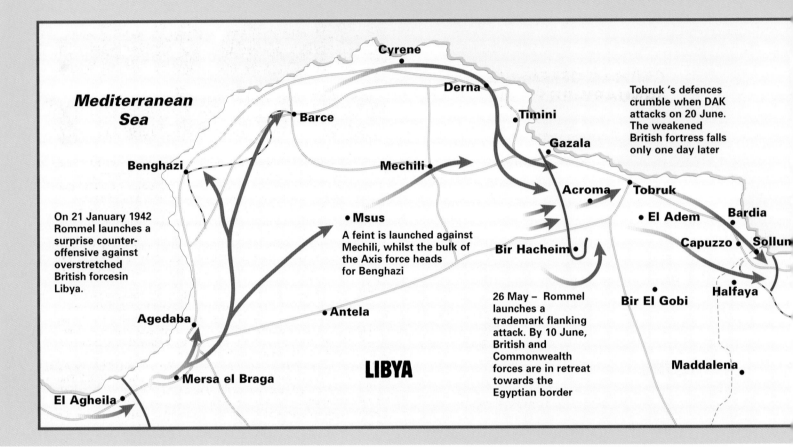

On 21 January 1942 Rommel launches a surprise counter-offensive against overstretched British forcesin Libya.

A feint is launched against Mechili, whilst the bulk of the Axis force heads for Benghazi

26 May – Rommel launches a trademark flanking attack. By 10 June, British and Commonwealth forces are in retreat towards the Egyptian border

Tobruk 's defences crumble when DAK attacks on 20 June. The weakened British fortress falls only one day later

Mediterranean Sea

LIBYA

The British defences consisted of a succession of fortified camps or 'boxes', occupied by infantry brigades with supporting artillery. Ensconced behind barbed wire, with some 500,000 landmines surrounding them, they served to break up and channel the enemy attack. Behind these lines the British armoured divisions waited, theoretically concentrated and ready to deliver a knock-out blow, but in reality scattered about the desert with confused command arrangements. Rommel believed the British just did not understand the most basic principles of war. In truth, his opponents grasped the theory: it was a failure of execution owing to the 'command by committee' syndrome still prevalent in the Eighth Army.

DESTINATION TOBRUK

Rommel had visited Hitler in March to obtain permission for a new offensive. His objective was Tobruk. He was to go no further, and was to return the Luftwaffe squadrons to Sicily within a month.

Rommel's own letters reveal greater ambition: he planned, even before the battle of Gazala, to break clean through to Egypt and the Suez canal, converting a hoped-for local success into a major strategic victory.

Rommel attacked on 26 May. Neither his plan nor that of the British survived first contact with the enemy. His feint at the centre of the British line failed to draw the British reserves; his predictable wide flanking manoeuvre was not intercepted by British tank divisions, which sat immobile while their commanders bickered.

General Cruewell, commander of the Afrika Korps, was shot down in his light aircraft and captured. This occurred just as Kesselring was visiting the command post and the Field Marshal (and former gunner) spent an enjoyable afternoon taking charge, as senior officer present, until Rommel arrived.

For a commander often criticised for not paying regard to logistics, Rommel turned the tables on the British by

Above: Hans Joachim Marseilles poses beside one of his 158 victims, all but seven of which were claimed in the Western Desert. He operated from Martuba, west of Tobruk and died on 27 September 1942 in an accident.

personally organising a night-time re-supply for 15th Panzer division. His tanks had broken through the British lines, but found themselves surrounded; the British commanders believed they had him trapped. It is one of the classic illustrations that commanders are only beaten when they themselves believe it. Rommel's confidence was supreme, as witnessed by a captured British officer who described Rommel directing this most confused of battles.

Hunched over a map in his command vehicle, headphones on, Rommel issued an endless succession of orders with quiet authority, his confidence, his grip on the battle in such dramatic contrast to the confusion on the other side.

There was no real front-line. Situation maps showed a hideously complex intermingling of forces. Victory went to the man who believed he would win, defeat to commanders who, deep down, believed themselves and

GERMAN OFFENSIVE JANUARY-JULY 1942

→ German attacks

— British Positions

Sidi Barrani

q Buq

Mersa Matruh

Fuka

El Dab'a

30 June – Rommel halted at El Alamein as Allies dig in

El Alamein

EGYPT

2 September – Axis attack on Alam Halfa fails

High tide of victory

FIELD MARSHAL KESSELRING and the Italian leadership had made cautious plans for the 1942 campaigning season. Rommel had other ideas. He was intoxicated by the Führer's vision of taking the Middle East in a giant pincer movement involving a drive south through the Caucasus and a race across the North African coast. He very nearly took the prize of Suez in a brilliantly executed campaign in the first half of 1942.

The *Deutsche Afrika Korps* and their often unsung Italian comrades executed a series of outflanking manoeuvres. They were brought to a halt by the Allied defensive line at El Alamein, which was flanked by the impassable Quattara depression.

Often outnumbered, Rommel was aided by his opponents: the British were overcommitted in the Far East, and had to withdraw Australian troops from the campaign at crucial moments. They were also handicapped by confused tactical thinking. Command was by committee, in stark contrast to the bullying, aggressive, but above all decisive nature of Rommel's staff meetings.

Rommel's relentless advance in 1942 was further aided by the Axis blockade of Malta, which protected the convoy route to Tripoli. The relief of the blockade marked the beginning of the end for Rommel; his reinforcements began to be destroyed in ever increasing quantities. Hitler was also being hard-pressed in Russia and could not afford to commit further supplies to Rommel until far too late.

AFTER THE TWO WEEKS of furious fighting south of Gazala the 8th Army withdrew, leaving Tobruk to be besieged. The DAK reached the port's perimeter on 20 June. Although it had a 30,000-strong garrison, Tobruk's defences had been weakened to defend the Gazala line, and armour was in woefully short supply.

The German attack went like clockwork. At 05:20 on 20 June Kesselring's bombers assaulted the south-east corner of the perimeter. Three hours later the 15th Panzer division punched through the British lines and fanned out. The Ariete and Trieste divisions exploited the gaping breach in the defences. The next day, after sporadic resistance Tobruk surrendered.

The spoils were fantastic. Two thousand vehicles, 5,000 tons of supplies and 2,000 tons of fuel were given up. Rommel now calculated that nothing could stand between him and ultimate victory. Nothing, that is, but the British defensive line at El Alamein.

Fall Of Tobruk 20/21 June 1942

→ German attacks	⇌ Batteries
→ Italian Attacks	◁ Airfield
····· British Minefields	XX Division
▨ Infantry Unit	X Brigade
▭ Armoured Unit	III Regiment
▧ Motorised Unit	II Battalion

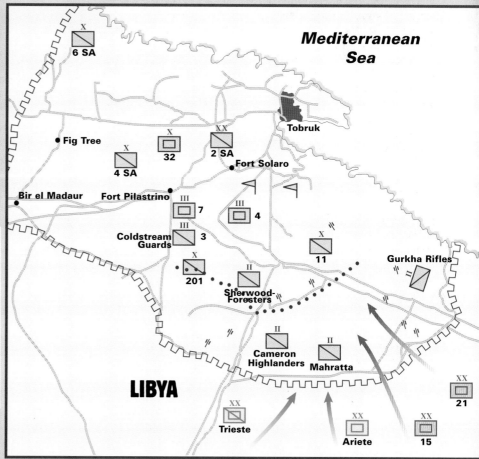

Mediterranean Sea

6 SA

Fig Tree

32

2 SA

Tobruk

4 SA

Fort Solaro

Bir el Madaur

Fort Pilastrino

7

4

Coldstream Guards

3

11

Gurkha Rifles

201

Sherwood-Foresters

Cameron Highlanders

Mahratta

LIBYA

Trieste

Ariete

15

21

Above: June 12 1942 – British armour is annihilated in 'the Cauldron'. Superior German training and tactical awareness overcame an enemy that was slow on the move, rash in the attack and indifferent in gunnery.

Above: In fast-moving armoured warfare awareness of the enemy forces disposition is particularly vital. Here a camera is being loaded onto a Messerschmitt 110 prior to a reconnaissance sortie.

Below: German medical orderlies operate a water purification plant. With water in short supply one German secret weapon was the jerry-can – the ultra practical metal liquid container which never leaked and from which every drop could be poured.

their system inferior. Fighting went in favour of the Germans around the 'Knightsbridge' box, held by the Guards brigade. The southernmost anchor of the line at Bir Hacheim was held by the Free French. It was attacked and taken after more than a week of epic resistance. The British withdrew, their retreat taking on the appearance of a rout as Rommel threw every last man and every precious litre of petrol into the pursuit.

Suddenly, Tobruk was under threat. Its mines lifted to bolster the Gazala defences, its artillery batteries similarly denuded, the so-called 'fortress' that had survived a protracted siege in 1941 fell in 24 hours. Churchill learned of the disaster while visiting President Roosevelt and his dismay was obvious. Roosevelt immediately offered all the assistance his nation could provide: even stripping his own nascent armoured forces of their tanks to help Britain in its hour of need.

RITCHIE SACKED

Auchinleck sacked Ritchie. Taking personal command, he stopped the retreat inside the Egyptian border at a railway station about 100 km west of Alexandria. It was called El Alamein. Identified even before the war as Egypt's crucial defensive line, it was one of the few places with a secure flank. Fifty km miles south of the coast the desert suddenly dips 700 feet into the impassable sand sea known as the Qattara depression.

At this point Kesselring favoured a consolidation of the Axis position and an invasion of Malta – the postponed Operation Hercules. But Rommel had something quite different in mind. Replenished by the large amount of captured supplies from Tobruk he advocated an immediate push on Cairo before the British recovered. Rommel received Hitler's backing.

On 26 June he delivered a none-too-successful right hook on the allied position at Mersa Matruh. But the British,

undefeated, pulled back to the prepared positions at El Alamein and Rommel followed in eager pursuit.

On 1 July Rommel tried to break through with a hasty attack, but was foiled. He re-grouped his exhausted vanguard a week later, but to no avail. Attack and counter-attack followed thick and fast. The British received reinforcements, the RAF made its presence felt; the Americans learned their diplomatic code was compromised, and from 29 June Rommel no longer read Fellers' reports. Auchinleck counter-attacked from 15-17 July and again on 21-22 July, the New Zealand division making excellent progress until assaulted in its turn by 21st Panzer division.

German reinforcements included the Ramcke parachute brigade, formed for the now abandoned attack on Malta. But the British were almost on top of their supply depots, and the RAF gained control of the air, pounding Axis supply columns before and during Rommel's next attack at the end of August. General Nehring was wounded, and von Bismarck, the commander of 21st Panzer was killed. But the British also suffered senior losses. The Eighth Army's designated commander, General 'Strafer' Gott was shot down and killed; General Bernard Law Montgomery was rushed out from England as a replacement.

The change in British fortunes from September 1942 has often been ascribed to the arrival of the ever controversial 'Monty', not least by Montgomery himself. Rommel thought he detected a change in the Eighth Army during August, while the Auk was at the helm, but the record of the unfortunate Gott suggests another disaster might have been on the cards had not Montgomery found himself in charge.

THE LAST ATTACK

The battle of Alam Halfa (30 August-2 September) decided the desert war. By mid-August, Rommel knew that he no choice but to make a fast, desperate bid

Italian Handicap

IT WAS GERMANY'S misfortune to be allied to Italy, a country which could neither produce nor deploy the new technologies demanded of modern warfare. Italy fought the entire war with the three mechanised divisions that she possessed in 1939. They were equipped with tanks that were obsolete and under-armed. Two of these divisions were destroyed at El Alamein. The remaining armoured division – the Ariete, was an outfit of some quality and was used most effectively at the Gazala breakthrough. It would later claim that it was the one Italian unit to never to have let Rommel down.

The rest of the forces were of varying levels of mediocrity and could be counted upon to fold like a house of cards. Italian units had dash and elan, but no endurance. Importantly, in the mobile warfare for which Rommel was so suited, the infantry divisions were not mechanised and so could rarely exploit the successes of the German armour. They did, however, prove reasonable effective if 'corsetted' at key points by intermingling with German units.

The Italian army was further compromised by indifferent leadership, due to the political appointment of senior officers. Although Rommel was nominally under the command of General Garibaldi, Graziani's replacement, he often showed his contempt for his allies in staff meetings. This was sometimes counter-productive: In January 1942 his arrogant conduct and perceived recklessness had led to the Italians holding back their tanks from operations around Agedabia.

If Italian armour was poor, the performance of most Italian infantry was risible. The British had, against odds of 10 to 1, almost kicked the Italians out of Africa in 1940. Only Rommel's intervention prolonged Italy's tenuous hold on her overseas empire.

The Fiat M13/40 was widely employed by the Italian armoured corps in the desert campaign. Balefully dubbed the 'mobile coffin' by its crews, it was cramped, unreliable and caught fire easily when hit by anti-tank rounds. Although the Axis had considerable armoured strength on paper, that strength was in reality undermined by the presence of such obsolete models.

The Italians thought as late as 1938 that there was still a future for the highly manoeuvrable biplane fighter in modern aerial combat. They were wrong. After initial success in a ground attack role, the Fiat Cr 42 suffered appalling losses in the Western Desert. The aircraft has the distinction of being the last biplane fighter ito serve in numbers in the front line with any major airforce of WW2.

to break through the Allied line in front of him and reach Suez. Otherwise sickness, exhaustion and shortage of supplies would so weaken his army that the enemy would have no problem in simply moving forward and steamrollering over his positions.

On 30 August as darkness fell two hundred panzers – including 26 of the new Mark IV Specials with the long 75-mm gun – and 243 Italian medium tanks moved off. By midnight they were attempting to cross a minefield which the British had sown between Himeimat and Deir el Munassib. There seemed to be more mines than they had been told to expect, and their problems were magnified by continual bombing from flights of Wellingtons. They were also engaged by British anti-tank guns firing from just in front. Despite what Rommel had said, it seemed that surprise was not on the side of the *Panzerarmee*.

By 8.00 a.m. the next morning, the bulk of the panzers were through the minefields, though divisional commander General Bismarck had been killed and corps commander General Nehring, had been badly wounded. Since they were now well behind schedule, they had to turn north along the line which led to the centre of the Alam Halfa Ridge, instead of further on towards Hamman. By 1.00 p.m. as they drew near the ridge, the panzers were running low on fuel – there sand had been much softer than was indicated on the captured British map they used, and both tracked and wheeled vehicles had run into trouble. But a welcome sandstorm cloaked them while the tanks were refilled; there was still no sign of the British armour, which by now should have offered itself for its usual destruction at the hands of the 88-mm Flak guns.

DEATH IN THE DESERT

It never did. The British tanks stayed out of range for the whole of this engagement, moving occasionally into place to act as mobile artillery. They added to the gradually increasing barrage of 25-pounder shells which crashed among the assembled panzers until the crews were blinded and deafened and longing for darkness. After this barrage,

precedent demanded that a decent silence should fall upon the battlefield, the British withdrawing into remote laagers, the Afrika Korps refilling their fuel tanks yet again and replenishing their ammunition racks.

But someone was making new rules. All that night the British artillery poured their shells into the area in which the panzers were now penned, while the RAF carried out a long session of pattern bombing which caught the supply and petrol echelons as they tried to come up.

When the morning of 1 September came, lack of fuel limited Rommel's forces to only one more attack, on the western end of Alam Halfa Ridge, and this was beaten back by the same implacable gunfire as before. That night the pattern was repeated, and the following day Rommel noticed yet another portent of the times ahead: amid the formations of aircraft which harassed and bombed his unfortunate formations were now appearing Mitchells and Liberators bearing the white star of the USAAF.

The incessant bombardment of Axis armour trapped below the Alam Halfa Ridge continued for another two days and nights

during which neither the panzers nor the guns gave each other much rest. During the night of 3/4 September, the Axis infantry filling the gap through which the panzers had passed had also to fight off New Zealand and British infantry attempts to close it. The gap remained open, however, and in the course of 5 September the remains of 15th and 21st Panzer and of the Ariete, Trieste and Littorio divisions withdrew through it, leaving behind many prisoners and the wreckage of a large number of Axis tanks.

ROMMEL RETIRES SICK

Rommel applied for leave. His attempt to fulfil 'Plan Orient', the grand pincer movement combining his invasion of Egypt and the German attack through the Caucasus, was postponed. Feted in Berlin, where he stayed with the Goebbels family, he disconcerted his replacement General Stumme with the statement that he would return if the British attacked.

And attack they would, even if they were taking their time about it. As Rommel confided to his staff, 'if I were Montgomery, we wouldn't still be here.' But Montgomery was about to make his move.

Above: Panzer IVs move forward towards the line at El Alamein. Between May and July 1942 German armour carried all before them. But in the process, their numbers and supplies were fatally depleted by the wear and tear of continuous battle.

Below: Even though the Afrika Korps was more civilised than German occupying troops elsewhere, for the North Africans the war was a great hardship. But no matter what the uniform, the same needs for luxuries and basic supplies alike offered unparalleled opportunities for trade.

GERMAN LOGISTICS CATASTROPHE

THE FIRST ESSENTIAL for any army to be able to stand the strain of battle is an adequate stock of weapons, petrol and ammunition. In fact, the battle is generally fought and decided by the quartermasters long before the shooting begins.

For all the brilliance of Rommel as an exponent of mobile warfare, his attempts to breakthrough at El Alamein depended upon the ability of his logistics staff to amass sufficient armour and supplies.

Malta was the vital lynch-pin in the arms race, and it became a frontline base in the fight against Axis aviation and shipping. The failure of the Luftwaffe in June to prevent significant numbers of Spitfires from being landed on the island, and the indefinite postponement of Operation Hercules – the planned airborne assault – meant that a revitalised island could once again prevent significant amounts of material from reaching the Axis forces. During the latter half of 1942, the Royal Navy increased the pace of operations against the Italian fleet, and two-thirds of the Italian merchant marine ended up at the bottom of the sea. As a result, the Axis forces in Africa were denied almost half their supplies and two-thirds of their oil.

Another issue was the length of the supply lines themselves. These, for either army, could be safely stretched about 500 km from its main supply base. However, if an army tried to stretch the elastic further, before intermediate bases could be established, then it would snap and the penalty was either a rapid gallop backwards to avoid defeat, or annihilation.

When the Germans reached El Alamein, it took a convoy seven days to complete the round trip from Benghazi – it took two weeks to get to the main port of Tripoli and back. By contrast, British and Commonwealth troops were only 60 km from replenishment.

Above: By mid-October 1942 the Allies enjoyed a superiority in tanks of 5 to 1. The British had been unable to come up with reliable armoured models of their own, but now half of their force was composed of American built Grants and Shermans. Only one in six of the Axis tank force was of comparable quality.

Below: Rommel's limited supplies were augmented wherever possible by captured allied booty. Here he enjoys some tinned Empire Selected Fruit on the hoof.

Above: Rommel's Afrika Korps had always been hampered by numerical inferiority. By the middle of 1942 the numbers did not stack up, and not even Rommel's dash could tip the scales. What few reinforcements that could be spared arrived piecemeal by plane, or risked being sunk to the bottom of the Mediterranean, courtesy of the RAF and Royal Navy.

Right: By late 1942 the Luftwaffe in Africa was being outclassed by its opponents, and for the first time lost air superiority. Rommel ruefully observed that "Anyone who has to fight, even with the most modern weapons, against an enemy in complete command of the air, fights like a savage against modern troops."

Russia 42
The Road to Stalingrad

In the summer of 1942, Hitler's armies unleashed an assault on the the oil fields of the Caucasus and Stalingrad. But Germany no longer had the resources to take on both targets simultaneously.

HITLER DECREED that Moscow would not be occupied after the German victory, but razed to the ground. Leningrad, cradle of the Bolshevik revolution was to be levelled too. The Red Army's December counter-attack saved the Soviet capital for the moment, but the great industrial centre of Leningrad was surrounded. Its population swollen to over three million by refugees flooding into the city ahead of the invaders, it was cut off by Germans to the south and to the north by the Finns, eager to avenge the Winter War.

Communist Party chiefs anxiously calculated their food reserves: on 1 November they realised there was only enough food for another week. And with winter approaching, there was so little fuel that buildings could not be heated and electricity was rationed to an hour a day. What followed was the most ghastly siege in history, a long drawn-out agony in which nearly a million men, women and children died of cold and slow starvation – three times the total war dead suffered by Britain or the USA in the whole of World War II. The German army made no attempt to storm the city. Heavy guns bombarded it daily, letting hunger and the bitter winter weather do the rest.

Elsewhere, Stalin ordered an ambitious series of attacks after the Red Army stopped the Germans at the gates of Moscow. His generals knew what happened to commanders who failed, and launched offensives all along the line. But despite tattered uniforms stuffed with straw and newspaper, weapons that jammed in the arctic temperatures and a grave lack of tanks or aircraft, the German army defended itself with extraordinary professionalism and courage. An attempt to relieve Leningrad was beaten off and counter-attacks not only restored the front, but trapped two Soviet armies behind the lines where they were destroyed in the spring.

NO RELIEF FOR LENINGRAD

The fluid fighting in early 1942 left German forces encircled too. The Soviet Northwest Front

Left: One of the problems facing the Germans was congestion: too many tanks using too few roads suitable for heavy armour.

The Wehrmacht's summer offensive in 1942 started out as devastatingly as the 1941 campaign. But this time the Germans knew that the Red Army would be a much tougher proposition.

> "4th Panzer Army could have taken Stalingrad without a fight in July, but it was sent south to help my army cross the Don. I did not need help: all the extra troops did was to congest the roads. By the time 4th Panzer returned to Stalingrad at the beginning of August, the Russians had moved in enough force to put up a serious fight."
>
> **Field Marshal Ewald von Kleist**

broke through in the Valdai hills, isolating several pockets of German troops who continued to defend their perimeters. In each case, the trapped divisions were clustered around an airfield, and the Luftwaffe flew in supplies until either relief was at hand, or – in the case of General von Seydlitz's six divisions at Demiansk – the Germans broke out to fight their way home. Seydlitz's men took a month to battle their way across the snow, their epic *katabasis* sustained by parachute drops and an iron determination never to surrender. In the euphoria that greeted their escape, the German high command overlooked the physical state of the survivors: months of combat on the frozen steppe, with inadequate rations,

medical and sanitary facilities left many men unfit for further service. The Germans also drew the comforting conclusion that they could keep encircled units supplied by air, an assumption that would be tested to destruction within a year.

CASUALTIES COMPARED

The German army suffered some 80,000 casualties in the Soviet winter offensive. It inflicted over 400,000 casualties in return, and many soldiers puzzled over the Red Army's ability to take such punishment. What the Soviets lacked in military skill, they made up for with fanatical – often futile – bravery. Goebbels damned them as mindless automata, an enduring image that survived long after 1945.

The spring thaw halted operations. With the German army still less than 300 km (190 miles) from Moscow, a distance the panzer divisions could cover in a week, the Soviets concentrated their forces around the capital. It was the obvious military strategy, and it was wrong. Hitler was looking south, to the Crimea, which he described as an unsinkable aircraft carrier within range of the Romanian oilfields – without which his panzers would go nowhere. The port of Sevastopol must be taken and the other Soviet foothold on the peninsula, the Kerch straits, must be seized as a platform for the next stage; the capture of the Caucasus and the Caspian oilfields 650 km (400 miles) beyond the front line.

Above: Oil supplies blaze at Kuban as Army Group A penetrates deep into the Caucasus. But a reorganised Soviet defence blocked further advances as Stalin issued his 'Not a step backward' order on 28 July.

Below: On 21 August the elite Gebirgsjäger *planted the* Swastika *flag on the summit of Mt. Elburus. Meanwhile, the rest of 49th Mountain corps advanced into the sub-tropical forests girding Sukhumi.*

The Wehrmacht had lost one million men in the east by the spring of 1942. Hitler demanded his allies make up the numbers, the Romanian and Italian armies supplying half a million men that year. By German standards they were poorly equipped and often badly trained, so they were mainly used to hold quiet sectors while the German formations led the attacks. By replacing German civilian labourers with slaves seized from eastern Europe, stripping battalions from divisions garrisoning western Europe, and calling up the next year's conscription class a year early, the Wehrmacht was able to assemble 2.7 million men on the Russian front. This accretion of strength could not be repeated, so Hitler was betting everything on one roll of the die.

RUSSIAN MIRACLE

Through the winter of 1941-42, hundreds of miles from the front line and invisible to the Germans, another army was labouring in impossible conditions. As the USSR's key industrial regions were over-run by the invaders, whole factories were uprooted and shipped to the Urals, to the deserts of Kazakhstan or the frozen tundra of Siberia. Over 1.5 million wagon loads made the journey, workers – many of them women – struggling to set up machine tools literally in the middle of nowhere. Not only did they get the factories working again, but they did so with unbelievable speed. The Yak fighter plant in Moscow was dismantled and taken to Siberia where production resumed in only a week. By early 1942 it was building more aircraft per month than it had done on its original site. From a far inferior base – Russia produced only a quarter as much steel as Germany – the Soviets were already out-building the invaders, supplying their armies with more tanks, guns and aircraft than the Wehrmacht was receiving.

The return of warmer weather was the signal for another Soviet offensive, an attempt to recapture Kharkov which failed dismally. Ten days' hectic thrust and counter-thrust in open country turned into a master class in *blitzkrieg*. The advancing Russians were outmanoeuvred by the superbly co-ordinated German air and ground forces. Marshal Timoshenko was summoned to Moscow to explain the loss of another three armies totalling over 200,000 men.

CRIMEA STORMED

As the German 6th and 17th armies shattered the Russian offensive at Kharkov, the 11th army broke through the heavily-fortified Soviet positions on the Kerch peninsula and drove the defenders into the Black Sea. Then it doubled back to storm Sevastopol, home port of the Soviet Black Sea Fleet.

Hitler moved his HQ to Vinnitsa in the Ukraine to oversee the next stage. Army Group South, re-named Army Group B (2nd and 6th armies, 4th Panzer army and 3rd Hungarian army) was to advance into the bend of the Don river then on to the Volga at Stalingrad. The other claw in a gigantic pincer movement would be a new formation, Army Group A (1st Panzer army, the 17th army and 3rd Romanian army) which would link up with Army Group B somewhere on the steppe west of the Volga, hopefully trapping another vast haul of Russian prisoners. Having gutted the Soviet armies again, Army Group A would then lunge east again to over-run the Soviet oilfields.

Six months after they had endured winter temperatures of -30°C, German soldiers found themselves on the Kuban steppe where the thermometer topped 40°C in the shade. Inside the tanks of 1st Panzer army the heat was simply unbearable. They captured the blazing wreckage of Maikop's oil installations, blown up by the Soviet rearguard. Shimmering in the distance like a layer of cloud, the Caucasus mountains were visible for miles

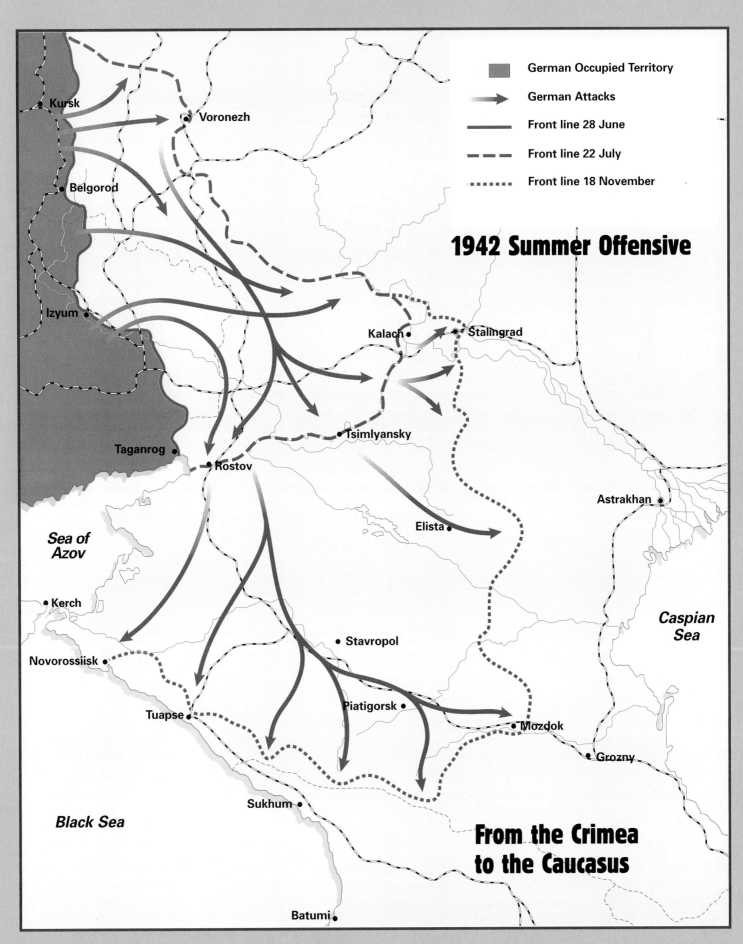

German Occupied Territory

German Attacks

Front line 28 June

Front line 22 July

Front line 18 November

1942 Summer Offensive

From the Crimea to the Caucasus

Kursk

Voronezh

Belgorod

Izyum

Kalach

Stalingrad

Taganrog

Tsimlyansky

Rostov

Astrakhan

Sea of Azov

Kerch

Elista

Caspian Sea

Novorossiisk

Stavropol

Tuapse

Piatigorsk

Mozdok

Grozny

Sukhum

Black Sea

Batumi

Above: Assorted vehicles of a Panzer division take a break from the fighting as Hoth's army breaks through the Soviet lines in July 1942. The Soviets had captured German plans for the drive on the Caucasus, but Stalin clung to the belief that the real target was Moscow.

Above right: Slovak infantrymen advance through the Ukraine. As the Axis forces closed on the Caucasus, they entered a land of minority peoples with little enthusiasm for Stalin. While the Red Army held back the Germans, the Soviet secret police, the NKVD, orchestrated a wave of terror against their own people lying in the path of the German advance.

before the Germans stormed the passes in August.

On the eastern side of the mountain range, the river Terek was the last obstacle facing *Panzergruppe* Kleist. Elements of the 16th Motorised division reached the edge of Astrakhan on the Caspian before the offensive finally ran out of steam at the end of September.

Russian resistance was stiffening, and the German forces were now hundreds of miles past the last railheads. Supplies of every kind were running out, and a desperate race followed, both sides hurrying forward ammunition, fuel, spare parts and more soldiers – always more soldiers – for one final battle before the *rasputitza* imposed nature's halt.

OFFENSIVE FALTERS

By any standards it was a remarkable achievement, but the German advance generated further discord at Hitler's HQ. Dissatisfied with Army Group A's pace of advance, he detached the 4th Panzer army from Army Group B, frustrating an attempt to pursue the retreating Russians all the way to Stalingrad. By the time the panzers were returned in August, the Soviet forces had rallied and were defending the outskirts of the city. The civilian population had been marched out to dig trenches and anti-tank ditches, and the prospect of taking the city by coup de main had passed. For the first time, the Germans did not have enough men to simply bypass the city with armoured forces and wait for it to fall, Stalingrad would have to be taken by frontal attack.

The headlong advance across open country to the Volga was spearheaded by the 6th army, a veteran formation led in Poland and France by General von Reichenau, one of Hitler's strongest supporters in the Wehrmacht.

RACE HATRED

A vocal anti-Semite, von Reichenau left his soldiers in no doubt as to their 'historic mission' to slaughter 'Asiatic inferiors' – fighting talk that won him command of Army Group South when Hitler sacked von Rundstedt in December 1941. He did not live long to enjoy his promotion to field marshal, dying of a stroke soon afterwards. But his influence permeated the army he had led to victory for two

FALL OF SEVASTOPOL

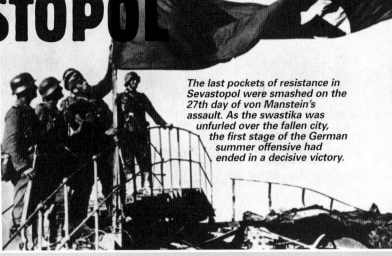

BY APRIL 1942 the Soviets had ferried 250,000 men into the Crimea, together with considerable tank and artillery support. But as in the previous year, the forces were committed piecemeal against the overwhelming German opposition. The Soviets were annihilated between 15 and 20 May, leaving von Manstein's 11th Army to move against the stronghold of Sevastopol.

Against Manstein's 200,000 men, 670 guns, 450 mortars, 720 tanks and 600 aircraft, the Soviets could field a mixed force of 100,000 marines, sailors and soldiers, plus 600 artillery pieces and insignificant forces of aircraft and tanks.

After an earth shattering five-day barrage, the German LIV Corps moved against the defences at the eastern end of North Bay. Throughout the first weeks of June, the Soviets defended magnificently every yard of territory, demonstrating a tenacity which would be repeated to resounding effect at Stalingrad later that year.

By the third week, Manstein was sufficiently worried, not only to throw in his last reserves, but to beg for reinforcements from the 17th Army. Eventually the sheer weight of material thrown against the Soviet defences began to tell. Not the least effective was the work of the huge German 80cm gun 'Schwere Gustav'. This gun systematically destroyed the main forts and the supposedly invulnerable underwater battery beneath Severnaya Bay.

The Germans finally breached the defences on the night of 28/29 June. During the next three days the Soviets organised a Dunkirk-style evacuation to rescue as many as possible of the men, women and children who had survived the 250 day siege.

Although von Manstein was awarded a Field Marshal's baton for taking Sevastopol, his 11th Army was so depleted that he would have to leave the drive on Stalingrad to the unimaginative General Paulus.

The last pockets of resistance in Sevastopol were smashed on the 27th day of von Manstein's assault. As the swastika was unfurled over the fallen city, the first stage of the German summer offensive had ended in a decisive victory.

Above and below: Manstein had guns of enormous calibre in his siege train. The opening barrage reminded some of the older members of the 11th Army staff of Verdun, 25 years before. The earth trembled with apocalyptic violence both when the shell was dispatched as well as when it landed.

Above: Armed to the teeth, three Soviet sailors pose for the camera. Naval personnel fought hard in defence of their base, and as the end approached some destroyed their guns as well as their own lives, rather than surrender.

Below: The huge Russian battery 'Maxim Gorky' was despatched using eight rounds of armour piercing and high explosive ammunition from the German 80cm rail gun. Fire was directed using a Fiesler Storch spotter plane.

years: the 6th Army cut a swathe of destruction across Russia as it smashed its way east. At its head was another of Hitler's favourites, General Friederich Paulus, whom the Führer intended to promote to chief-of-staff of the OKW in place of General Jodl after the summer offensive had been won.

The plan to capture Stalingrad was simple enough. Weiterheim's XIV Panzer Corps would form the northern flank, five of Hoth's panzer and motorised divisions would form the southern flank, while nine infantry divisions would fill the centre. They were all across the Don in 24 hours and to the delight of Berlin, Weiterheim's panzers reported that they had reached the banks of the Volga and the northern suburbs of Stalingrad by the 23 August.

It seemed that only one more heavy blow would secure victory, but the dogged Soviet defenders of the city had other ideas. The battle to come would mark a turning point in the war in the east and would seal the fate of Adolf Hitler and the Third Reich.

Above: In the six months following June 1941, the Soviet economy was transferred to a war footing. 1,500 Soviet factories representing 33 percent of the country's industrial output were moved east, to areas secure from Nazi air attack. In spite of the disruption, production had doubled by the end of 1941.

Below: German troops enter the outskirts of Stalingrad following the large-scale incendiary and dive-bomber attacks on 23/24 August. The 'final' assault on the city began on 13 September, and Goebbels' propaganda machine promised the German people victory by the end of 1942.

Partisan War

WHEN THE GERMANS first overran the Ukraine in 1941, they were welcomed as liberators. This goodwill was quickly squandered through the brutality of the *Einsatzgruppen* and the SD. In fact, German brutality was counter-productive: instead of cowing the Russian people into submission, it drove large numbers out into the forests and onto the steppes, where they joined the partisan armies which fought a no-quarter war with the occupiers.

It was a brutal war fought without any human feeling. Buildings were torched, livestock killed, women and children driven out into the snow to die. The merest hint of resistance to the Germans triggered acts of hideous barbarity, and it was one 18-year-old girl's fate to symbolise the partisan war that winter.

Zoya Kosmodemianskaya came from the Moscow Komosol (Soviet youth movement) and was caught setting fire to German stables in the village of Petrishchevo. Paraded through the streets with a placard around her neck, she was tortured then hanged, her young body mutilated to underline the lesson for the villagers. Her frozen corpse was found and cut down by the advancing Red Army.

Zoya became a national heroine. Her fate, so typical of that meted out by the German army was taken to heart by the Russians, as German soldiers would later discover when they tried to surrender, and German women would discover in 1945 when their homes were broken into by Russians bent on vengeance.

It has been estimated that the partisans in the period 1941-1945 killed, wounded or captured 1.5 million members of the German and axis forces. 21,000 troop and supply trains were derailed, 12,000 bridges were brought down and 1,100 aircraft destroyed at German airfields.

Above: "No German participating in combat action against guerrillas or their associates is to be held responsible for acts of violence either from a disciplinary or judicial point of view." Hitler's directive gave the German soldier in Russia carte blanche to rape and to murder, and all too often he took full advantage of it.

Right: In January 1943, 57,500 partisans were fighting in Belorussia; by November of that year the number had grown to 122,600. At the beginning of 1944, more than 250,000 Soviet partisans were operating behind German lines. They caused enormous problems for army units and contributed of the collapse of Army Group Centre in 1944.

Left and below: Many parts of captured Russian territory were only nominally occupied. Outside the main towns it was a no-man's-land, where the Germans had to use heavily armed and armoured trains to discourage partisan attacks in these areas. Even so, attacks continued, and German troops had to be ready to respond instantly.

DIE ROLLENDE

FESTUNG

The End in Africa

The last Panzer to appear in North Africa was the massive Pzkpfw VI Tiger, with its thick armour and deadly 88-mm gun. Only one battalion of these behemoths was sent to Tunisia.

IN APRIL 1943 Hans von Luck, the commander of an Afrika Korps reconnaissance battalion, was flown to Germany on the orders of General von Arnim, commander-in-chief of Axis forces in North Africa. Perhaps, where Rommel and Arnim had failed, this highly decorated young officer could succeed. Perhaps the Führer would listen to a frontline soldier.

It was a dangerous flight from Tunis to Sicily: he travelled in a Heinkel He 111 flying at wave top height to avoid detection and the inevitable swarm of Spitfires. Von Luck reached Berchtesgaden, where he met the recently reinstated *Generaloberst* Heinz Guderian, now inspector of panzer forces. He got as far as the office of General Alfred Jodl who forbade him to see Hitler. The mere mention of another retreat would send Hitler into a rage and his entourage were terrified of the Führer's anger.

So Rommel's plan for a systematic withdrawal of Axis forces in North Africa was turned down. Tunisia was to hold out, postponing an Allied assault on Italy for as long as possible. There was to be no 'German Dunkirk' as Rommel described it. Instead, there was another Stalingrad – dubbed 'Tunisgrad' by the bitter survivors. For the second time in three months, Hitler delivered over 100,000 German soldiers into enemy hands.

BEGINNING OF THE END

To understand how this catastrophe came about, it is necessary to go back to the autumn of 1942, when Rommel's Afrika Korps was compelled to hold its ground – by Hitler's express order – and be pounded to pieces by Montgomery's Eighth Army.

On 8 November 1942 British and American forces landed in Morocco and Algeria. It was the most ambitious amphibious operation up to that time: 35,000 US troops were shipped straight across from America; another 49,000 from their bases in Britain, together with 23,000 British and Commonwealth soldiers. Nearly 400 transport ships were involved, escorted by six battleships, eleven aircraft

The German adventure in Africa came to an end in a defeat as total as had occurred at Stalingrad, three months before.

The DAK fought with stubborn efficiency to the bitter end, but Hitler was deaf to all pleas to evacuate Tunisia. His refusal doomed 250,000 Axis troops to captivity, including 100,000 German veterans with irreplaceable experience.

"Ammunition shot off, arms and equipment destroyed. In accordance with orders received, DAK has fought itself to the condition it can fight no more. The German Afrika Korps must rise again. Heia Safari!"

General Cramer last commander of the Deutsche Afrika Korps May 1943

carriers, fifteen cruisers and over a hundred destroyers and anti-submarine vessels.

Algeria was a French colony, administered by the Vichy regime and many units of the French garrison resisted the Allied landings. Only two years before the British had attacked the French fleet in Algeria, killing over a thousand French sailors. Opposition at Oran, scene of what many Frenchmen saw as British perfidy, was especially fierce. At Casablanca, the incomplete French battleship *Jean Bart* had to be overpowered

by the USS *Massachusetts,* and several French submarines were sunk by US carrier aircraft as they attacked the troop transports. But the French colonial army was too small, too poorly equipped and internally divided: it could only impose a brief delay before the Algeria's ports were in Allied hands, and Allied troops were heading east along the coastal plain. Ahead lay Tunisia and 1500 km beyond in Libya, Rommel's Afrika Korps. Caught between two fires, the 'Desert Fox' was doomed.

Or so the Allies thought.

General Walter Nehring had been wounded in August while in command of the Afrika Korps at Alam Halfa. Recovering in Germany, he was surprised to be ordered not to resume his command but to fly to Tunisia and hold it for Germany.

IMPROVISED DEFENCE

He reached the city on 16 November. There he found two battalions of German paratroops, a parachute engineer battalion, a reconnaissance company and a battery of 88 mm anti-aircraft guns. There were two battalions

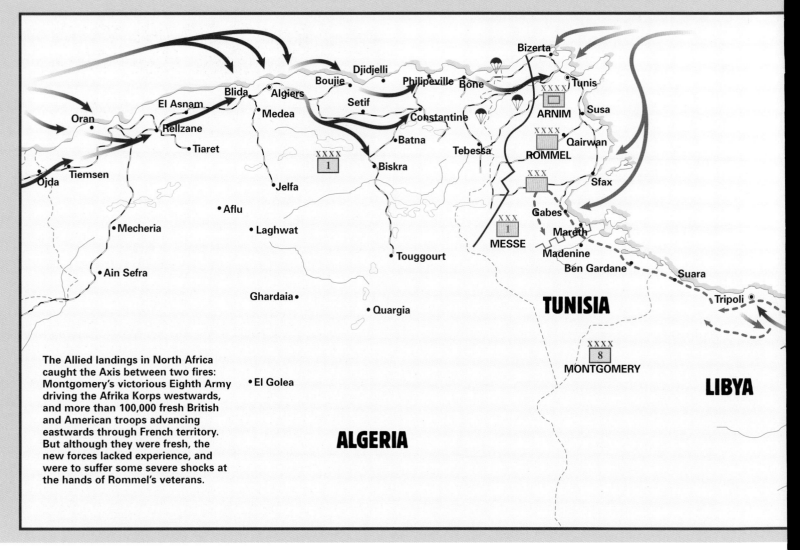

The Allied landings in North Africa caught the Axis between two fires: Montgomery's victorious Eighth Army driving the Afrika Korps westwards, and more than 100,000 fresh British and American troops advancing eastwards through French territory. But although they were fresh, the new forces lacked experience, and were to suffer some severe shocks at the hands of Rommel's veterans.

of Italian naval infantry ashore at Bizerta, with a couple of S-boats off the coast. Some 14,000 French colonial troops were stationed in the area, their loyalty and intentions uncertain.

QUICK REACTION

Within 48 hours American armoured cars were reported crossing the frontier, passing through the French units in the area unopposed. Nehring improvised a number of *kampfgruppen* as additional German forces flew into Tunis, despatching them into the hinterland to create as large a bridgehead as possible. A pupil of Rommel's, he acted in the correct belief that a company on the spot today is worth a battalion there tomorrow.

German aircraft were shuttled over from Sicily, and on

19 November, after the expiry of an ultimatum to the local French forces, they bombed French positions between Beja and Medjez El Bab.

In mainland France, German forces poured into the Vichy rump state, their primary target Toulon where the French fleet lay at anchor. But the SS armoured columns were too late: on Admiral Darlan's orders, the warships were scuttled. The French army of Tunisia was disarmed by the Germans, but many men, often in formed units, fled westwards to the Allies.

France's definitive African regiments, the *Chasseurs d'Afrique,* began the campaign in Algeria by taking on the Americans, but ended it fighting in a composite French division on the Allied side.

On the coast road, the German

airborne engineers blocked the leading echelons of the British 78th division and the 2nd *Fallschirmjäger* regiment stopped the US advance on Medjez.

The Germans rushed their men into Tunis faster than the Allies could advance from their beachheads in Algeria. Within three days of the Allied landings, there were a thousand extra Axis soldiers in Algeria; a week later, 4,500. Some 20,000 German troops arrived over the following ten days, brought over from Sicily by some 673 transport aircraft.

The transports flew in *pulks*, close formations of 30 to 40 aircraft escorted by a handful of fighters and staying no more than 50 metres above the water in order to minimize the chance of radar detection.

Sometimes they were too

late. A drop on one airfield was cancelled with the planes in the air: British parachutists had seized it that morning. On 25 November, an American armoured column overran Djedeida airfield.

Nevertheless, by 1 December 27,550 Axis troops had taken up defensive posuitions in Algeria, and the Allied advance had stalled. General von Arnim arrived on 8 December to take command of all Axis troops in what was now designated 5. *Panzerarmee.*

ROMMEL IN TUNISIA

Rommel's *Panzerarmee Afrika* did not withdraw into Tunisia until 13 February – two years and a day since the arrival of the Afrika Korps in Tripoli. His retreat across Libya was harried from the air, but efforts to

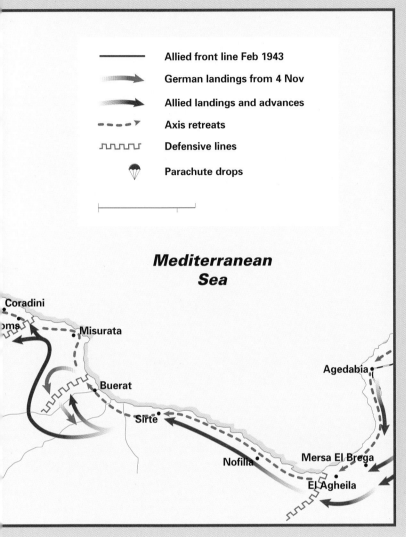

Allied front line Feb 1943

German landings from 4 Nov

Allied landings and advances

Axis retreats

Defensive lines

Parachute drops

Mediterranean Sea

Coradini

oms

Misurata

Buerat

Sirte

Nofilia

Mersa El Brega

El Agheila

Agedabia

Retreat to Tunis

AFTER EL ALAMEIN The Desert War for the Afrika Korps was one long series of retreats and defensive actions, until inevitably they were thrown out of Africa in May 1943. But Rommel and von Arnim had bought the Germans enough time to prepare their defences in Sicily and more importantly Italy, where the Allies were committed to striking next.

The Anglo-American landings in North-West Afica on 8 November 1942 were a gamble. Designed to take Axis forces in Libya from the rear, they partly depended on the attitiude of the Vichy French authorities for their success. Intense negotiations with French Admiral Darlan came to nothing and some of the landings were opposed. Only after intense fighting were Oran and Casablanca taken.

The German response was swift, with reinforcements, including elite parachute formations, being sent from Sicily on 9 November. Vichy France itself was occupied on 27 November. The Allies nearly succeeded in catching the Axis forces in Tunisia by surprise, but they failed to consolidate their successes before strong German forces were in place to oppose them. The Allied offensive had ground to a halt by mid-December.

In mid-January, following a meeting between Churchill and Roosevelt at Casablanca, the Allied commander General Eisenhower began to concentrate on planning future Allied operations in Italy, leaving the Tunisian battle to General Sir Harold Alexander.

Within a month Rommel had linked up with Axis forces in Tunisia, and, holding the Allies down on the newly-constituted Mareth line turned his attentions on the Americans.

On 14 February 10th Panzer Division attacked the US at Sid Bou Zid in the Dorsal Mountains. The Americans withdrew to Kasserine where they were ferociously attacked on 20 February. But when they fell back Rommel could not press home his advantage, and Allied forces quickly plugged the gap to stop any further German advance.

overtake and trap him on land were ineffective. There was a half-hearted attempt to repeat the British triumph of February 1941, when they reached Beda Fomm before the retreating Italians. But German rearguards were alert. Rommel reached El Agheila, then continued to pull back westwards, through Homs, until he evacuated Tripoli on 19 January.

LAST CHANCE SALOON

The bulk of Rommel's troops dug in on the Mareth line, where the coastal plain narrows opposite the island of Djerba. His premier tank formation, 21st Panzer Division was detached to von Arnim, where, undetected by the Allies, the Germans planned an audacious assault against the American forces around Kasserine. The German offensive – the last in

North Africa – caught the Americans off-guard. But the success was local: Axis forces were exhausting themselves swimming vainly against the tide that was engulfing them. The Allies were too numerous and too well supplied. US rations were so generous they included oranges, shipped from California and consumed among Tunisia's fruit farms. Early American weaknesses were unlikely to be repeated now they were under the command of the swashbuckling General Patton.

Rommel returned to the Mareth line, where the British had closed up and were preparing to attack. On 6 March Rommel anticipated the British with an offensive of his own: straight down the coastal road to Medenine. It was doomed from the start. Montgomery had

Operation Torch transports, silhouetted by the slanting rays of the sun, wait off-shore during landing operations at Mers-El-Kebir in the Oran area of Algeria.

Above: By early 1943 the Luftwaffe had lost the battle for air superiority. As long as weather permitted Allied aircraft could attack Axis positions without fear of Luftwaffe response. Ground forces had therefore to be self-reliant in protecting themselves against air assault.

Above: The North African war was not always fought under the heat of a burning sky. The campaigning year was limited to the dry season as the rains made the desert tracks impassable. For the Germans in the winter of 1942/43 the bad weather came as a welcome respite.

Below: Some of the US troops landed in Africa during Operation Torch had travelled non-stop from America. Many of these inexperienced, over-confident men had bought a one-way ticket. America was to learn the hard way not to underestimate German fighting men.

ample warning from ULTRA and prepared a gigantic ambush: the sort of *Pakfront* that had taken such a toll of British armour in the earlier days of the desert war. In a personal letter, Montgomery explained Rommel's actions to Field Marshal Sir Alan Brooke: 'He is trying to attack me in daylight with tanks, followed by lorried infantry. I have 500 6-pdr anti-tank guns dug in on the ground: I have 400 tanks; and I have good infantry, holding strong pivots, and a great weight of artillery. It is an absolute gift, and the man must be mad.'

It was over in 24 hours. Of the 141 tanks in Rommel's three panzer divisions, 52 were left on the battlefield. On 9 March Rommel handed over command to von Arnim and flew to Rome for medical treatment. Officially, he would return when fit, but he knew in his heart he would not see Africa again.

Montgomery duly battered his way through the Mareth line, characteristically recommending his defensive action at Medenine and the breakthrough at Mareth as models for future study by the Staff College.

MONTGOMERY ON THE OFFENSIVE

In fact, his attack did not conform half so neatly to expectation as he proclaimed. Arnim withdrew to Wadi Akarit, a natural barrier north of Mareth where on flank rested on the steeply sloped jebel, the other on the sea. The British balked at the idea of bouncing the Germans out of the position before they had a chance to fortify it.

Instead, Montgomery launched a night attack with two infantry divisions on 5 April. Elements of the 4th Indian division overran German positions in the hills, attacking in complete silence, the stealthy tactics of the North-West Frontier proving a match even for German veterans. A ferocious infantry battle took place on the plain before the

Germans were driven back, but despite the Allies' overwhelming advantage in armour the Germans still managed to break away without being shattered by a tank attack.

VON LUCK LUCKLESS

On 10 April the British Eighth and First armies met. Arnim presided over a dangerously shallow bridgehead around Tunisia and the end was no longer in doubt. Yet neither his pleas for a withdrawal order, nor Rommel's personal meeting with Hitler persuaded the Führer to give up Africa before it was too late. Hence von Luck's futile mission to Berchtesgaden. Arnim faced the biggest concentration of British troops yet seen in World War II: three tank and seven infantry divisions. Together with the Free French and the US 2nd Corps (three infantry and one tank divisions) the odds were overwhelming.

PATTON IN CHARGE

America's best fighting general of the war, George S. Patton transformed 2nd Corps. "Go until the last shot is fired and the last drop of gasoline is gone and then go forward on foot," he was quoted as saying. He led from the front, like Rommel, getting strafed by the Luftwaffe twice on the opening day of his offensive at El Guettar on 21 March. Minutes after he left one frontline position, it was struck by a German artillery salvo. When a night air raid on his headquarters was reported as a ground attack, Patton burst out of his tent, carbine in hand.

GIs in the 9th division were surprised to find a three-star general in their midst one night during another German attack – and amused by his loud order to "get those staff officers out of those holes and up here where they can be shot at". Patton's scorn for the Allied tactical air forces in North Africa, commanded by a an RAF Air Vice Marshal, came close to causing an international incident.

Masterclass at Kasserine

Above: German armour at Kasserine was, outnumbered, as was often the case in Africa. This Panzer IV mounts a long-barrelled 75 mm gun which was more than a match for Allied tanks, and the crew members have attached spare track wherever possible along the hull front for added protection.

BY EARLY 1943, the Axis were being squeezed between the pincers of the Eighth Army driving north and the Americans driving east. Germany needed a miracle to avoid being swept from Africa.

General Arnim favoured a modest counterstroke, aimed to win time. Rommel – even a desperately ill Rommel, haunted by his long retreat and the loss of Hitler's favour – designed a knock-out blow. His plan involved cutting off the leading British and American divisions with an all-out offensive that swept from Kasserine to the Mediterranean.

The attack broke over the heads of General Lloyd Frendenall's US 2nd Corps. Frendenall has been described by military historian Carlo D'Este as "one of the most inept senior officers to hold a high command during World War II." US forces were scattered over a wide front, their commander 65 miles behind the lines where he ordered his combat engineer battalion to build him an underground bunker complex. His subordinates were little better. As one GI put it, "never were so few commanded by so many from so far away."

For the last time Rommel was in the thick of battle, having shattered an enemy. Piles of high quality booty drooped into his hands, and bewildered American prisoners poured in. Rommel's actions were assisted by poor weather. Though it meant that he had no Luftwaffe support, it also meant that the Allied air superiority could not count.

But it did not last. Fatally, Rommel split up his forces, claiming that "by deploying troops at several danger points I hoped to split the enemy forces up more than my own". It was contrary to the principle of concentration that had served him so well in the past, and it did not work. Given interception of Rommel's coded signals the Allies could place just enough of a holding force against the German probing attacks. The assault eventually ground down.

The delay gave the Allies time to rush up reserves, and by the evening of the 22 February Rommel had to accept that his grandiose counterstroke could not work, and called off the assault.

Above: The last triumphs in North Africa were led by a strongly reinforced Panzer arm. If these up-gunned and more heavily-armoured vehicles had been allocated to Rommel earlier in the 1942 campaigning season he might have taken Cairo and Suez.

Below left: The terrain in Tunisia was perfect for defensive operations. Advancing armour inevitably had to be channelled down the passes between the mountains and could be easily ambushed.

Below: The US II Corps was lured to destruction in the same way that British armour had often been before El Alamein. American confidence had taken a shattering blow, though it soon recovered.

Above : A Ju 52 is strafed, one of its crew members lying dead under the wing after having been forced into an emergency landing. This lightly-armed and lumbering mainstay of the Luftwaffe resupply units was a sitting-duck to Allied fighters.

Below: A Jagdpanzer 38(t) Hetzer is knocked out by an American with a 2.75 inch anti-tank rocket launcher. The simplicity and effectiveness of the 'bazooka' impressed the Germans and they soon produced similar weapons themselves.

On 23rd March Patton shattered a counter-attack by 10th Panzer Division, then went on to drive the Germans out of their defensive positions. A month after Kasserine, American self-confidence was restored.

SINK, BURN, DESTROY!

Ground down by the British and resurgent Americans, Hitler's Army Group Africa experienced grave shortages of fuel and ammunition as its air bridge came under attack by Allied fighters. Allied naval forces swept the coast, obeying Admiral A.B.C. Cunningham's unambiguous orders to 'Sink, burn, destroy! Let nothing past!' The Luftwaffe ran out of fighter aircraft and many 'pulks' of Ju 52s were intercepted by Allied aircraft – even being attacked twin-engine bombers on one occasion.

By April no more personnel were allowed to fly into Africa, so von Luck was unable to return to his command. Casualties among German transport squadrons were severe, coming as they did in the wake of the Stalingrad debacle. A total of 177 Ju 52s and six Me 323s were shot down. As the Luftwaffe had already pressed its flight instructors and their more experienced pupils in the frontline squadrons, it was unable to replace them.

The final battle began on 6 May. Organised resistance collapsed that morning, Arnim's weak divisions having so little fuel that counter-attacks were no longer possible. By the afternoon of the following day, British troops were on the outskirts of Tunis and the defence had fragmented into isolated pockets. Arnim was captured on 12 May, and the surrender of the remaining Axis forces ordered that day.

Over 100,000 German soldiers were taken prisoner as well as 90,000 Italians. General Alexander signalled Churchill in triumphant mood, "It is my duty to report that the Tunisian campaign is over. All enemy resistance has ceased. We are masters of the North African shores."

British losses in Tunisia included over 6,000 dead and 30,000 wounded and missing – even when outnumbered and outgunned, the German army was an unforgiving, ruthlessly professional opponent.

Hitler had clung too long to his African enclave, but deserves credit for flinging troops into Tunisia at the end of 1942, when professional advice was to withdraw to Europe. The campaign kept the Allies away from Italy until the Autumn, by which time the Wehrmacht would have vastly increased its strength in the country and made its conquest much more difficult.

Below: Headed by 'Old Glory' American troops set off for the aerodrome at Maison Blanche outside Algiers. American landings here, unlike the rest of the operation, were virtually unopposed. Only two destroyers were lost and a few infantrymen were hit by die-hard snipers. The landings marked the beginning of the end for Panzerarmee Afrika.

LAST STAND OF THE AFRIKA KORPS

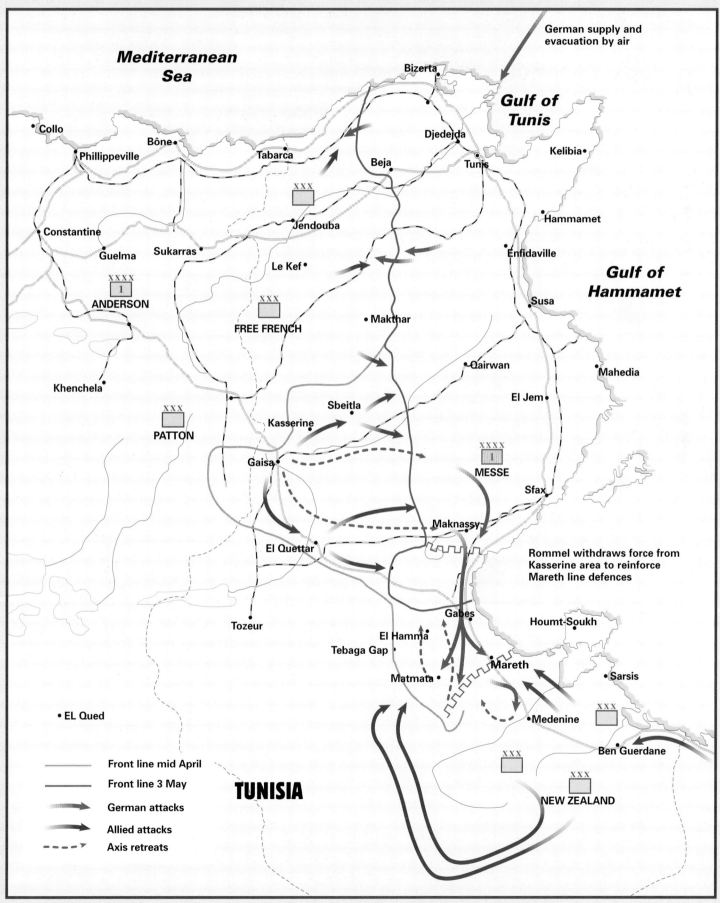

German supply and evacuation by air

Mediterranean Sea

Gulf of Tunis

Gulf of Hammamet

Collo
Bône
Phillippeville
Tabarca
Bizerta
Djedejda
Beja
Tunis
Kelibia
Hammamet

Constantine
Guelma
Sukarras
Le Kef
Enfidaville
Susa

XXXX
1
ANDERSON

XXX
Jendouba

XXX
FREE FRENCH

Makthar

Qairwan
Mahedia

El Jem

XXX
PATTON

Khenchela

Sbeitla
Kasserine
Gaisa

XXXX
1
MESSE

Sfax

Maknassy

El Quettar

Rommel withdraws force from Kasserine area to reinforce Mareth line defences

Tozeur

Gabes
Houmt-Soukh

El Hamma
Tebaga Gap
Mareth
Sarsis

Matmata

Medenine

XXX

• EL Qued

Ben Guerdane

XXX

XXX

TUNISIA

XXX
NEW ZEALAND

Front line mid April
Front line 3 May
German attacks
Allied attacks
Axis retreats

Stalingrad

The German Sixth Army had forced its way into Stalingrad expecting a quick victory and another triumph for the Third Reich. But the fighting grew harder and harder as autumn inexorably turned to winter.

No battle in history was as significant as Stalingrad. Before the fight for the city on the Volga, the Germans were winning the war. After the battle, their final defeat was inevitable.

IN THE SUMMER OF 1942 it seemed nothing could stop the 6th Army. The largest of the 12 German armies on the eastern front, it broke through the Soviet defences and the Red Army's retreat became a rout. The panic was as bad as anything seen the previous summer. Stalin responded with typically brutal vigour. Order No. 227, known for its key phrase 'Not a step back!' not only imposed the death penalty on men retreating without authorisation, but also called for retribution against their families. A return to Bolshevik-style 'discipline of the revolver' saw more than 13,500 executions carried out by the NKVD before the end of 1942.

Soviet resistance hardened as the 6th Army reached the Volga. Stalin's draconian measures played their part, but there was a genuinely popular spirit of resistance animating the defenders. Soviet soldiers' letters reveal a keen sense that the invaders were now 1500 kilometres inside Russia. If they could not be stopped here, where could they be stopped? And by mid-1942 all Russia knew what German rule meant for people designated 'racial inferiors' by the self-appointed master race. It was time to win or die.

Stalingrad was named after the Soviet dictator to commemorate a Civil War victory credited to his leadership. Stretching for nearly 25 km (15 miles) along the west bank of the Volga, it consisted mainly of wooden houses. However, there were three new manufacturing plants, the Red October steel works, the Barrikady ordnance factory and the Stalingrad tractor factory. These massive complexes were transformed into fortresses by Red Army engineers and by German bombing.

The fury of the German onslaught disguised the fact that the *Ostheer* was actually weaker than in 1941. There had been few city fights then, as the panzer divisions had by-passed places like Minsk, Kharkov and Kiev. But in 1942 there was little armour to spare for Stalingrad. A large part of the Wehrmacht's panzer strengh remained on the central front, to hold down the major Russian forces guarding Moscow. Kleist's 1st Panzer Army was by now nearing the Caspian Sea. The first three SS formations were re-equipping as fully-fledged panzer divisions, but they had been sent to France after the Allied attack on Dieppe was taken to herald a possible cross-Channel assault. As a result, new tanks were in short supply in the East, since the SS had priority. All this meant that when Hitler demanded his army take Stalingrad, it had to be done the hard way, by frontal attack.

SIXTH ARMY ATTACK

Supported by 2,000 guns and 500 tanks, 6th Army smashed into the heart of the city on 13 September. The 71st infantry division reached the river, cutting Stalingrad in two and bringing the crucial landing stages under fire. The Russians now had to run a gauntlet of machine-gun and mortar fire to get reinforcements and supplies into the city – and to extract the endless flow of wounded. 13th Guards division was rushed across from the east bank and suffered 90 per cent losses in a series of counter-attacks. Stalingrad's railway station was reduced to rubble as it changed hands four times on 14 September.

The Germans were fighting under the umbrella of 1,000 sorties a day flown by VIII *Fleigerkorps*. In face of that German air superiority, the Soviets developed a new tactic – they kept as close to the German front line as possible, making it harder for the Germans to rely on airstrikes.

The 6th Army's commander was summoned to Vinnitsa in the Ukraine on 12 September. At Hitler's field headquarters, known as *Werwolf*, the Führer demanded the immediate fall of the city for 'world historic reasons'. *Generaleutnant* Friederich Paulus had originally estimated that it would take ten

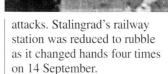

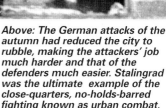

Above: The German attacks of the autumn had reduced the city to rubble, making the attackers' job much harder and that of the defenders much easier. Stalingrad was the ultimate example of the close-quarters, no-holds-barred fighting known as urban combat.

days of hard fighting with a period of re-grouping to follow, and he stuck to his original estimate.

GENERAL PAULUS

Paulus was a brilliant staff officer, formerly Reichenau's chief-of-staff, but this was his first independent command. From the moment he returned to the front, he was subjected to an incessant stream of signals from Hitler. His staff noticed a nervous tic appearing above one eye, and he suffered a recurrence of what German soldiers called 'the Russian sickness' – dysentery.

Above: An infantryman peers warily from his defensive position in a ruined Stalingrad building. The Soviets used such rubble as fortifications, often emerging from by-passed cellars to attack the Germans from behind.

Above: Stalingrad was a key industrial city, but it sprawled for tens of kilometers along the west bank of the Volga. Occupying the city proved to be much harder than the German high command had anticipated.

Above: German armour had proved decisive in the sweeping advance through the Russian steppes, but once bogged down in the ruins of Stalingrad the panzers proved vulnerable to determined attacks by defending infantrymen.

Hitler continued to goad Paulus throughout September and into the following month as the 6th Army pushed painfully through the ruins of the city. The amount of ground taken each day seemed always smaller than the last, and Soviet counter-attacks, especially by night, enabled them to cling to a small bridgehead on the west bank of the river. Tempers flared at Hitler's headquarters. On 24 September Hitler sacked General Franz Halder, chief of the Army General Staff.

TURN OF THE TIDE?

It was at this point, before the Soviet counter-attack, before the blizzards, before the shrinking Axis bridgehead in North Africa was overwhelmed, that Hitler sensed he had lost the war. General Warlimont confided to his diary after a visit to Vinnitsa, 'he has realised his fatal gamble is over, that Soviet Russia is not going to be beaten in this second attempt.' Hitler had told his generals that if he failed to take the Caucasian oilfields he would have to make peace. By October 1942 it was plain that Army Group A's lunge towards the Caspian had come to a halt. Attrition of men and vehicles had been heavy and the panzer divisions had outrun their supply lines. But worse was to come – winter was only weeks away.

Hitler did not make peace. Instead he focused more and more on that city by the Volga, named after his greatest enemy. Previously, he had ordered the 6th Army to occupy enough of the bank to stop river traffic. Now he demanded total conquest of Stalingrad.

By coincidence, Soviet generals Rokossovsky and Zhukov were in Moscow on the same day that Paulus flew to meet Hitler. They presented Stalin with an ambitious plan. The 6th Army's front ran for about 200 km (130 miles), from just south of the city, north west across the Don bends, to the Volga north of Rynok. Paulus had eight divisions inside Stalingrad, 11 manning the front and a single one in reserve.

THE SOVIET PLAN

Zhukov intended to attack the German front line either side of Stalingrad, cutting off the forces fighting for the city. By feeding in just enough replacements to sustain resistance in Stalingrad itself, the Soviets planned to hold the 6th Army in place while they assembled their best formations opposite Paulus' flanks. Since these were held by Romanian, Hungarian and Italian units, they lacked the weaponry or skill to deal with a massed tank attack.

Even as Paulus launched his final all-out effort to take the last sectors still in Soviet hands, German intelligence identified a threat to 6th Army's left flank.

As nine of his depleted divisions attacked the familiar ruins of the Red October factory on 11 November, 48th Panzer Corps was ordered to move behind the line of the Don. A corps in name only, it could call on one German panzer division with just 45 tanks and a Romanian armoured division with a similar quantity of obsolete vehicles. The 6th Army held 90 per cent of Stalingrad, but would never occupy the whole city.

For those German and allied divisions out on the bare steppe, the Stalingrad campaign was reminiscent of World War I. They remained in their trenches, exchanging the occasional artillery bombardment with the Russians. Aircraft sometimes joined in, but the majority were assigned to the fight for the city. Most of the German and all of the allied formations relied on horse transport; the Italians and Romanians had field guns dating

Sixth Army Attacks

IN SEPTEMBER 1942 General Friederich Paulus finally launched the Sixth Army's main attempt to capture Stalingrad.

But the time for taking the city by coup de main had passed. Hitler's diversion of Hoth's 4th Panzer Army to the Caucasus had delayed the drive on the Volga, and even when ordered to turn back the Panzers had to fight their way through stiffening Soviet resistance.

TOO LATE

Von Paulus's makeshift attack could only have succeeded if it met an enemy that was not only beaten but whose morale was extremely low. The delay had given the Soviets time to reinforce the city. From the very first engagements it was clear to the Germans that the Russians had recovered beyond anyone's expectations, and that the Russian slogan "The Volga has only one bank" was no empty boast.

The town had half a million inhabitants, and much of the civilian population had been marched out to dig trenches and anti-tank ditches. But that was not the only German worry. German intelligence had not warned the units taking part that Stalingrad sprawled for more than 30 kilometres along the Volga and that, in places, the western edge of the city was more than eight kilometres from the bank of the river.

LOW GERMAN MORALE

Generaloberst Von Richtofen, commander of Luftflotte IV, complained of the lack of spirit in the 6th Army. On 22 September he wrote "In the town itself progress is desperately slow. The 6th Army will never finish the job at this rate. Above all because it is threatened from the North by the Russians and because reinforcements arrive only in dribs and drabs. We have to fight endless engagements, taking one cellar after another in order to gain any ground at all".

Russian soldiers, spurred on by patriotic propaganda, were now fighting in circumstances in which their own natural talents were an advantage, and their lack of armour and mobility did not matter.

They fought from holes burrowed in rubble, from the blackened caverns of burned-out offices, from behind parapets of gaunt tower blocks; they fought for every yard of every street and every alleyway in the city.

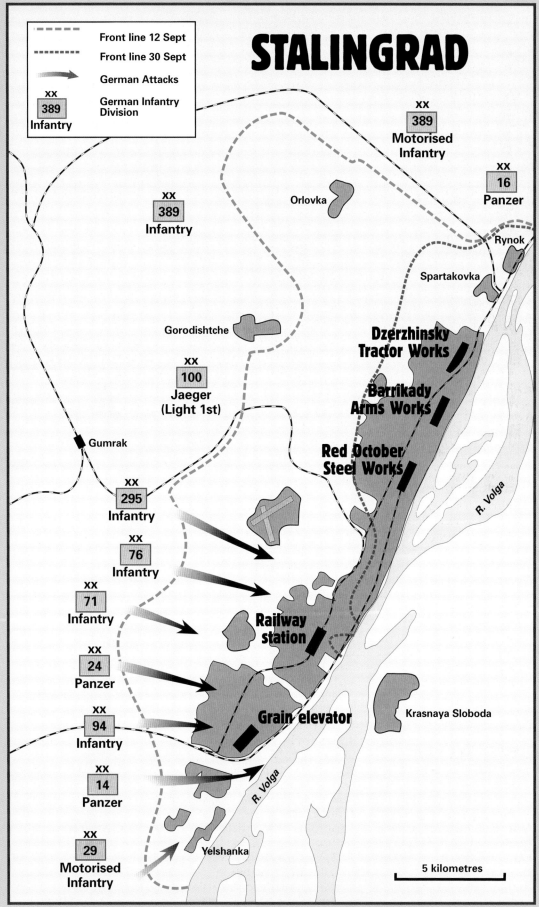

Above: Soviet troops on the east bank of the Volga engage Axis forces on the west bank with a PPSh 41 sub-machine gun and a Degtyarev light machine gun. Fierce Red Army resistance meant that the Sixth Army never established a bridgehead on the Soviet side.

Below: A Bersaglieri runs for cover across the iron-hard steppe. The large Italian Eighth Army guarded the German northern flank, but proved no match for the Soviet 1st Guards and 5th Tank Armies.

Below: Winter brought new horrors to the Germans. Cold-weather gear, while of better quality than the year before, was nevertheless in short supply – and Goering's promise that the Luftwaffe would be able to supply the Sixth Army from the air proved to be disastrously wrong.

from the First World War. As the blistering 50 degree heat of the Russian summer turned into autumn, rain filled the trenches and the soldiers endured a miserable existence.

SOVIET OFFENSIVE

On 19 November Paulus received alarming signals from his divisions on the steppes. Soviet forces were attacking in unbelievable strength from their bridgeheads over the Don. Division after division reported massive artillery barrages, intense air attack and wave after wave of tanks. Some units were already failing to respond to radio calls from 6th Army headquarters. Then the Soviets attacked in the south too. By 23 November the encirclement was complete. Some 300,000 German and allied soldiers were trapped. And the 6th Army's winter clothing was still in storage at the Tatsinskaya depot, 200 km away.

Paulus reported that he had only enough food for a week and that fuel and ammunition was running low. His subordinates begged him to order a break out, but Paulus' superior, Field Marshal von Manstein, refused to hear of it. Hitler insisted that *Festung Stalingrad* hold out until relieved. The expression 'fortress' gave false comfort: the troops had no proper fortifications, just the holes in the frozen ground they had managed to excavate with their remaining explosives.

GOERING'S BOAST

At this critical moment, Hermann Goering intervened fatally. Smarting from humiliation – the RAF was making a mockery of his proud boast that Germany would never be bombed – he announced that the Luftwaffe would fly in enough supplies to keep the 6th Army fighting.

Most of the senior officers involved in the airlift assumed that this was to be for a very limited period until the army broke out or a relief force went in. In fact, any staff officer with the 6th Army's order of battle

and a pencil could work out just how ridiculous Goering's promise was.

It is usually stated that the 6th Army's minimum supply requirement was for 500 tonnes per day. However, 500 tonnes was in fact the requirement for Seydlitz's 51st Corps alone. The German 6th Army could not have survived on anything less than 1500 tonnes of supplies: the airlift only managed an average of about 100 tonnes. To keep 6th Army going would have required more than the entire Luftwaffe could fly in.

WINTER HELL

The temperature sank remorselessly. Blizzards swept across the steppe. Huddled in underground bunkers, the 6th Army counted the days until a relief operation rescued them. Fighting rations were reduced to 200 grammes of horsemeat and 200 grammes of bread per day. Support troops received half that, and there was nothing at all for Soviet prisoners held inside the pocket. Yet the ordinary soldiers believed, against mounting evidence to the contrary, that Hitler would get them out.

Staff officers, privy to Paulus' indecision and teleprinter messages from Army Group Don, suspected the worst. Although Paulus' headquarters continued to pass on Manstein's promise to save them, the female nurses in the base hospital were flown out of the pocket on the first evacuation flights.

Manstein failed. He sent *Generaloberst* Hoth to blast a way through the Soviet lines on 12 December, and in a week of desperate fighting, his panzer corps got close enough to see the horizon lit up at night, flares rising and falling over the pocket. His mission had been anticipated by Zhukov, who had already taken steps to counter any relief attempt. Within days, the Soviets attacked the Italian and Romanian armies along the river Chir, north west of Stalingrad. Another great breakthrough was achieved, and Hoth's relief force

Defenders of the Krasny Oktiabr steel works watch as a flight of Ilyushin Il-2 Stormoviks pass low overhead on their way to attack nearby German positions. The first Wehrmacht assault on Red October started on Sunday 27 September 1942, and over the next three months the complex was to host some of the most bitter and costly fighting of the war in the east.

Red October

THE SPRAWLING HULK OF Stalingrad spread out along the banks of the Volga was stiffened by a spine of huge industrial plants, notably the Dzerzhinsky tractor works, the Barrikady ordnance works, and the huge *Krasny Oktiabr* (Red October) steel works.

The first German attack, on 27 September, was mounted by the 389th Infantry Division, the 100th Jaeger Division and the 24th Panzer Division. Over the next two weeks the Germans ground their way through the tractor factory and on to the Barrikady plant. There was a lull before the the attacks continued, on 14 October.

The battle for Red October became a bloody stalemate, made worse by the coming of sub-zero temperatures and the fact that German units had been ground down to ten percent of their nominal fighting strength. The last major push, on 11 November, was brought to a halt when Zhukov launched his great counter attack on 19 November.

Above: Stalingrad's industrial sector was perfect for ambushes. A German MG34 team engages snipers on the roof of a factory.

Right: The German bombardment of Red October turned the steel works into a massive rubble heap: hard to attack across, but offering the defenders countless fighting positions.

Above: On 19 November, a massive Soviet barrage opened up on the Rumanian divisions to the north of the Sixth Army. This was followed by the overwhelming attack of no less than six Soviet armies, spearheaded by the 1st Guards and 5th Tank Armies.

Below: The Soviet plan was simple: penetrate the Axis defences at their weakest points, then drive deep behind the bulk of the enemy forces. Attacking with considerable verve, the two arms of the Soviet pincer met on 23 November. Hitler's Sixth Army was trapped.

Below: Italian troops on the Don front fall back in the face of overwhelming Soviet power. Short rations, low ammunition, sickness and above all the intense cold meant that the Axis forces around Stalingrad had to retreat or be annihilated.

was compelled to turn away and meet the new threat. The 6th Army was abandoned.

The airlift collapsed on Christmas Eve when an enterprising Soviet tank commander drove his T-34s to the limit of their endurance. The tanks over-ran Tatsinkskaya airfield just as the last Ju-52s scraped off the runway. The 6th Army fought on, but as autopsies revealed, the men were starving to death. Sentries committed suicide. After Christmas was celebrated, with an odd mixture of foreboding and acute sentimentality, some officers shot themselves.

To stiffen his soldiers' resolve, Paulus had 364 of his men executed for cowardice.

NOWHERE TO GO

Stalin ordered the pocket crushed in January, and a renewed Soviet blitzkrieg broke into the perimeter west of the city. The survivors fled into the city where every cellar became packed with wounded men. Typhus and dysentery swept through the ranks of emaciated, frost-bitten soldiers. The scale of suffering was outside the Germans' experience, but was even worse for the Soviet prisoners-of-war held inside the pocket. The handful of survivors found by the Red Army had been forced into cannibalism to stay alive.

The last airfield inside the pocket was at Pitomnik, and hideous scenes ensued as the Soviets approached. Thousands of wounded men crawled

MARSHAL Rokossovsky's Don Front launched Operation Uranus, attacking the Romanian Third Army at 07.30 on the morning of 19 November. Vatutin's South West Front followed half an hour later, broadening the attack to a width of more than eighty kilometres. Over half a million troops and about a thousand tanks quickly brushed the Romanians aside. At 10.00 the next day, Yeremenko's Stalingrad Front joined the attack, and the two huge pincers met near Kalach on 23 November, sealing off the German Sixth Army.

SW Front *Vatutin*
1st Guards Army
5th Tank Army
21st Army

338,631 men
2,201 artillery pieces
4,300 mortars
628 rocket launchers
730 tanks

Don Front *Rokossovsky*
65th Army
24th Army
66th Army

292,000 men
1,838 artillery pieces
3,937 mortars
435 rocket launchers
180 tanks

Stalingrad Front
Yeremenko
62nd Army (in Stalingrad)
64th Army
57th Army
51st Army

383,000 men
2,500 artillery pieces
3,300 mortars
337 rocket launchers
650 tanks

through the snow and desperate fights broke out to get aboard the last aircraft.

Hitler had forbidden generals or party leaders to use their powers to extract friends and relatives; some men were nevertheless spirited out. Albert Speer's brother discharged himself from the field hospital where he was being treated, and was eventually posted missing. Hitler's nephew Leo Raubal was a captain in the engineers, and survived to be taken prisoner. Hitler would later offer Stalin his son Iacob in exchange for Leo, but the Soviet leader refused.

Some 25,000 sick and wounded were evacuated, and a number of specialists and officers ordered home before Stalingrad surrendered, but a far

Sixth Army Encircled

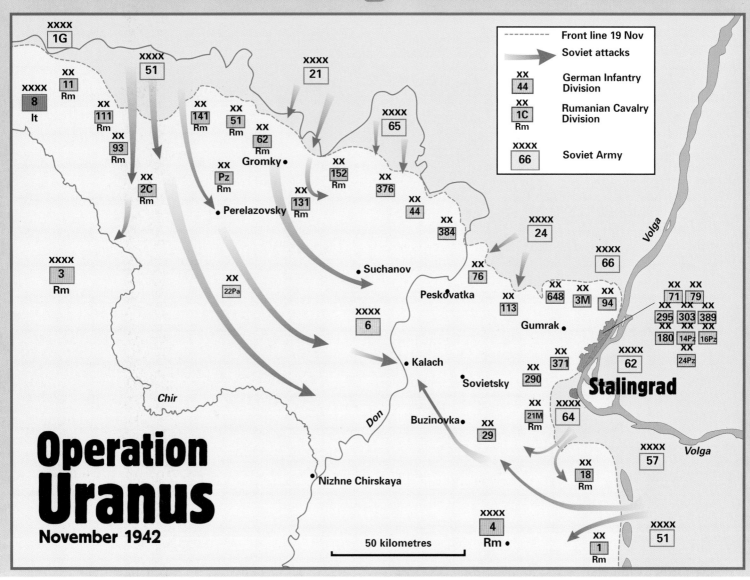

Operation Uranus
November 1942

Legend:
- – – – – Front line 19 Nov
- → Soviet attacks
- XX / 44 — German Infantry Division
- XX / 1C Rm — Rumanian Cavalry Division
- XXXX / 66 — Soviet Army

Map labels: 1G, 51, 21, 11 Rm, 8 It, 111 Rm, 141 Rm, 51 Rm, 65, 93 Rm, 62 Rm, 2C Rm, Pz Rm, 152 Rm, 376, 131 Rm, 44, 384, 24, 3 Rm, 22Pa, Suchanov, Peskovatka, 76, 66, 113, 648, 3M, 94, 71, 79, 295, 303, 389, 180, 14Pz, 16Pz, 24Pz, 6, Kalach, Gumrak, Gromky, Perelazovsky, Sovietsky, 371, 290, 62, Stalingrad, Buzinovka, 21M Rm, 64, 29, Nizhne Chirskaya, 18 Rm, 57, Volga, 4 Rm, 1 Rm, 51, Chir, Don

50 kilometres

greater number of men died as frost-bitten limbs and wounds turned gangrenous. Anaesthetic ran out. No rations were given to the wounded after 11 January.

SIXTH ARMY FALLS

Hitler promoted Paulus to Field Marshal, on the tacit understanding that no German Field Marshal had ever been taken alive. But Paulus refused to kill himself and surrendered on 30 January. Ironically, it was the anti-Nazi old soldier, Strecker, commander of 11th Corps, who held out longest. He surrendered his isolated pocket in the north of Stalingrad on 1 February. Small parties broke out on to the steppe, trying to make their way back, and were spotted from time to time by Luftwaffe reconnaissance flights. None made it.

For the families and friends of the men involved, Stalingrad was more than a defeat: it was a betrayal. Hitler gave his word that the 6th Army would be saved. Instead, the soldiers were sacrificed to Hitler's crackpot strategy and Goering's vanity.

Of the 300,000 men in the pocket, 91,000 survived to surrender, and half of them were dead before spring. Curiously, since they had beheaded the Polish army in 1941 by shooting 15,000 officers, the Soviets treated the 6th Army's officers with relative forbearance: 95 per cent of them would survive the war. But 95 per cent of the ordinary soldiers died in Soviet POW and labour camps.

Below: Romanian General Demetriou, Lieutenant General Edler von Daniel and XIV Corps commander General Helmuth Schlömer are seen after the surrender of Stalingrad. Grim though their imprisonment will be, it will be nothing to the hell ordinary German soldiers will suffer.

An oil-covered survivor from a torpedoed merchantman. He is one of the lucky ones: hundreds of ships sunk meant the death of thousands of seamen, from drowning, burning, or exposure in the bitter Atlantic waters.

Iron Coffins
The Defeat of the U-Boat

By the beginning of 1943, it seemed that the U-boats were winning the battle of the Atlantic. More boats were operational, and Allied ship losses rose catastrophically.

THE SECOND U-boat 'happy time' occurred during the first seven months of 1942. On 13 January, U-boat commanders lying off the American coast received orders to commence hostilities with the USA. Co-ordination between US Army, Navy and civilian administrations was poor: ships were silhouetted by the lights of American towns where 'blackout' was unknown. U-boats remained on the bottom by day, surfacing at dusk to inflict repeated losses on merchant ships still sailing singly and often fully illuminated.

The US authorities took a long time to profit from hard-won and freely-offered British experience. It took until April 1942 for the US Navy to beat back the onslaught, conducted by no more than a dozen submarines at any one time. Monthly losses averaged over a hundred merchant ships totalling 500,000 tons.

U-BOAT STRANGLEHOLD

Imports to Britain continued to decline during 1942, partly because the U-boats were inflicting such heavy attrition in the Atlantic, but also because large quantities of shipping were diverted for the invasion of North Africa (Operation Torch) in November. At the same time the US counter-offensive in the Pacific absorbed considerable quantities of US hulls. From a pre-war total of 50 million tons a year, British imports fell to 42 million in 1940; 31 million in 1941; and 23 million tons during 1942 – which was too little to keep the country going.

Although Hitler's armies ended the year on the ropes in both Russia and North Africa, the citizens of Great Britain faced even more stringent rationing and British war industries were threatened with a lack of raw materials. Prime Minister Winston Churchill remained highly concerned about the U-boat threat, and it was agreed at the highest levels that the Allies' top priority for 1943 was

the defeat of the U-boats. Until they were mastered, the build-up of US forces in Britain was in peril and the prospects for a successful invasion of mainland Europe remote.

ATTACK THE BASES

From the autumn of 1942 U-boat bases in France and shipyards in Germany were targeted with great energy by RAF Bomber Command and the US 8th Air Force. Enormous destruction was caused to the ports, which were easier to locate than cities inland. Lorient and St Nazaire were levelled; but, secure in their concrete pens, the U-boats were unharmed. This effort was criticised at the time (and since) as a waste of effort: diverting a fraction of the four-engined bombers to anti-submarine patrols would have had far greater effect.

To be fair, the success rate of ASW aircraft had not been great, with hardly a kill confirmed since the beginning of the war, so the bomber chiefs' argument that it was better to attack the U-boats in their lair, rather than search for them mid-Ocean seemed to make sense at the time. Doenitz shared the view that submarines at sea could avoid air attack. Neither party knew that developments in airborne radar, depth charges and homing torpedoes were poised to make aircraft the greatest threat to the U-boat.

HARD FACTS

In fact, the cold arithmetic of the Battle of the Atlantic was already turning in the Allies' favour. In the summer of 1942 the average number of merchant ships sunk had fallen to less than one per U-boat sortie. And the U-boat hit rate dropped from 0.91 ships per sortie in July/August to 0.65 in September and 0.63 in November. Half of all U-boat sorties produced no results at all. The Type VII and Type IX submarines required urgent modernisation or, better, replacement by more modern designs.

Admiral Doenitz planned one more major effort to break the

Above: The U–boat war was one of move and countermove, with both sides bringing in new weapons to counter the last enemy ploy. But Allied air power was the one thing which the Kriegsmarine could not match.

Below: A damaged merchant ship, unable to keep up with its convoy, is sunk by gunfire. U-boats pounced on such stragglers like wolves, but increased Allied defences meant that such surface attacks were very risky.

Atlantic lifeline with his older boats, before refitting them with new weapons and sensors. However, Hitler ordered him to attack the Allied landings in North Africa. U-boats were ordered into the Mediterranean, which Doenitz regarded as a lost cause. Twenty-five U-boats of the Atlantic force were sent to North African waters, where the Allies had concentrated their air and surface ASW forces to protect the troop transports. Eight U-boats were damaged and three lost with all hands in exchange for just eleven Allied ships. The submarines failed to disrupt the amphibious assault, which overran Algeria and soon reduced Axis presence in North Africa to a bridgehead in Tunisia.

Most U-boats that sailed in January 1943 carried improved torpedoes. The G7a could be set to run in a pattern, looping around inside a convoy until it hit something. A few carried the G7e which homed in on the sound of a ship's propellers. The T-5, which entered service that summer, was a faster version, capable of 24 knots and intended as the standard anti-escort weapon. Deck guns were removed in favour of increased anti-aircraft armament. Passive sonar, capable of detecting ships at up to 20 miles was fitted in an array along the port and starboard bow sections.

However, the Allies were poised to counter with new types of airborne radar, undetectable

Left: When it came to detecting the enemy, the U-boats were at a disadvantage. Allied sub-hunters could find U-boats with radar and HF radio direction-finding equipment, but to find convoys the U-boat had primarily to rely on radio messages from France and the Mark I human eyeball.

Right: Fuel-efficient diesel engines enabled U-boats to range far and wide in the search for victims, but their need for air also tied the boats to the surface for long periods.

Below: Merchant seamen at least had a chance of reaching lifeboats when hit by torpedoes: a depth-charged U-boat crew had far less chance of survival.

by the Germans' Metox FuMB warning gear (the 'Biscay Cross'). Additionally, High-Frequency Direction-Finding equipment (HF/DF or 'Huff-Duff') would enable Royal Navy escort vessels to run down a line of bearing to catch U-boats making the long radio transmissions that were such a feature of 'Wolfpack' tactics.

The *Kriegsmarine* was woefully behind the Allies in the use of radar at sea and it was not until mid-1943 that some U-boats received a primitive search radar, a conversion of a Luftwaffe system. Defensive measures were more advanced: U-boats were provided with Aphrodite, a radar reflecting balloon that moved across the surface of the sea, and Thetis, a radar-reflecting buoy designed to draw the enemy's attention while the U-boat slipped away.

In winter 1942-43 technology took second place to the elements in the North Atlantic. It was the worse winter in living memory. Convoys had to heave-to in

ferocious gales that could last a week or more. U-boats pitched violently on the surface, the watch peering into binoculars while clinging to the bridge, trusting to the safety harness to save them when green water swallowed the whole boat. U-boats sought relief from the mountainous seas by diving deep below the tempest, but they could find no targets there.

90 BOATS AT SEA
As the winter gales finally subsided, the U-boat arm at last achieved the numbers Doenitz had demanded before the war to achieve the economic blockade of the UK. The Atlantic force rose from 157 boats to 186 by May 1943, with numbers at sea rising from 61 in January to 90 in April. Four convoys were attacked with particular effect in March 1943: 39 out of the 200 merchantmen were sunk.

Doenitz scented victory – though exaggerated claims by his skippers contributed to a sense of triumph which was premature. By

contrast, Churchill was dismayed, though President Roosevelt responded by allocating 150 new ships from US yards for British use. The British Official History would refer to this time as the 'crisis of crises' in the Atlantic.

The U-boats sank a total of 84 merchant ships in the Atlantic during March, as well as the escort *Harvester*, sunk by *U 432*. Eleven ships were sunk in the Indian Ocean by long range Type IXDs, 12 in the Mediterranean and three in the Arctic. Doenitz, who focussed entirely on tonnage sunk, chalked up some 750,000 tons, though the true figure was 635,000 tons.

The secret war was also going the German way. German *B-dienst* (signals intelligence) teams were reading the Allied naval codes, enabling Doenitz to position his patrols across the paths of the convoys. At the same time, changes to the German Enigma code procedures left the Allied codebreakers at Bletchley Park blind, so chillingly described in Robert Harris's

novel *Enigma*. U-boat captains concentrated their attentions on the 'air gap' southeast of Greenland where, apart from a handful of RAF Coastal Command B-24s in Iceland, no Allied aircraft had the range to cover. The presence of two Type XIV U-boat tankers (*U 461* and *U 463*) enabled many Type VII boats to remain on station for longer than usual.

TURN OF THE TIDE
The sudden rise in U-boat successes ended as quickly as it began. The weather improved, enabling the escort carriers attached to ASW groups to get their aircraft into the sky. Four such groups were in the mid-Atlantic by May, and many more land-based ASW aircraft roved above the convoys. Radar and HF/DF sets enabled escort vessels to engage submarines more often, and torpex-filled depth charges, more than 50% more powerful than conventional munitions, made attacks more lethal. Forward-firing mortars

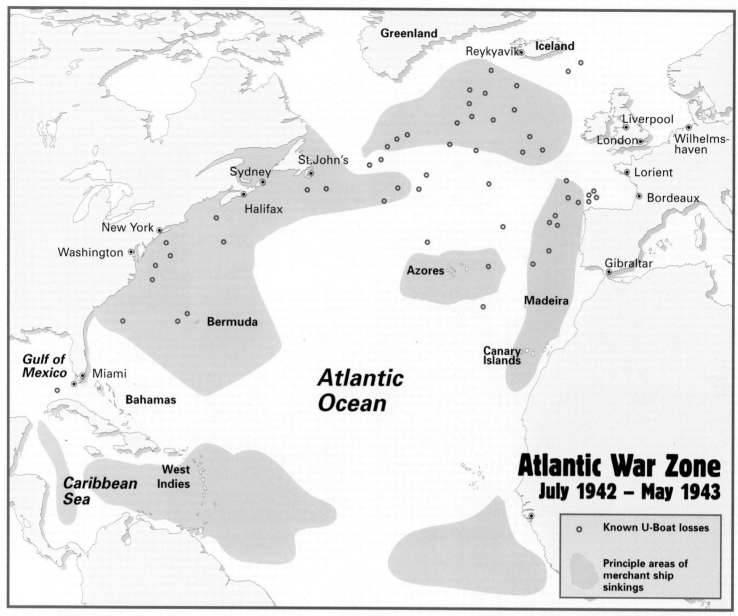

Greenland
Reykyavik • Iceland

Liverpool
London • • Wilhelms-
haven

St.John's • Lorient

Sydney • Bordeaux
Halifax

New York •

Washington • • Gibraltar

Azores

Madeira

Gulf of
Mexico • Miami

Canary
Islands

Bahamas

*Atlantic
Ocean*

West
Indies

Atlantic War Zone
July 1942 – May 1943

*Caribbean
Sea*

| ○ | Known U-Boat losses |
| | Principle areas of merchant ship sinkings |

Climax in the Atlantic

There were more than 200 convoy routes designated by the Allies during World War II, about half of which were attacked by U-boats. Most were known by two letters often indicating the starting and finishing ports. Each of the important routes was used by more than 100 convoys before 1945.

AS	USA - Freetown	JT	Rio de Janeiro - Trinidad	SG	Sydney - Greenland
BRN	Brazilian coastal	JW	Loch Ewe - Kola Fjord	SL	Sierra Leone (Freetown) - UK
BT	Bahia - Trinidad	KG	Key West - Guantanamo	SQ	Sydney - Quebec
BTC	UK coastal	KJ	Kingston - Europe	TA	UK - USA
BX	Boston - Halifax	KMF	UK - Mediterranean (fast)	TAG	Trinidad - Aruba - Guantanamo
CU	Caribbean - UK (tankers)	KMS	UK - Mediterranean (slow)	TAM	Gibraltar - UK
DN	Durban - North	KRS	UK - North Africa	TB	Trinidad - Bahia
EBC	Channel	KS	Casablanca - Brest/St Nazaire	TBC	UK coastal
ECP	Channel (Invasion convoys)	LMD	Lorenco Marques - Durban	TJ	Trinidad - Rio de Janeiro
EMC	Channel (Invasion convoys)	MH	UK coastal	TM	Trinidad - Gibraltar
ET	North Africa - Gibraltar	MKF	Mediterranean - UK (fast)	TS	Takoradi - Freetown
ETC	Channel	MKS	Mediterranean - UK (slow)	UC	UK - Caribbean
FN	Freetown - Natal	NG	New York - Guantanamo	UGF	USA - Gibraltar (fast)
FXP	Channel (Invasion convoys)	OA	UK - Outward (N. America)	UGS	USA - Gibraltar (slow)
Gibr	Canaries - Gibraltar (coastal)	OB	UK - Outward (N. America)	UR	UK - Reykjavik
GTX	Gibraltar - Tripoli - Alexandria	OG	UK - Gibraltar	UT	USA - UK
GUS	Gibraltar - USA (slow)	ON(F)	UK - North America (fast)	VWP	UK coastal
HA	Tripoli - Augusta	ONS	UK - North America (slow)	WAT	Key West - Aruba - Trinidad
HG	Gibraltar - UK	OS	UK - Freetown	WEG	UK coastal
HN	Bergen - Methil	OT	New York - North West Africa	WS	UK - Middle East
HX	Halifax/New York - UK	PG	Panama - Guantanamo	XB	Halifax - Boston
		PK	Petsamo (Kirkenes) - Kola Fjord	XK	Gibraltar - UK
		PQ	Iceland - North Russia		
		QP	North Russia - Iceland		
		QS	Quebec - Sydney		
		RA	Kola Fjord - Loch Ewe		
		RB	St. Lawrence - UK		
		RS	Gibraltar - Sierra Leone		
		RU	Reykjavik - UK		
		SC	Sydney - UK		

Right: Karl Doenitz was one of the few senior Nazis who knew how to defeat the British, but he could not match the resources thrown into the Battle of the Atlantic by the Allies.

('Hedgehog') and a 2,000 lb (900 kg) torpedo tube-launched 'super depth charge' further increased the chance of a 'kill'. Allied aircraft patrolling over Biscay, caught new U-boat skippers on their first patrol and tired crews on their way home after gruelling weeks at sea. The code-breakers cracked Enigma again, and in June, the British abandoned naval code no. 3 after positive proof it was compromised.

U-boat losses soared: in the first three weeks of May, 15 were sunk and another 15 damaged and compelled to abort their patrols. In April/May, 58 boats were lost – 53 in the Atlantic. Doenitz' youngest son Peter was among the 1,500 U-boat crewmen killed.

At the Admiral's headquarters consideration was given to abandoning the campaign; decorated skippers Erich Topp and Reinhard Suhren argued that there was no prospect of success, at least, not with the submarines currently in service.

In his memoirs, Doenitz describes it as a 'bitter decision' to fight on. His objective was to force the Allies to continue to devote resources to convoy defence, and to train crews for the next U-boat generation. In other words, he would continue sending out crews to almost certain death, while promising future 'wonder weapons' to reverse the tide of war.

His once towering reputation among his men was diminished; some of the more jaded officers wondered if Doenitz, now commander-in-chief of the Kriegsmarine, had not spent so long with Hitler he became infected. One disillusioned propaganda writer survived a disastrous U-boat patrol to write the famous novel Das Boot. (Although perversely, it is set in 1941 when U-boat morale was at its highest.) Others unwisely spoke out at the time. Doenitz once intervened to save the reputation, if not the life of one Ritterkreuz holder, Heinrich Bleichrodt who resigned his commission in U 109 mid-Atlantic. But the 25-year-old commander of U 154, Oskar Heinz Kusch was shot by firing squad for making disparaging remarks about Hitler. Erich Topp wondered whether Doenitz was "so naïve he did not know what people were saying in the U-boat messes about the Party and the Grofaz' (Grosstes Feldherr in Alles Zeit – an early propaganda description of Hitler as the Greatest Military Commander of All Time used scornfully later in the war). As an admiral in the Bundesmarine after the war, Topp tried to get Kusch rehabilitated, but die-hard elements in the naval veterans movement were able to stop him.

MOST CONVOYS ARE SAFE

The heavy losses suffered by Halifax 228 and 229 and slow convoys 121 and 122 obscured the fact that eleven other convoys arrived safely. In the first quarter of 1943, 95% of shipping completed the Atlantic run. The U-boats sank 264 ships during this period, totalling 1.5 million tons; meanwhile US shipyards built 546 ships totalling 3.5 million tons.

From then on, the graphs at Doenitz's headquarters and the Admiralty charted a remorseless drop in U-boat sinkings. The campaign would continue until the last day of the war, but the Type XXI 'electroboote' did not enter service until 1945, largely due to the Allied strategic bombing campaign. The schnorkel, introduced to enable TypeVIIs and Type IXs to remain submerged for most of a patrol, never worked successfully. 'Snorting' U-boats made so much noise, they could not detect a convoy – or an escort thundering down having detected the radar reflection from the schnorkel.

In March 1945, 29 Type VII U-boats sortied from their bases in Norway to attack shipping around the UK, 15 of them new boats on their maiden patrol. They accounted for nine ships, but 17 of the submarines were sunk; 54 crew men were captured, 746 killed. The dedication of Hitler's U-boat fleet outlasted that of the Führer himself, but it had lost the war more than two years earlier.

Below: Having produced sufficient vessels to give every convoy a close escort, the Allies then developed specialised anti-submarine groups, often based on escort carriers, whose sole function was to chase down and sink U-boats.

An American-built Consolidated PBY Catalina in service with RAF Coastal Command drops a depth charge. Anti-submarine aircraft were the biggest threat to U-boats: they could cover an enormous area of sea on a patrol and attack with greater speed than a surface vessel.

Hunter Killers

Above and left: Depth charges dropped by a Sunderland flying boat ring a Type IX U-boat, ripping through its pressure hull and forcing the crew to take to the water in their life jackets.

Right: Crew at least had the chance to escape from U-boats on the surface: once underwater, chances were almost nil. Survival depended on being somewhere near an escape hatch, with underwater breathing gear, and getting out before the boat sank too far. Very few managed it.

Assault on
Dismembering the Axis

Left: Troops from Montgomery's Eighth Army land on Sicily. By now, the veteran desert army consisted of four infantry divisions, three armoured brigades, and three further divisions in reserve.

HITLER'S insistence on pouring men into Tunisia enabled the Axis bridgehead in Africa to survive another six months. But its fall was inevitable once the US Army was ashore in strength and the British 8th Army advanced across Libya.

Hitler assumed that the Allies would follow up their victory with an immediate assault on his Italian ally. In fact, there was a bitter and protracted debate over what to do next. The US Army wanted to land in western Europe; they and the Russians demanded a 'second front' in 1943. Only the British insisted on attacking Italy.

They argued that the Italian army would disintegrate if the

Allies landed. Germany would be compelled to divert men and resources to defend Italy – forces that would otherwise be fighting in Russia or preparing to resist the eventual Allied landings in France. And the British sincerely doubted the ability of the western Allies to take on the Germans in 1943. Subsequent events suggest their misgivings were justified.

Most Italians were reluctant German allies. In the First World War Italy had fought against Germany; British and French divisions had fought to stop a German invasion of Italy in 1917. The experience of 1940-42 hardened Italian attitudes. Mussolini's war had led to the loss of Italy's African colonies and the destruction of the Italian 8th Army alongside the Germans at Stalingrad.

Occupation duties had highlighted the differences between the Italians and Germans. Nazi demands to

Italy

With the defeat of the Axis in North Africa, it would only be a matter of time before the Allies moved again. But Germany and her Allies had to defend a coastline stretching from North Cape to the Turkish border. Where would the Allies strike?

Main picture: A German MG34 team watches over a stretch of the Sicilian coast. This was just one of a number of beaches on which the British and Americans could land – but it was the closest to Africa.

Below: A German officer spots an advancing Allied column in Sicily. Once the British and Americans had a foothold ashore, the Axis high command knew that it would only be a matter of time before they would have to evacuate.

deport the Jewish populations of Greece and Yugoslavia to the extermination camps confirmed to many Italians that their allies were barbarians. Only Mussolini and a diminishing band of die-hard Fascists still believed in his 'new Roman Empire'. Most ordinary people – and the military high command – recognised it was time to break with the Nazis.

MULTI-FRONT FEARS

Doubts over Italy and fear of an Allied assault across the Channel left Hitler anxious over his planned summer offensive in Russia. His generals intended to chop off the Kursk salient, shortening the front line and hopefully inflicting another stinging defeat on the Red Army. The German army had never failed to shatter the Russians in summertime. With no snow or mud to impede the panzers, and sunny skies for the Luftwaffe, there was every expectation of

success. To guard against nasty surprises south of the Alps, Hitler sent General Rommel to Italy where he was tasked with contingency planning in case of Italian defection.

Allied invasion plans were masked by a successful deception operation. German intelligence believed there would be an attack on Sardinia or on Greece. A body dressed as a British officer, washed ashore in Spain, provided clinching (but faked) evidence – later the subject of the book and film, *The Man Who Never Was*.

On 10 July 1943 US, British and Commonwealth forces invaded Sicily. A divisional scale airborne assault supplemented the amphibious landings; involving 180,000 men and over 2,500 ships, it was the largest amphibious attack of the war apart from D-Day. Only two German formations, the *Hermann Goering Panzerdivision* and 15. *Panzergrenadierdivision* were

there to hold off eight Allied divisions. Nobody expected the quarter of a million Italian troops to fight with any heart.

The airborne element of the Allied invasion suffered grievous losses. A combination of strong headwinds and inexperienced tow pilots led to premature glider launches: many of the powerless craft and their occupants crashed into the sea miles short of land.

GERMAN RESISTANCE

Divided into small battlegroups or *Kampfgruppen*, the Germans resisted with exemplary professionalism. Tenacious rearguards held up vastly larger forces. Sharp counter-attacks won local victories that kept the Allies off balance. Some Italian formations fought hard, but others melted away. German reinforcements arrived: the elite 1. *Fallschirmjager* division and 29. *Panzergrenadierdivision*.

Field Marshal Montgomery's 8th Army made slow progress up

> **"In February, the Italian empire ceased to exist. Today, we have captured our first slice of the Italian homeland. We have knocked Mussolini off his perch, the enemy is hemmed in, and now we will drive the Germans out of Sicily."**
> **Field Marshal B.L Montgomery**
> **30 July 1943**

the eastern side of the island, while the dynamic General Patton was sent on a roundabout route to the north coast. The only 'thruster' of the campaign, he took grave risks, suffered one shock defeat, but stampeded towards Messina once past Palermo.

It was clear that Sicily would soon fall, and Hitler conceded

Left: Luftwaffe paratroopers were mostly used as conventional infantry during the Sicilian campaign. 1.Fallschirmjäger Division – formerly the pioneering 7 Flieger Division – was flown to Catania in response to the Allied landings, and fought hard against British and American paratroopers.

Right: The landings in Sicily persuaded a large section of the Italian government that it was time for Mussolini to go. Ousted from power, he was replaced by Marshal Pietro Badoglio.

Below: German suspicions of Italian intentions were confirmed in the Sicilian campaign. Privates like these surrendered to the Allies, while their officers plotted Mussolini's overthrow. In turn, the Germans planned to occupy Italy should it prove necessary.

that only a timely withdrawal would avoid a second Tunisia debacle. Stubborn defensive fighting held the Allies back until the beginning of August when Field Marshal Kesselring, Commander-in-Chief South-West, ordered the evacuation.

On the night of 11-12 August every available vessel was used as a ferry. Despite ample warnings, the Allies failed to intervene; 40,000 German troops and their equipment got clean away. Some 60,000 Italian troops were also shipped over, but their role in the war was almost over.

Mussolini's position was precarious. Two Fascist factions plotted his overthrow, both intending to fight on. However, it was the king and a cabal of

military officers who prevailed, and they wanted either neutrality or to change sides. The Fascist Grand Council, which had not met since 1939, was convened on 24 July. A motion against Mussolini was carried by 19 votes to 8. The dictator was arrested in the name of King Victor Emmanuel and Marshal Pietro Badoglio appointed head of a new government.
The Fascist regime that had dominated Italy for twenty years evaporated overnight.

TALKING TO BOTH SIDES
Badoglio assured the Germans that Italy would remain faithful, but Rommel's 'Operation Alaric' was ready to be implemented just in case. Pressed by the

British and Americans to surrender immediately, the Italian leaders prevaricated, giving the Germans time to transfer additional troops to Italy, mainly from the East. Far away on the Steppes the battle of Kursk had begun badly for Germany. It was already coming to an end when news reached Hitler's headquarters that the Allies were ashore in Sicily. The end of offensive operations at Kursk on 13 July enabled some units to be withdrawn. These included 1. *SS-Panzerkorps*, which was sent by train to northern Italy.

The Allies wanted Italy to co-operate in surrender: they demanded that the Italian fleet sail to Malta and that Italian

army units support an airborne drop on Rome. At length, weary of Badoglio's manoeuvrings, the Allies conducted an amphibious assault on the beaches at Salerno, south of Naples, on 9 September. Simultaneously, Montgomery blasted his way across the straits of Messina to arrive at the toe of Italy; naval units ferried British airborne troops to seize the naval base of Taranto.
Italy belatedly surrendered.

FLEET SURRENDER
The Italian fleet sailed to join the Allies, but was attacked by German bombers equipped with some of the world's first air-to-surface guided missiles. The battleship *Roma* was sunk with heavy loss of life.

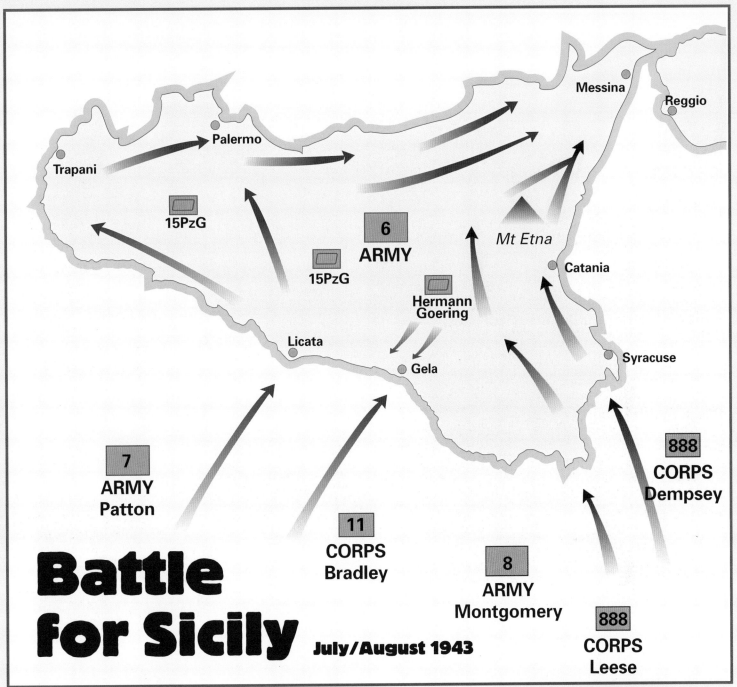

Trapani

Palermo

Messina

Reggio

15PzG

6
ARMY

15PzG

Mt Etna

Catania

Hermann
Goering

Licata

Gela

Syracuse

7
ARMY
Patton

888
CORPS
Dempsey

11
CORPS
Bradley

8
ARMY
Montgomery

888
CORPS
Leese

Battle for Sicily

July/August 1943

THE ALLIED INVASION FORCE taking part in Operation Husky, the invasion of Sicily, involved 180,000 men and 2,600 ships. The Axis defenders of the island numbered about 300,000, including 40,000 German veterans in the 15th Panzergrenadier Division and the 'Hermann Goering' Panzer division. Although the Axis forces outnumbered the invasion force, they had to cover every potential landing ground along the hundreds of kilometres of coastline – and in any case, a large proportion of the Italian strength was made up of men whose hearts were no longer in the fight.

The fact that the Allied landings took place under the cover of bad weather added to the surprise factor – though it was to cost the 1st British air-landing brigade dearly when only 54 out of 109 gliders landed on the island: many of the rest crashed in the sea, and several hundred troops drowned. An American airborne drop fared little better: at least the paratroopers were mostly dropped over land, but only 200 out of 3,500 were anywhere near their objectives.

Nevertheless, by 08.00 on the morning of 10 July advance units of the British 5th Division were ashore and driving towards Cassibile. Further to the west, General Patton's 7th US Army was facing stiffer opposition. The biggest problem was at Gela, where the Hermann Goering Division counter-attacked on 11 July. This could only hold the Allies, however, and Patton was soon driving hard for Palermo while Montgomery pushed through Syracuse and Catania. The British advance was slow, however, due to the difficult terrain, and the campaign became a race for between the two Generals for Messina.

Above: Once the Allies had a secure beachhead on Sicily, they could use their command of the Mediterranean to funnel in supplies and reinforcements. With the Italians lukewarm, the Germans could not match Allied resources, and eventually abandoned the large island.

Above: Field Marshal Rommel planned to seize control of Italy should the Italian government falter in its commitment to the Axis. Italy surrendered on 8 September, and the next day German troops disarmed Italian units all over Italy. Here, an SS Sturmbannführer *interrogates an Italian officer who the day before had been an ally.*

Below: The day after the Italian surrender, General Mark Clark's US Fifth Army, which included the British Tenth Corps, began landing in force on the Italian mainland, at Salerno to the south of Naples.

Above: Italy still possessed a powerful fleet, including fast modern battleships like the Vittorio Veneto*. Although the Italian Navy had done little with these assets during the Mediterranean campaign, the Germans knew that if they fell into British hands it might be a different story.*

Below: As the Italian fleet steamed south from Livorno, on its way to be interned at Malta, it was attacked by Dornier Do 217s. The battleships Italia *and* Roma *were hit by Fritz-X guided glider bombs, the latter breaking in half and sinking after a bomb detonated in her magazine.*

Some Italian troops were able to surrender to the Allies, but the surrender was a disaster for most Italian soldiers. Across Italy, the Balkans and Greece, German garrisons turned on neighbouring Italian units. They were disarmed and hauled off to Germany for use as slave labour. In some cases, now immortalised by the best-seller *Captain Corelli's Mandolin*, they were massacred.

Mussolini's captivity did not last long. His location on the Gran Sasso was an open secret, and his jailers assumed escape from a remote mountain resort was impossible. Il Duce was spirited away on 8 September, after a daring glider assault by *SS Obersturmführer* Otto Skorzeny and a crack team of paratroops. Mussolini survived to preside over a short-lived Fascist republic in northern Italy.

RISKY LANDING

General Patton was not involved in the Salerno landings, code-named Operation 'Avalanche'. But he was shown the plans. Patton was a larger-than-life character, but underneath the bluster lay a first class military mind. He pointed to the river Sele that runs into the Gulf of Salerno. It was marked as the boundary between the British 10th Corps and US 6th Corps

He predicted, before a shot was fired, that the Germans would counter-attack there. Within a week, German 10th Army commander General von Vietinghoff proved him right

British commandos and US Rangers seized Salerno itself while the British advanced inland to occupy the airfield at Montecorvino . On the south bank of the Sele, two raw US infantry divisions occupied a bridgehead some 5 km deep and 15 km across.

The only forces available for immediate defence of the area were regimental sized *Kampfgruppen* formed from the 16.*Panzerdivision*. These held up the Allied advance just as they had in Sicily: German rearguards seemed much stronger than they

were, while the slightest tactical error by an Allied battalion was punished by a ferocious local counter-attack. The Texas National Guardsmen of the US 36th Infantry Division came badly unstuck, but so too did several British county regiments.

Sluggish tactical progress was matched by equally torpid generalship. The Allies failed to expand or reinforce their bridgehead, while the Germans rushed in every available mechanised formation.

Despite frequent air attacks, forcing them to move at night, and a fuel shortage that was never fully overcome, the Germans moved fast. Within a week the Germans had six armoured or motorised divisions in place against four Allied infantry divisions. On 12 September they commenced an all-out attack on the landing beaches.

Vietinghoff's orders from Hitler, via Kesselring, were to eliminate the beachhead. Had the *Leibstandarte* panzer division been sent south, as Kesselring requested, the Germans might very well have succeeded. As it was, the counterstroke penetrated the Allied lines just where Patton had said it would.

The commander of the Allied 5th Army, General Mark Clark, already had his eyes on Rome when panic-stricken soldiers appeared at the water's edge. The Germans were rumoured to be just behind them. That night, Clark issued a warning order to the fleet: prepare for evacuation.

ALLIES CLOSE TO DEFEAT

Clark subsequently defended his decision as a routine precaution, but Allied landing craft were not capable of re-embarking heavy equipment, only soldiers. Had such a retreat been ordered, the 5th Army would have had to abandon its artillery, tanks and transport. The two British divisions hunkered down, their corps artillery supplemented by naval bombardment; the US divisions were driven back, but held on short of the beach.

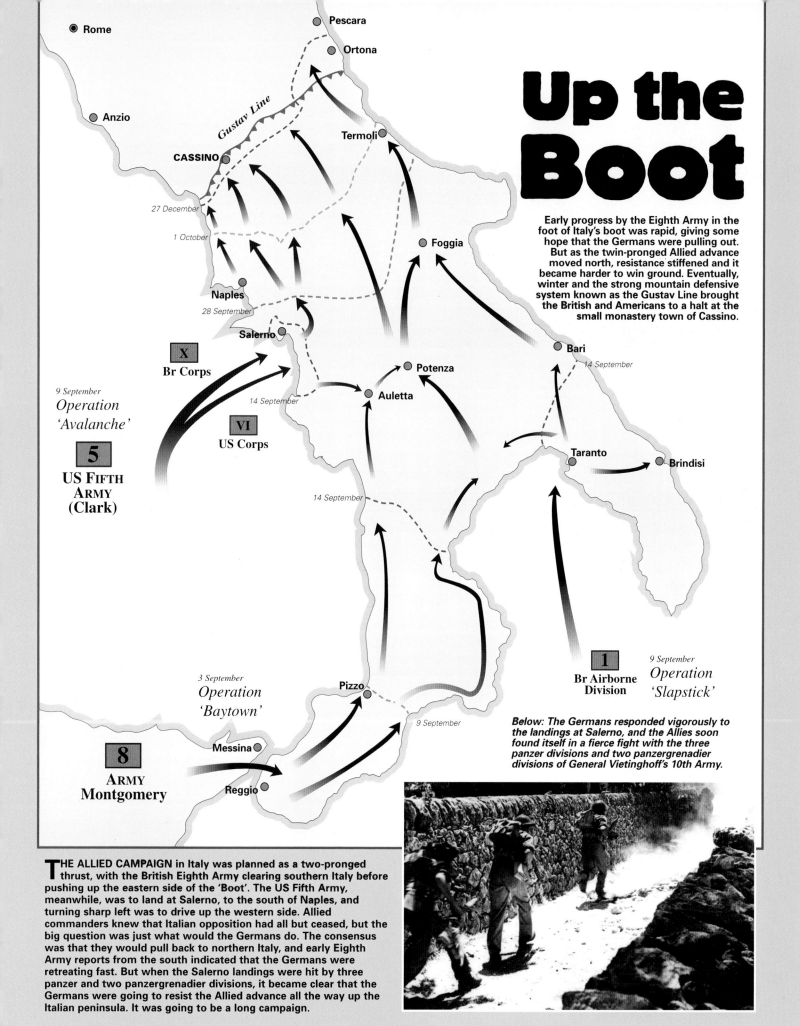

Rome

Pescara

Ortona

Gustav Line

Anzio

Termoli

CASSINO

27 December

1 October

Naples

28 September

Foggia

Salerno

X

Br Corps

Potenza

9 September

*Operation
'Avalanche'*

Auletta

14 September

VI

US Corps

Bari

14 September

5

**US Fifth
Army
(Clark)**

14 September

Taranto

Brindisi

1

**Br Airborne
Division**

9 September

*Operation
'Slapstick'*

3 September

*Operation
'Baytown'*

Pizzo

9 September

Below: *The Germans responded vigorously to
the landings at Salerno, and the Allies soon
found itself in a fierce fight with the three
panzer divisions and two panzergrenadier
divisions of General Vietinghoff's 10th Army.*

8

**Army
Montgomery**

Messina

Reggio

Up the Boot

Early progress by the Eighth Army in the
foot of Italy's boot was rapid, giving some
hope that the Germans were pulling out.
But as the twin-pronged Allied advance
moved north, resistance stiffened and it
became harder to win ground. Eventually,
winter and the strong mountain defensive
system known as the Gustav Line brought
the British and Americans to a halt at the
small monastery town of Cassino.

THE ALLIED CAMPAIGN in Italy was planned as a two-pronged
thrust, with the British Eighth Army clearing southern Italy before
pushing up the eastern side of the 'Boot'. The US Fifth Army,
meanwhile, was to land at Salerno, to the south of Naples, and
turning sharp left was to drive up the western side. Allied
commanders knew that Italian opposition had all but ceased, but the
big question was just what would the Germans do. The consensus
was that they would pull back to northern Italy, and early Eighth
Army reports from the south indicated that the Germans were
retreating fast. But when the Salerno landings were hit by three
panzer and two panzergrenadier divisions, it became clear that the
Germans were going to resist the Allied advance all the way up the
Italian peninsula. It was going to be a long campaign.

All eyes turned south to Calabria, where Montgomery's 8th Army was making an extraordinarily leisurely promenade up the coast. The prickly Field Marshal's greatest admirers, including his most recent biographer, Nigel Hamilton, have not troubled to defend Montgomery from the accusation that he tarried deliberately. He loathed Americans in general and Clark in particular. He wanted to be called to ride to the rescue. War correspondents managed to drive in civilian vehicles from his most advanced units all the way up to the Salerno bridgehead, but Montgomery's ponderous advance failed to pick up speed even while German battlegroups cut and slashed at the 5th Army.

REINFORCEMENTS

The US 82nd Airborne division had been held in reserve to land near Rome and seize the Italian capital. Instead, it was flown into the Salerno bridgehead, once the British had driven back the German assault and secured

Above: Men of the 2nd Battalion, 6th Queen's Regiment pass a knocked-out Panzer IV in the country near Salerno. A German counter attack on the beachhead failed, though it did inflict heavy losses on the Allies.

Right: The landings south of the city were the signal for a popular rising against the Germans in Naples. Soon Italians would be fighting alongside the Allies.

Montecorvino airfield. More ground troops were rushed in, the British departing from centuries of tradition by transferring some 8th Army veterans on their way back to their own regiments and into units in the bridgehead instead. The result was a small scale mutiny: an incident as ugly as it was needless and one still controversial over 50 years later.

Lavish air support and continued shore bombardment by the warships offshore helped sustain the battered defenders. Vietinghoff knew he could only delay the inevitable, and Kesselring recognised that to persist with the attacks risked defeat. On 16 September the Germans withdrew into the

surrounding mountains as suddenly as they had come. The same day, US patrols in the south encountered elements of the British 8th Army. Montgomery set up a photo opportunity: he had himself driven up to Mark Clark, who was standing outside his headquarters, and tried to shake hands before climbing down from his vehicle. But Clark stepped back so the two men were pictured side-by-side.

GERMAN WITHDRAWAL

While the Allied commanders indulged in such points-scoring, the Germans pulled back north of Naples, which rose in revolt on 27 September before the Allies entered the city. The prospect of taking Rome before winter had

disappeared. Field Marshal Kesselring toured the likely front line in person, impressing on every man the necessity of holding the Allies as far south as possible. The terrain lent itself to defence, with towering mountain ranges dominating narrow valleys. Winter weather would nullify the Allies' air power. From coast to coast, the Germans dug themselves in.

At the heart of their defences, barring the way to Rome, lay the impressive medieval monastery at Monte Cassino. Beneath its majestic walls a handful of German paratroops dug foxholes, occupied firing points, positioned their range-finders and high-powered binoculars and watched and waited.

The Commanders

Above: Montgomery was the natural choice to command the British forces making the first invasion of Axis soil. His Eighth Army were veterans, and he knew how well the Germans could fight. However, his rivalry with Patton caused some problems in Sicily.

Above: The tall figure of Mark Clark led the American side of the war in Italy. Patton having been removed in temporary disgrace, it fell to Clark to command the Salerno landings. After a very close-run battle, he was determined to be the first Allied commander to capture an Axis capital.

Above: Albert Kesselring proved to be a commander of genius, marshalling his sometimes limited forces to deny the Allies the quick victory they wanted in Italy. It took two years of hard fighting to force his armies back as far as the Austrian border.

Above: Erwin Rommel was made commander in Northern Italy early in 1943. After the Italian surrender he advised the abandonment of southern Italy, withdrawing all German troops to the Po valley. However, Kesselring preferred a more resistant strategy.

The End of Blitzkrieg
Russia 1943

Weary German troops march through Kharkhov, scene of the German army's last great triumph in Russia. Although man-for-man, the German soldier was still the best in the business, years of battle and superior enemy numbers had taken their toll.

The collapse at Stalingrad marked the turn of the tide in the East. Never more would the massed Panzers of the Wehrmacht wreak havoc: from now on, the Red Army was the master of the battlefield.

TRAPPED IN THE frozen hell of Stalingrad, by 1 January 1943 the soldiers of the German 6th Army knew they were doomed. Reduced to some 150,000 men, up to a third of them were severely ill with typhus and dysentery; all suffered from malnutrition. Deaths from hypothermia were a daily occurrence. But still they held on, without hope of relief. The reduction and final destruction of the Stalingrad pocket occupied seven Soviet armies until the last day of the month: armies that would otherwise have joined their Red Army comrades in a massive drive west.

The Soviet breakthrough at Stalingrad tore a gap in the German front line that was longer than the entire western front in the First World War. Within days of Paulus' surrender, Soviet tank battalions raced across the open steppe west of the river Donets, their wide tracks and low ground pressure enabling them to overtake scattered groups of retreating Germans. Ahead lay the Dnieper crossings and giant hydro-electric plant at Zaporezhe; north, and about to be surrounded, lay the industrial city of Kharkov. The latter was abandoned by its SS garrison on 14 February, ignoring Hitler's orders to hold fast.

COUNTER ATTACK

Kharkov was the first Soviet city to be liberated. Eighteen months of Nazi occupation had reduced its population by 25 per cent: some 100,000 young men and women had been deported to Germany as slave labourers. Many people, mostly the old and very young, had died during the winter: As Hitler and Goering had both boasted, Russian civilians would be allowed to starve. About 15,000 people had been shot out of hand: the teachers at the university, Communist party members, Soviet government officials and all Jews. A Quisling-style administration was set up in Kharkov, a combination of Ukrainian nationalists, gangsters and adventurers. Schools were closed, but the black market flourished. The *Burgomeister* and his mistress fled with the SS when the city was abandoned.

With chilling symmetry, the NKVD took over the Gestapo headquarters and its basement torture chambers. A letter box was attached to the building for people to denounce their neighbours anonymously as collaborators. Starving Russian soldiers wandered the streets, released from a nearby POW camp but liable to arrest by the NKVD which regarded all ex-prisoners as traitors for having surrendered. BBC correspondent Alexander Werth was stunned at the indifference shown to these living skeletons, slumped near to death in the snow.

HITLER AND MANSTEIN

Hitler flew to Zaporezhe to confer with his commanders. At quiet moments in the conference the sound of Russian artillery could just be made out. Field Marshal von Manstein persuaded the Führer to let him conduct the battle his way, instead of the rigid defence Hitler favoured. The result was a tactical masterstroke, still studied in military academies today.

Manstein let the Soviet advance continue while he assembled a powerful striking force on its flanks. SS panzer divisions *Leibstandarte*, *Reich* and *Totenkopf,* combined with five army panzer divisions and the *Grossdeutschland* division counter-attacked with massive support from a newly reinforced Luftwaffe. In what he dubbed his 'backhand blow', Manstein drove east to cut off all the Russian forces that had broken over the Donets. The SS panzer corps stormed Kharkov in mid-March. The four Soviet tank corps strung out between the Donets and Zaporezhe were annihilated.

The Battle of Kharkov stabilised the front just as the spring thaw imposed its annual

Above: Panzers move through the outskirts of Kharkhov as von Manstein's Army Group Don retakes the city in March 1943.

Below: An SS officer urges his troops on outside Kharkhov. Without interference from Hitler, Manstein was able to fight the Soviets in a fluid style, drawing the Red Army in traps and then counter-attacking with vicious efficiency, destroying the Soviet 3rd Tank Army in the process.

halt on military operations. The startling recovery of the *Ostheer* after the Stalingrad disaster unsettled Stalin, who made a tentative diplomatic approach to Hitler via Swedish diplomats. But the Führer was still set on decisive victory and the extermination of what he persisted in regarding as the Jewish-Bolshevik threat. Hitler's army was outnumbered 2:1 in men and by 5:1 in tanks and guns, but training and tactical leadership were far superior to that of the Red Army. If the odds were too unfavourable for a third successive summer offensive in 1943, the German army high command was nevertheless

Above: The mighty Tiger spearheaded the German attack, supported by the new Panther and swarms of upgraded Panzer IIIs and Panzer IVs. The Tigers were dominant when they could be brought into action, but they were slow and lacked range. The Panthers promised much, but premature use meant that they were unreliable, and many broke down

Below: The boundless Russian steppe offered perfect tank-fighting terrain, but the long lines of sight also helped the thousands of Red Army anti-tank guns dug in around the Kursk salient.

Below: The two sides were evenly matched numerically, but the Germans still had the advantage in training and experience, and upgunned versions of the Panzer IV were well able to take on the Soviet T-34. But the Russians were fighting from defensive positions, and the Germans ran into a wall of anti-tank fire.

determined on an attack.

There was little thought of knocking Russia out of the war, however much Hitler clung to the dream of final victory. His generals wanted to attack in order to cripple the Soviet army. With the loss of North Africa, it was only a matter of time before the Allies attacked Italy or even landed in France. Unless the Red Colossus could be smashed before then, the nightmare loomed of a two-front war that Germany could never win.

KURSK SALIENT

The objective was a salient projecting 150 km into the German lines between Belgorod and Orel. Centred on the town of Kursk, it was about 200 km wide at its base. Initial orders for the offensive were issued by OKH on 13 March: Army Group Centre would attack from the north with a massively reinforced panzer group, while Army Group South struck from the opposite side of the salient. The Soviets had never previously managed to halt a determined German assault short of the strategic depths of their vast hinterland. The German high command assumed – and the Soviet generals feared – that it would be no different this time. The panzers had to break through little more than 100 km to cut off all Soviet units in the salient; further exploitation might take them back to the Don at Voronezh. In fact, the follow-up operation envisaged by OKH was Operation *Parkplatz*: the storming of Leningrad. Nine divisions were earmarked for the assault and the superheavy siege artillery

used to batter Sevastopol into submission was en route north. It was not destined to arrive.

Kursk was such an obvious objective that the Russians began fortifying it almost as soon as the Germans decided to attack it. However, the Red Army planned new offensives of its own, north and south of Kursk, scheduled to open the moment the German attack stalled. Stalin and his most senior commanders gambled that they could hold Kursk against the elite panzer divisions, absorb the full strength of the German blow, then unleash a multi-front offensive that would liberate the Ukraine. However anxious some of his frontline commanders were, Marshals Rokossovsky and Zhukov were confident the Red Army of 1943 was far more proficient than the stumbling giant of 1941 or the gallant amateurs of 1942.

ZITADELLE POSTPONED

Hitler postponed his attack several times in order to employ the latest heavy tanks now in production. When the offensive, code-named *Zitadelle* finally opened on 5 July, it was spearheaded by 147 Tiger Is, 200 Panthers and 89 Elefant assault guns. The bulk of the panzer battalions were still using the older medium tanks, 844 panzer IIIs and 913 panzer IVs took part. However, the Soviets had made excellent use of the delay and had some 700 JSU-152 'animal killer' tank destroyers lurking among their nine lines of entrenchments. Russian infantry dug deeply into the black earth of central Russia: networks of

Battle of Kursk

July 1943

THE GERMAN ATTACKERS taking part in Operation Citadel were disposed in two large army groups. To the north was Army Group Centre, commanded by Field Marshal Gunther von Kluge and based around the three Panzer Corps of *Generaloberst* Walther Model's powerful Ninth Army. Von Manstein's Army Group South was composed of *Generaloberst* Hermann Hoth's Fourth Panzer Army, spearheaded by XLVIII Panzer Corps and II SS Panzer Korps, comprising the best units Germany could field. The plan was for the two great arms of a pincer movement to cut off the salient around Kursk. Nearly a million men in 50 divisions, 16 of them armoured, were poised to wipe out the Red Army.

GOOD INTELLIGENCE and German delays meant that the Soviet High Command was well prepared for the attack. Between them, Rokossovsky's Central Front and Vatutin's Voronezh Front massed 20,000 artillery pieces to stand off the attack, and a series of huge defensive lines tens of kilometres in depth were constructed. Equipped with large numbers of anti-tank weapons, these defences were sure to give the Germans greater difficulty than they had encountered in the summer campaigns of previous years. To the rear, Konev's powerful Steppe Front acted as a strategic reserve, its Tank Armies ready to shore up the defences, to blunt any German penetrations and to counterattack should the chance be offered. On 12 July, 5th Guards Tank Army threw back II SS Panzer Corps in the largest armoured battle in history, with over 1,000 tanks in bloody combat around the little village of Prokhorovka

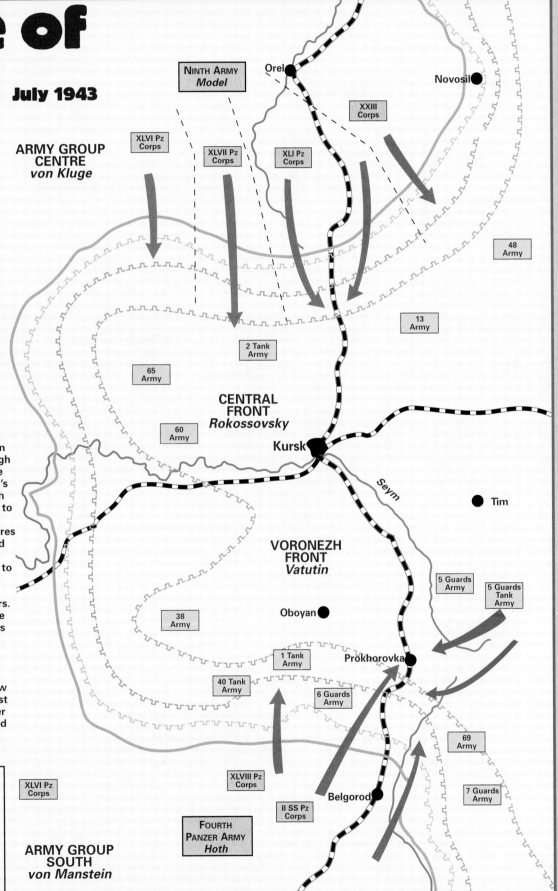

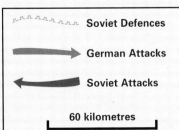

Soviet Defences

German Attacks

Soviet Attacks

60 kilometres

Above: Troops and tanks of the 3rd SS Panzer Division Totenkopf head into the cauldron at Kursk. Along with the Leibstandarte and Das Reich divisions, Totenkopf formed the II SS Panzer Corps. Under the command of Obergruppenführer und General der Waffen SS Paul Hausser, the corps spearheaded Hoth's 4th Panzer Army.

Below: The SS nearly broke through the Soviet defences, only being stopped by a fierce counter attack launched on 12 July by General Rotmistrov's 5th Guards Tank Army.

Below: Soviet prisoners are taken at Kursk. Compared to the campaigns in 1941 and 1942, their numbers were tiny. In place of the sweeping movements of previous summer campaigns the Germans managed to penetrate less than 30 kilometres in a week.

underground bunkers connected by trenches were defended by clusters of concealed anti-tank guns. Over 3,000 mines were laid per kilometre of front. And the Russians were sufficiently forewarned to fire an artillery bombardment on the Germans' jumping-off points two hours before the German preliminary barrage began.

24 HOUR WARFARE

The German 9th Army, commanded by the brilliant *Generaloberst* Model, made little headway into the northern shoulder of the salient. In savage fighting that barely let up over the short summer nights, his men advanced barely 10 km. On 12 July Army Group Centre was attacked all across its front by Soviet forces bent on liberating Orel; the ground won at such terrible cost had to be abandoned as 9th Army pulled back to defend its own flank.

Zitadelle went better in the south, where the SS panzer corps smashed remorselessly through each line of defence. Again, the fighting went on 24 hours a day. The intense summer heat triggered thunderstorms by the end of each afternoon. Both sides were very active in the air, the Luftwaffe only able to dominate selected areas of the front, the Soviets flying thousands of bomber sorties against German supply routes. The tank battles culminated in the celebrated action around the small town of Prokhorovka on 10-12 July; the SS vanguard, led by *Totenkopf* tore through the Soviet 1st Tank Army, overrunning the 71st Guards Rifle Division. Stalin sat at his desk in the Kremlin day and night, demanding hourly situation reports. He consented to the release of 5th Guards Tank Army and the 5th Guards Army from the reserve: they moved up, ready to counter-attack.

As the Soviet reserves counter-attacked at Prokhorovka, Hitler summoned Field Marshals Manstein and Kluge to Rastenburg. Kluge reported that Army Group Centre could not

maintain the offensive: 9th Army had suffered 20,000 casualties in a week and the Russians' own offensive was so powerful Orel might be lost. Manstein argued for one more supreme effort, arguing that if he committed his last reserves, he might yet break through to Kursk.

ON THE BACK FOOT

Hitler called off Zitadelle and ordered the SS panzer corps to be transferred to the west. The *Ostheer* would go over to the defensive and contain the Russian drive on Orel. What he and his generals failed to realise was that the Red Army was poised to launch the greatest offensive it had yet undertaken.

Model was unable to prevent the loss of Orel, which was liberated on 5 August. The Soviet Briansk and Kalinin Fronts began new offensives in the north, liberating Smolensk in September. Another major attack developed south of Kursk, forcing Manstein back to the scene of his triumph in the spring. This time there was no power available for a backhand blow: all the Germans could do was fight a succession of rearguard actions as they withdrew, giving up Belgorod on 5 August and eventually abandoning Kharkov itself. Army Group South retreated to prepared positions running from Zaporezhe to the Black Sea. The Soviets reached the isthmus connecting the Crimea to the mainland. The German 17th Army was isolated.

RED ARMY SETBACK

By the end of September the Red Army had reached the Dnieper north and south of Kiev. An ambitious airborne operation was mounted in order to capture the crossings at Kanev and Bukrin, some 90 km downstream, but poor intelligence resulted in one of the three parachute divisions landing right on top of 10th *Panzergrenadier* division. The paratroopers were destroyed and the hard-won bridgehead at Bukrin eventually abandoned.

Commanders of Genius

Manstein
Adolf Hitler described Erich von Manstein as, "Perhaps the best brain that the General Staff Corps has produced." He was creator of the plan to conquer France in 1940, he smashed Sevastopol into submission, and he was the general who used the brilliant counter attack at Kharkhov to show that there was still bite in the Wehrmacht after Stalingrad. Manstein favoured the Kursk offensive, but only if it could be carried out quickly. In the event delays meant that the Soviets built massive defenses, and Manstein's forbodings proved accurate.

Kluge
Gunther von Kluge, whose Army Group Centre provided the northern wing of the Kursk attack, had little faith in the plan and left most of the operational control to Model. Kluge was a very bright but less than direct man, prone to play both sides of any argument. Although he persuaded the Führer to delay the offensive at Kursk, he also complained in writing about the delay – probably to cover himself against blame if the offensive failed. Kluge toyed with the opposition to Hitler, but never whole-heartedly. He committed suicide in Normandy in 1944.

Model
Walther Model was known as 'the Führer's Fireman', always sent to where the battle was hottest. It was Model who persuaded Hitler to delay the offensive at Kursk, waiting until everything was ready and his units had re-equipped with the newest heavy tanks like the Tiger and the Panther, which had yet to be fully tested in battle. Model's battle went badly from the start, and he eventually had to withdraw in the face of massive Soviet counter-attack towards Orel. However, Model's failure did little to effect the Führer's faith in his General.

Hoth
An infantry commander who switched to tanks, Hermann Hoth was one of Germany's leading armoured experts. His major achievements came in Russia, commanding a Panzergruppe during operation Barbarossa before taking command of 4th Panzer Army in June 1942. He held open the corridor which enabled Kleist's Army Group to escape after Stalingrad, and in the battle for Kursk his Panzer Army almost broke through the Soviet defences. When Hoth urged withdrawal after the Soviet Autumn offensives, he was retired by Hitler.

Zhukov
Former Red Army cavalryman who rose to become one of the most outstanding military commanders of World War II. After his successful defence of Moscow in 1941, Zhukov became Stalin's military deputy. He spent much of the time at the various fronts, and his influence can be seen in the successful defence of Leningrad and in the battles of Stalingrad and Kursk. These were massive hammer blows from which the German invaders were never to recover, and led directly to Zhukov's greatest triumph – the German surrender in Berlin.

Rokossovsky
Of Polish descent, Konstantin Rokossovsky survived arrest by the NKVD in Stalin's pre-war purge of the Soviet army, and returned to active service in 1940. An extremely competent field commander, his abilities were highly respected by his German opponents. Rokossovsky commanded the Central Front at Kursk, and the immense line of defences he created blunted the attacks of Model's 9th Army. At the end of the War his 2nd Belorussian Front swept across north Germany to link up with Montgomery's 21st Army Group.

Vatutin
One of the brightest of all Red Army commanders, Nikolai Vatutin was a pre-war staff officer who, apart from a spell at Leningrad, spent the first year of the war on the General Staff. Appointed to command the Southwestern Front at the end of 1942, he was soundly defeated by Manstein at Kharkhov. He more than made amends at Kursk, where he commanded the Voronezh Front. By 1944 Vatutin was proving to be a very capable field general, but his career was cut short when he was killed by Ukrainian partisans.

Konev
Ivan Konev had been tasked with the defence of Moscow in 1941, and as the Germans advanced Stalin wanted him arrested and executed. Zhukov stood up for Konev and saved one of Russia's greatest commanders. Konev's Steppe Front was the strategic reserve for the battle of Kursk, his armies supporting Vatutin and Rokossovsky. After the battle Konev and Vatutin worked in tandem, driving deep into the Ukraine. At the end of the war, Konev and Zhukov were rival commanders chasing the greatest prize of the war – Berlin.

Above: For once, Stalin listened to his generals and accepted a defensive strategy. Men and weaponry were poured into the Kursk salient, ready for the German attack. But Stalin was worried. He had a right to be: the Red Army had never yet beaten off a German summer offensive.

However, a tiny enclave on the west bank at Lyutlezh, 20 km north of Kiev was secretly reinforced by 3rd Tank Army. On 3 November the German forces surrounding the bridgehead were shattered by some 2,000 guns. Russian tanks broke through to threaten Kiev with encirclement and the city was abandoned three days later.

RED TIDE

The front continued to roll westwards during November as the Red Army recaptured Zhitomir and Korosten. Once again, Manstein bided his time, fending off Hitler's demands for immediate action. The Russians became over-extended as their mechanised units out-ran their supply columns. Their air support diminished because it took time to repair captured airfields – although the Germans abandoned their practice of burying mines on the runways when they learned that the Russians used

German prisoners to clear them. Manstein counter-attacked and re-took both towns, re-establishing the direct rail link with Army Group Centre. However, a Soviet breakthrough at Cherkassy combined with Hitler's refusal to retreat from the one stretch of the Dnieper still under German control, left a dangerously exposed salient jutting into Russian territory by the year's end.

Holding the Germans at Kursk, then attacking at Orel and Kharkov cost the Red Army 863,000 casualties; the tactical superiority of the German army still compensated for its numerical disadvantage. German losses in the Kursk offensive were 50,000 men and 500-700 tanks and assault guns. While the panzer divisions were not wiped out, it was the last time Germany would be able to assemble such an armoured striking force. The initiative now lay with the Russians.

Top: In spite of their new weaponry, the German attack was little more than a battering match, and in a war of attrition the Soviets had the upper hand. The Red Army's magnificent T-34 was just as good as most German tanks – and its artillery was better and much more numerous.

Above: The repulse of the German offensive at Kursk and the successful Soviet counter offensive which retook Orel finally removed any German threat to Moscow. It also proved to ordinary Russian soldiers that they could beat even a full-strength Wehrmacht.

Right: Surviving members of the elite Leibstandarte division show the strain at the end of the battle for Kursk. In spite of their ferocious attacks, the SS Panzer Corps suffered catastrophic losses during Operation Citadel.

Eastern Front

AFTER KURSK had stripped them of so much equipment and so many men, the Germans were faced with a new and disturbing situation: the Soviets, who had suffered similar losses, had no apparent difficulty in replacing them immediately. Only a few days after the Citadel operation was called off, the Soviets took the offensive, taking Orel and finally relieving Kharkhov by the end of July.

NON-STOP OFFENSIVES

The offensives continued, one beginning as its predecessor slowed, giving the Wehrmacht no time to regroup. Rokossovsky and Vatutin smashed forwards towards Kiev, while the Kalinin Front aimed to retake Smolensk. In the south Malinovsky aimed for the Dnieper alongside Konev, and Tolbukhin's Southern Front threatened to cut off Kleist's forces on the Kerch peninsula and in Crimea.

By mid-September, every Soviet front from Smolensk southwards was on the move. To the hard-pressed Germans, fresh tanks and men seemed to be appearing out of a limitless well. After a pause for the autumn mud, the offensives continued over the frozen ground. By the beginning of November armies were grinding their way across the river, and 2,000 guns were pounding the Germans around Kiev. The only pause came at the end of the year, when the Red Army paused to consolidate. But nobody on the German side was in any doubt: the New Year would see the Red Army steamroller on the move again.

Below: The catastrophic German losses at Kursk decisively shifted the balance of power in the East: the Wehrmacht no longer had the capability to hold back the resurgent Red Army

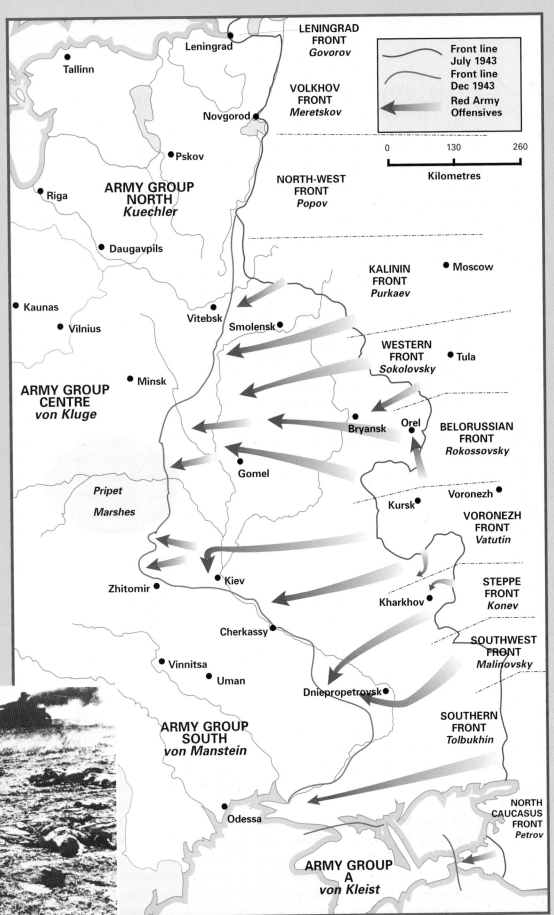

LENINGRAD FRONT *Govorov*

VOLKHOV FRONT *Meretskov*

NORTH-WEST FRONT *Popov*

| Front line July 1943 |
| Front line Dec 1943 |
| Red Army Offensives |

0   130   260
Kilometres

Leningrad
Tallinn
Novgorod
Pskov

ARMY GROUP NORTH *Kuechler*

Riga
Daugavpils

KALININ FRONT *Purkaev*

Moscow

Kaunas
Vilnius
Vitebsk
Smolensk

WESTERN FRONT *Sokolovsky*

Tula

ARMY GROUP CENTRE *von Kluge*

Minsk

Bryansk
Orel

BELORUSSIAN FRONT *Rokossovsky*

Pripet Marshes

Gomel

Voronezh
Kursk

VORONEZH FRONT *Vatutin*

Zhitomir
Kiev

Kharkhov

STEPPE FRONT *Konev*

Cherkassy

SOUTHWEST FRONT *Malinovsky*

Vinnitsa
Uman

Dniepropetrovsk

SOUTHERN FRONT *Tolbukhin*

ARMY GROUP SOUTH *von Manstein*

Odessa

NORTH CAUCASUS FRONT *Petrov*

ARMY GROUP A *von Kleist*

The Nightfi

Germany was defended by huge numbers of flak guns in 1939. Effective as these were, the Luftwaffe soon realised that a specialised night-fighter force was needed to protect the factories, and, increasingly the civilian population.

ghter War
Darkness of Death

The Junkers 88 was the Luftwaffe's most adaptable aircraft. The G-series went on to become Germany's most succesful night-fighter type. Its long endurance, good performance and plethora of electronics wreaked havoc among the RAF's bombers.

For five years the Luftwaffe and RAF fought without quarter in the night skies over Europe. It was a battle dominated by material resources and scientific innovation – a battle which Germany ultimately lost as her cities burned.

IN JULY 1940, as Britain braced itself for a German invasion, British Prime Minister Winston Churchill determined to hit back. "There is one thing that will bring Hitler down," he wrote to Lord Beaverbrook, "and that is an absolutely devastating, exterminating attack by very heavy bombers from this country upon the Nazi homeland." Strategic bombing had been advocated with great passion by many senior officers in the RAF before the war. After the defeat of France and the evacuation of the BEF, it was the single offensive method left to Britain.

NIGHT BOMBING

Like most major powers in the 1930s, Germany had developed a civil and military system to protect itself against air attack. Some 12 million German civilians had undergone limited training in civil defence. Pride of place in the defensive network were 2,600 anti-aircraft guns –

more than any other nation. There was a chain of radar stations looking out across the North Sea, but unlike its British equivalent, there was no central command authority to coordinate the defending aircraft on the basis of the radar reports. German defences were essentially local; two special zones were created for the defence of the vital Ruhr industries and Berlin itself. Only a handful of fighter aircraft were involved in the air defence of Germany.

The German defences inflicted prohibitive losses on daylight raids mounted by the RAF. British fighters were too short-ranged to reach Germany and the unescorted bombers' defensive armament was too weak to protect them. The British switched to night bombing, which was discovered – after a year of operations – to be incredibly inaccurate. The 1941 Butt Report exposed the embarrassing fact that less than a tenth of the bombs fell

within three miles of their targets. The revelation provided further stimulus to those officers who favoured the indiscriminate bombing of major urban centres. Churchill himself stated that an attack on German civilian morale was a worthwhile objective. What the British thought they were aiming at was in any case irrelevant from the German point of view. During 1941 and 1942 Germany was subjected to a succession of night raids on her big cities. Hitler assumed, and Goebbels proclaimed, that the intention was 'terror bombing' as practised by the Luftwaffe on Belgrade and Rotterdam.

ZERSTÖRER SQUADRONS

The Luftwaffe had a ready force to counter the bombers. The Messerschmitt Bf-110 *Zerstörer* had proved too vulnerable to single-seat interceptors to continue its intended role as a long-range fighter. When Oberst Josef Kammhuber was selected to command the first dedicated night fighter wing –

NJG or *Nachtjagdgeschwader* 1, the majority of his aircraft were Bf-110Cs. They had no specialist equipment and relied on the keen eyesight of the crew to spot British bombers in the eerie glow cast by searchlights on the clouds. The Bf-110 had a good margin of speed to overhaul any bomber it encountered, and a powerful cannon and machine gun armament made short work of the Blenheims, Whitleys and the other twin-engine medium bombers that made up the bulk of RAF Bomber Command.

Additional night fighter units were created by re-assigning several *Zerstörer* squadrons. Converted medium bombers were also pressed into service: Dornier Do 17s and Do 215s, as well as the ubiquitous Junkers Ju 88 were fitted with cannon in the nose or in gunpods beneath the fuselage.

The aircraft were painted black all over, which was believed to be the most effective camouflage at night. It seems logical, but it was wrong. Werner

Streib, *Geschwaderkommodore* of NJG 1, had his Ju 88 painted pale grey and later flew an almost white-coloured He 219. Mottled grey camouflage schemes proved better than black, which tended to reflect the glow of fires and searchlights and show up clearly against clouds.

The newly formed night fighter units were coordinated by a radar system perfected by Kammhuber, who was promoted 'Air Officer for Night fighters' on the Luftwaffe staff. A chain of Wurzburg radar stations ran from Denmark to Paris, with the coverage of each set slightly overlapping that of its neighbours.

Up to half-a-dozen fighters could orbit the radio beacon co-located with the radar sets, although it was often only one. Radar operators plotted the movement of 'their' fighter with a blue light on a frosted-glass screen; others used a red light to chart the course of the bomber.

The fighter control officer watched both flight paths, marking them in crayon and relaying instructions to the fighters. Vectored on to their target, the fighter either shot down the bomber or it was passed on to the next station along for the next team to deal with. To the Germans, the system was known as the *Himmelbett* (Heavenly Bed), but the British knew it as the Kammhuber Line.

KAMMHUBER LINE

The night fighters took a steady toll of RAF bombers as they made their way, individually, to and from their targets. The bombers' defensive armament was weak – one or two .303 machine guns was usually all they could bring to bear against an opponent armed with 20 mm cannons.

From July 1941, German fighters began to carry radar of their own. The FuG 202 Lichtenstein set could detect aircraft at up to 4000 metres. This proved an effective supplement to the ground radar, despite reducing aircraft speed.

The Stars

Left: Heinz Wolfgang Schnauffer is seen here on 16 October 1944 having been awarded the Diamonds to his Knight's Cross with Oak Leaves and Swords. The tribute was awarded for his 100th kill. Dubbed the 'night ghost' by the British, Schnaufer achieved all of his victories in a Messerschmitt Bf 110. He served with Nacht-Jagdgeschwadern 1 and 4. His final tally stood at 121 nocturnal victories when he was captured in Denmark by the British in May 1945.

Right: Hauptmann Prinz Heinrich zu Sayn-Wittgenstein, Gruppenkommandeur of IV/NJG 5, is pictured with his Junkers 88 on the Eastern Front in the summer of 1943. Of the 29 kills displayed on the tail, 24 are for RAF aircraft – the remainder for Soviet machines. Linked bars represent multiple victories on the same night. Though killed eighteen months before the war's end, the Danish-born aristocrat – descendant of a famous Russian field marshal – remained the Luftwaffe's third highest scoring ace with 83 kills.

Right: Helmut Lent was a career pilot. Joining the Luftwaffe in 1937, his first victory came in a Zerstörer on 2 September 1939. He joined the embryonic night-fighter arm when refused a request to transfer to single-seater fighters. With a final tally of 110 victories (eight by day) he led the night-fighting Experten through most of the war. Hitler had been impressed by Lent on the occasions that they met, and had ear-marked him for the post of Inspector of Night Fighters. But fate intervened and Lent was killed in 1944 on a routine flight to a neighbouring airfield.

Below: Single-seaters were unsuited to early types of night-fighting. Pilots caught in a search-light could be blinded and directionless for minutes. The Messerschmitt Bf 110 was much better, as the navigator could take over if the pilot was disorientated. The aircraft also needed a new role after its mauling by day in 1940.

Right: Werner Streib, dubbed 'the father of the Night-Fighters' for his pioneering efforts in the field of all-weather interception, was the sixth-highest scoring night fighter ace with 65 victories. He claimed the night fighter arm's first victory in German airspace, on 20 July 1940, and was the second Nachtjäger to be awarded the Knight's Cross. In June 1943, he was appointed technical advisor to Ernst Heinkel to assist in the development of the He 219 and was the first to use one of these new craft in combat. On his first sortie he shot down five bombers in half an hour. After the war he joined the reformed Luftwaffe, and went on to command a flying school in Ladsberg.

Below: German night fighters caught in the open by day were easy prey for the Allied single-seaters which roamed the length and breadth of Germany during the final year of the war. In this gun-camera picture, a Ju 88C weaves desperately in an unsuccessful attempt to escape a P-51.

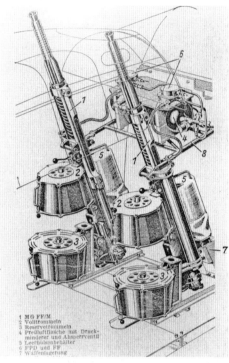

Left: Night fighter tactics by necessity differed from those employed by day fighters. Given visibility problems it was vitally important to get a kill on first contact. In 1941 Rudolf Schönert of NJG1 came up with the concept of upward-firing cannon, but these were not finally introduced until 1943, when fitted to Bf 110s of NJG5. The guns were fixed at an angle of 70° from the horizontal. Now the fighter only had to keep station below the unprotected belly of the target and open fire. Known as Schräge Musik – 'Slanting' or 'Jazz' music – the system proved highly effective, eventually being fitted as standard to every type of night fighter.

1 MG FF/M
2 Volltrommeln
3 Reservetrommeln
4 Preßluftflasche mit Druck-
minderer und Absperrventil
5 Leechülsenbehälter
6 FPD und FF
7 Waffenlagerung

Above: The Ju 88C-series was conceived of as both a Zerstörer and Nachtjäger, with fixed forward-firing armament in a solid nose. Eventually some 3,200 were delivered exclusively for the night-fighting arm. The dummy glazed nose was intended to confuse enemy interceptors into thinking the heavily-armed aircraft a bomber.

Below: During the early part of the war German night-fighters often operated over flak-defended areas, with the occasional inevitable loss. One such was this crash-landed Bf 110.

Kammhuber's system had limitations. When the new chief of Bomber Command, Air Chief Marshal Sir Arthur Harris, launched his '1000 bomber raid' on Cologne in May 1942, the bombers flew in a dense stream; all aircraft attacking within a 90 minute period. The Kammhuber Line was swamped. Airborne radar assumed greater importance for the night fighters from then on.

WINDOW OPENS

There was one way of disabling German radar both on the ground and in the air, but neither side dared use it. Strips of metal, cut to half the wavelength of a radar set would flood the screen with thousands of echoes, effectively blinding it. German research had been halted when it was realised that it would confer a once-only advantage: with the secret revealed, the other side would use it too. But by summer 1943, with little serious German bomber force to fear, the British felt confident enough to unleash this novel weapon, code-named 'window'.

On the night of 24-5 July 1943, 791 bombers attacked Hamburg. As the bomber stream entered German airspace, they released millions of strips of tin foil, 270 mm long, which cascaded down to leave a fuzzy mess on the Wurzburg and Lichtenstein radar screens.

German reaction to the Hamburg raid was imaginative, but late. Bomber pilot Oberst Hajo Herrman established three squadrons of single-seat fighters to supplement the dedicated night fighters. Lacking radar, they relied on a continuous commentary relayed over multiple channels by radars operating on different wavelengths. These *Wilde Sau* (Wild Boar) operations were incorporated into an integrated defence of the Reich, *Luftflotte Mitte*.

Belatedly, the Germans had recognized that the US daylight bomber campaign was not a temporary phenomenon.

The Allied 'Combined Bomber Offensive' confronted Germany with a serious problem. It was more than 'terror bombing': it systematically tore the heart out of German industry.

Whereas the German heavy bomber programme had been cancelled on the eve of the war, the British persevered. From 1942 Halifax and Lancaster four engine bombers replaced the earlier types. Flying at greater altitudes and carrying heavier bombloads, they inflicted considerably more damage; with the introduction of aluminised explosive in 1944 the effects were even greater.

Factories established by Albert Speer to galvanize Germany's sluggish war industries were destroyed; surviving operations had to be dispersed. For the night fighter force the consequences were severe. Its numbers remained static at 300-400 aircraft, while the British and American bomber fleets repeatedly staged raids by twice as many bombers.

ELECTRONIC WARFARE

The Luftwaffe's maintenance and repair units were overstretched and would remain so. Airborne radar sets were even more temperamental – Germany lost the world's first 'electronic warfare' battle. German airborne radar had only a fraction of the scientific resources applied to it as Allied electronic systems. Allied radar sets were superior and their electronic counter-measures more effective. The SERRATE system enabled British night intruders to track the German night fighters by their radar emissions. The later PERFECTOS system triggered German IFF transponders, providing the British with the target's bearing and range.

The intruders – Beaufighters, then Mosquitos – turned the hunters into the hunted. Wing Commander Bob Brabham took some significant scalps in his 29-victory career. Flying a Beaufighter VIF in 1943, he accounted for three German aces

Wilde Sau

Nothing could stem the tide of ever-growing numbers of Allied bombers. The Luftwaffe, stretched on all fronts, could sometimes blunt but never stem the Allied strategic bombing campaign.

Above: The Bf 110's offensive armament increased considerably during the war. Originally armed with two cannon and four machine guns, late-war weapons fit might include as many as six forward-firing cannon, with two upward-firing Schräge Musik guns in the rear fuselage.

Above: A rare gun-camera image shows the destruction of a British twin engined bomber. The date is unknown, but predates the second '1,000 bomber' raid on Cologne (1/2 June 1942), as the pilot of the interceptor was killed in that action.

THE GREATEST PROBLEM faced by a night-fighter crew was how to find your target. The Luftwaffe attempted several different techniques to maximise the chances of making a contact. Before the radar defence line, established by Josef Kammhuber coud have any real effect, a fighter's chances of hitting a bomber stream were based on an educated guess. In 1940/41 many units simply operated in the sky over a suspected target area, and used the light offered by a full moon or a search-light battery to home in. The chances of making an interception were slim, and the dangers to the aircrew great.

In 1943 with the Kammhuber Line paralysed by Operation Window, Herman Goering gave the go-ahead for Major Hajo Hermann's *'Wilde Sau'* plan to create a large force of roaming single-engined fighters. Desperate times called for desperate measures – independent of any ground control, they were free to attack bombers as they found them.

Above: For most of the war, the primary method of night air defence required the use of searchlights, usually grouped into batteries of nine, to illuminate targets for huge numbers of anti-aircraft guns. In 1939, more than two-thirds of the Luftwaffe's manpower served in the Flak arm.

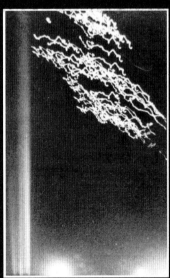

Above: To help night fighters find their way over a blacked-out land, a number of visual aids were introduced. One was to identify major cities by search light configurations mixed with starshells of prearranged colours. Nuremberg employed three vertical beams, side-by-side.

Above: The Wilde-Sau or 'Wild Boar' night-fighting technique called for fighters without radar, but with extra fuel, to operate over the RAF bomber target area. Pilots relied on searchlights to pick out a victim. Pilots were often blinded by the lights or shot down by friendly fire.

Above: The end of the line: a view of Grove airfield in Denmark, as recorded on 9 May 1945 by the British. Junkers Ju 88s of NJG 3 are parked with their propellers removed and canopies and engines covered. A number of Messerschmitt Bf 110s can also be seen, together with standard Ju 88 bombers.

Below: Searchlights and flak reach up to a damaged British bomber which turns back over a German city with one engine on fire. A crippled bomber, as a straggler, was a particularly easy target for night fighters. But the possibility of limping back to safety was always better than the certainty of death or capture which came with bailing out.

from NJG 1: Hauptmann August Geiger (53 kills), Oberfeldwebel Georg Kraft (14 kills) and Feldwebel Heinz Vinke (54 kills). Mosquitos proved even deadlier, accounting for 249 German aircraft, including 83 Bf-110 night fighters, for the loss of 84 of their own to all causes.

NIGHT FIGHTER BY DAY

The night fighter force suffered a steady stream of casualties. Even if a night fighter crew failed to find a British bomber, they might equally well fail to find their own airfield. It was all too easy, in the excitement of an interception, to stray over a flak concentration. There were inevitable instances where night fighters were shot down by other night fighters, although such 'friendly fire' errors became less common once the British twin-engined bombers were replaced by four engined types. Landing accidents and mid-air collisions accounted for others.

One avoidable source of losses was Goering's insistence on sending up specialist night fighters against daylight raids. Stung by Hitler's criticism, he forced the *Nachtjagd* to take part in the interception of particularly heavy raids by the US 8th Air Force. Gun camera footage of delighted P-47 pilots record the last moments of a number of Bf 110s and Ju 88s that stood little chance if caught by single-seater fighters.

WEAPONS UPGRADE

In early 1943 the *Nachtjagd* strength comprised 310 Messerschmitt Bf 110s, 80 Junkers Ju 88s and ten Dornier Do 217s. The Bf 110F had been supplanted by the G model, specifically designed for nightfighting. Its DB 605B engine provided more power to compensate for the weight and drag of the radar set; double dampers reduced the telltale glow of their exhausts. Since inexperienced crews often opened fire at long range, giving the bomber a chance of evading, and attacks from below were

easier as the bombers could seldom bring their defensive armament to bear, the Germans reinvented an idea from the First World War. Dubbed *Schräge Musik* (Jazz music) the installation consisted of one or two 20 mm cannon in the fuselage, angled to fire upwards. By 1944 over 50 per cent of the kills were being scored with this system. The bombers never realized they were under attack until it was too late. *Schräge Musik* proved so successful it was even mounted on some Focke-Wulf FW 189 reconnaissance aircraft, pressed into service as night fighters at the end of the year.

EXPERTEN

The German *Moskitojäger*, the wooden Focke-Wulf Ta-154 was a disappointment and the controversial Heinkel He 219 was cancelled after a very short production run, but there was one German aircraft capable of challenging de Havilland's 'wooden wonder.' The first jet *Nachtjagdgeschwader* was established in December 1944, using Messerschmitt Me-262s. Most were single seaters without radar, but a few appeared in 1945 sprouting Neptun radar aerials and some two-seat versions saw combat in the closing months of the war. The Me-262 was handicapped by its speed: as contacts took place at relatively close range, the jets had little time to take aim and fire before they overshot. Perversely, the Mosquito's own speed made it vulnerable to the Me-262s which did not experience this problem when intercepting one of them.

As with day fighter operations, a tiny fraction of night fighter pilots inflicted most of the losses. The top 20 aces accounted for 1,245 bombers between them: 17% of the kills claimed by the *Nachtjagd* over the course of the war. Two pilots, Heinz-Wolfgang Schnaufer and Helmut Lent scored over 100 kills; 23 others shot down 50 or more bombers.

Kammhuber Line

During the Hamburg raids on 24/25 July 1943 the RAF unleashed its latest secret weapon in the radar war. 700 bombers released 46,000 bundles of small aluminium strips. Known as 'Window' they completely paralysed the German radar system.

Above: Generalmajor Josef Kammhuber, a tremendous leader and organiser, was given the impossible task of clearing the skies of Allied bombers. Goering made him the scapegoat for the destruction of Hamburg in 1943.

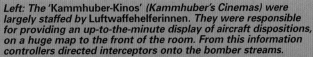

Left: The 'Kammhuber-Kinos' (Kammhuber's Cinemas) were largely staffed by Luftwaffehelferinnen. They were responsible for providing an up-to-the-minute display of aircraft dispositions, on a huge map to the front of the room. From this information controllers directed interceptors onto the bomber streams.

Centre left: A Ju 88 with an early type of Lichtenstein radar. Alongside the Kammhuber Line, the Luftwaffe sought to explore the possibilities of on-board radar. This would make the night-fighter much less dependant on ground control, with its own ability to track and intercept bombers.

Below left: Day and night operations were controlled at Jagddivision (fighter division) level from massive bunkers such as this one in Stade, northern Germany. General of Day Fighters Adolf Galland called them 'Battle Opera Houses' due to their tiered interior lay-out.

Right: The Himmelbett control stations tracked both the target and intercepting aircraft. The Würzburg-Reise units (below right) tracked single aircraft, while the Freya radar tower, with a range of 160 km provided a bigger picture. The problem was that one radar could only guide one fighter. Such a system was easily swamped as the British launched larger and larger raids.

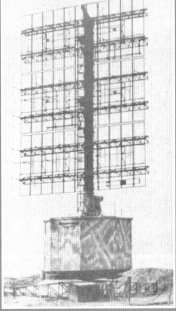

To the Gustav Line

Italy 1943/44

German theatre commander Albert Kesselring was determined to deny the Allies an easy victory in Italy. Whilst scratch forces kept the invaders at bay in the south, he built up a near impregnable barrier across the peninsula – the Gustav line. The way north to Rome was barred.

RESCUED FROM his mountain gaol by SS commando leader Otto Skorzeny, Benito Mussolini was re-established in northern Italy. Yet this was not the *Duce* of old. He had his son-in-law, Count Ciano shot for siding with the Grand Council that voted him out of office, but real power in Italy lay with the Germans. It would remain so throughout the short life of the so-called Republic of Saló. Although the 'Italian Social Republic' continued to field an army and air force, Mussolini spent most of his time with his mistress Clara Petacci. When it came at last to peace negotiations in 1945, the German commanders in Italy dealt with the Allies without informing Mussolini – or Hitler.

GERMANY ALONE
At the end of 1943 however, there were few thoughts of surrender. Field Marshal Albert Kesselring was appointed Commander-in-Chief of the newly established Army Group 'C'. His brief was to hold the

The sun sets on the German defences. The Italian terrain lent itself perfectly to a determined defender – the mountains and narrow passes were worth several divisions to an experienced commander.

The American misconduct of the Anzio landings afforded German propaganda virtually its last opportunity to parade masses of captured Allied troops. Three months after this photo captive and captured would reverse roles.

Allies as far south as possible; if British and American bombers could operate from Italian air fields, the strategic bomber offensive against Germany would become more dangerous and the Allies would be able to exploit the Adriatic to their advantage. The guerrilla war in Yugoslavia was already tying down large bodies of troops: with the Allies able to sustain Tito's partisan army, the drain on German resources would accelerate. A new guerrilla war was beginning within German-occupied Italy too. It was no

more than a nuisance at first, but a nasty cycle of ambushes and atrocities would gather pace over the next 12 months.

German forces consisted of two armies, the 14th (*Generaloberst* von Mackensen) and 10th (*Generaloberst* Vietinghoff). They held the winter defence line built in the wake of the Salerno landings, a succession of entrenchments, minefields and bunkers running from Gaeta in the west through Cassino and up the valley of the river Rapido, through the Maiella mountains and then along the

river Sangro to the Adriatic coast. The Germans called it the 'Gustav' line, which the Allies knew; it was also known as the 'line of no retreat,' which the Allies didn't.

HOLDING THE LINE

South of the Gustav line the Germans created a number of other fortified lines, each intended to delay the Allied advance. The ground was ideal for the defence: mountain passes and narrow coastal plains were blocked by determined rearguards. There was often no

alternative but to make a frontal attack, and the Germans would always slip away at the last minute rather than fight to the last. Booby-traps and minefields discouraged energetic retreat. Aggressive night patrolling – by both sides – made this a 24-hour-a-day war for the frontline infantry.

The southern-most German defences, the 'Viktor' line was penetrated in October. Campobasso was taken by the 1st Canadian Division, while Termoli fell to an amphibious assault. The 'Barbara' line was

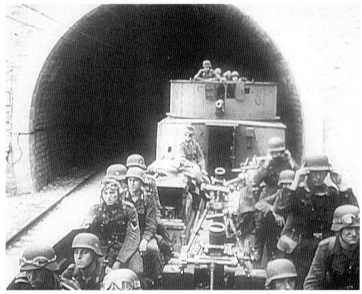

ruptured in November when Mondragone was captured and British and American troops crossed the river Trigno. General Herr's LXXVI *Panzerkorps* contested the Adriatic coast yard-by-yard and fell back in good order to the 'Bernhardt' line, the last defensive positions before the 'Gustav' line. General von Senger und Etterlin's XIV *Panzerkorps* did the same on the west coast.

BRITISH SNAILS

To attack the 'Bernhardt' line, General Montgomery first had to cross the river Sangro, its waters in full spate after heavy autumn rains. Bridgeheads were established in the teeth of sharp German counter-attacks, and by 22 November the British were across in strength. The river Foro was crossed on 8 December, but the city of Ortona was thoroughly fortified by German paratroops. The Canadian division's attack bogged down in a maze of medieval streets, defended with stubborn courage and diabolical skill. A building, captured after a hard fight, blew up shortly afterwards, wiping out a whole Canadian infantry platoon. The Germans had concealed explosives in the cellar, converting it into a giant time-bomb. Other buildings had rearmost walls removed: if the

buildings were captured, the Germans could fire anti-tank rockets directly into the rooms and retake them. The Canadians copied the time-bomb trick to lure 20 German paras to their doom, and employed 17-pdr anti-tank guns to pick off enemy strongpoints. Batteries of 25-pdr field guns blew the roofs of buildings which were then attacked with mortars, lobbing their bombs into the enemy-held rooms.

NO WAY FORWARD

Orsogna, further inland, required three divisional-scale assaults before the Germans were ejected. The end of 1943 found LXXVI *Panzerkorps* still holding Pescara, and the British commander General Alexander despairing of achieving anything on the eastern coast.

On the western side of Italy, Lt.-General Mark Clark's 5th Army captured Monte Camino in December. Alexander re-deployed his forces to give Clark 12 divisions while a much reduced British 8th Army had six, of which only one was British. General Montgomery flew home to prepare for D-Day; command of the 8th Army passed to General Leese. Mark Clark was ordered to crack the Gustav line at Monte Cassino and attack up the line of the

Death of a Monastery

Above: On the morning of 15 February 1944, 142 four-engined and 87 twin-engined American bombers flew over Monte Cassino in three waves. They dropped 453 tons of high explosive and incendiary bombs. The Abbey was reduced to a total ruin, which the Germans then took over.

Right: The rule of mountain warfare is that whoever is master of the hill is master of the valley. The Allied plan was to storm down the Liri Valley towards the Anzio beachhead. To do this they needed to take the high ground on both sides. This they succeeded in doing, but it took them five months.

TO ALLIED COMMANDERS surveying the killing grounds in front of the town of Monte Cassino, it must have seemed that the Abbey of St Benedict was mocking them. Standing stolidly atop the 560 metre hill, the Allies thought it was at best used as an artillery observation post and at worst as an arms repository. In fact the Germans had respected the sanctity of the Church and only three soldiers were stationed anywhere near it. They were three MPs stationed there to keep soldiers out.

Eventually the Allied command opted to destroy the monastery prior to the next assault. Although Allied air and ground attacks succeeded in reducing much of the monastery and its outer walls, the shelling did not destroy the subterranean chambers, which were to provide excellent shelter for the defenders. They would emerge from these time and again to repel determined but suicidal Allied assaults.

Right: The Abbey of St Benedict was a religious foundation of great importance in which the body of St Benedict was preserved. The Germans managed to evacuate the Abbot and his monks together with the Abbeys treasures to Rome as the bombing started.

Below: The destruction of both the Abbey and the town was a boon to defenders and a massive headache for the attackers. The Allies could not use their numerical and armoured superiority, and every pile of rubble became a defendable position. The Germans had been forced to learn this bitter lesson at Stalingrad.

Above: The Allies may finally have decide to bomb the Abbey due to a misinterpreted radio message. A German voice had been heard asking:"Wo ist der Abt? Ist er noch im Kloster? (Where is the 'Abt'? Is it still in the monastery?)" Abt is the German abbreviation for Abteilung (section). Unfortunately Abt also means Abbot, to which the conversation actually referred.

*Above:
To his credit General Mark Clark did not believe that the Germans were using the Abbey for military purposes. He wholeheartedly opposed the act of needless vandalism wrought on one of the great Abbeys of Medieval Europe.*

Above: The Allied advance stalled in front of the Gustav line. The only way forward was by a simultaneous flanking manoeuvre with an amphibious landing at Anzio together with a renewed frontal assault on Monte Cassino.

Below: Contrary to popular perception Italy is not all blue skies, sunshine and Chianti. The winters were long and savage. Roads through the mountains were few and were turned to rivers of mud with heavy rain and the weight of traffic passing over them.

rivers Liri and Sacco. To draw off German reserves, a new amphibious landing would be made some 100 km behind the front. To prepare for the main attack, another bitterly contested river crossing had to be made, over the Rapido, but by 10 January, the plans were laid to combine an assault on the Gustav line with a landing at Anzio. The Monte Cassino position would be isolated and Kesselring's men caught between two fires. Alexander and the British hoped to trap a major proportion of the defenders in their positions, but Clark had a different agenda.

WILD CAT TAMED

A Royal Navy captain involved in Operation 'Shingle' noted, "We were briefed for the landing at Anzio. This was going to be the great thing: tanks would go mad on the plains of Rome and cut off the Germans; the Germans would surrender and the bottleneck at Cassino would be broken. The only thing was, the Germans must have had the same briefing…"

Kesselring kept a powerful force in reserve, anticipating an attack from the sea. When it came on 22 January, he reported it as the landing – the expected Allied invasion of western Europe. Whether he believed this, or the initial reports were wildly exaggerated, or the canny Marshal just wanted the reinforcements, Kesselring immediately received panzer and *panzergrenadier* divisions stationed in France. Together with his own mobile reserve, he was able to despatch significant reinforcements to the Cassino front as well as concentrate troops for a major counter-attack at Anzio.

GRASPING THE NETTLE

Kesselring thought the landing zone around Anzio could sustain a good four divisions or so, and prepared his counterstroke accordingly. Yet the Allies had only landed two, fearing that it would be difficult to supply a

Anzio Annie

Right: The 28cm Kanone 5 was one of the finest artillery pieces ever produced. It was used extensively from the Atlantic Wall to the siege of Sevastopol. The complete unit weighed in at 218 tonnes and the gun could propel a 255kg shell up to 62km.

Below: A near perfect firing point for the guns was established in a tunnel on the main railway line connecting Rome to Nettuno. Although there were two tracks at the site it was deemed safer to operate only one gun at a time with the other gun kept in another tunnel further to the North. The gun emerged from its excellent cover only to retire again after firing.

IF THE GERMANS were unable to throw the Allies back into the sea as Hitler had demanded, then neither were the Allies able to widen the beachhead established at Anzio. The Germans placed a ring of steel around the Allied positions and attacked them day and night.

Among the ordinance deployed were two railway guns that had originally been sent to Italy for shipment to Tunisia. They were eventually sent south to Anzio from Milan in January 1944. For four months the guns between them made life hell for the entrenched Allies. A constant drizzle of 28cm shells were scattered all over the Allied positions, in concert with an unceasing bombardment from lighter artillery pieces. The guns, known collectively as 'Anzio Annie' remained in action until the breaching of the Gustav line in May 1944. So rapid was the Allied advance after the breakthrough that the escape route of the guns was cut off and they were captured almost intact and ready to move out.

larger force. General Lucas found himself almost unopposed, but contented himself with digging in on a broad front and awaiting events. Within a week, there were four German divisions in the surrounding hills and 2. *Panzerdivision* was on its way to join them. Prodded by his superiors, General Lucas ventured a modest advance on 30 January. German pioneers blew many of the bridges over the Mussolini Canal then 26. *Panzerdivision* and *Panzerdivision Hermann Goering* struck back. Two battalions of US Rangers were ambushed near Cisterna, only 6 men escaping back to the beachhead.

The Germans counter-attacked on 3 February, but the British 1st Division maintained a coherent front at the cost of heavy

casualties. The main German effort came on 16 February, spearheaded by one panzer, two *panzergrenadier* and two infantry divisions. The US 45th and British 56th Divisions bore the brunt of the shock, and thanks to heavy artillery and air support, they were able to hold their perimeter despite terrible casualties. The lavish and timely intervention by sea and air was no accident: Kesselring's plans were known to the Allies in detail thanks to Ultra intelligence. German losses were over 5,000 men that day. General Lucas was sacked on 22 February and it fell to his former deputy, General Truscott to repel the last German effort on 29 February. With the Allies now pouring troops into the beachhead, the prospects of driving them into the sea had

long vanished. The Germans went over to the defensive, ushering in a grisly period of First World War-style trench warfare.

BATTLE FOR CASSINO

The fortified town of Cassino and Monastery Hill that overlooked it stood between Clark's 5th Army, Anzio and Rome. On the night of 11-12 January, the French Expeditionary Corps broke into the German defences in the mountains, reaching as far as Atina. The US 2nd Corps fought to take a series of rocky heights adjacent to Monastery Hill, coming 'within a bare 100 metres of success' according to *Generalleutnant* von Senger und Etterlin whose men still held their ground when the fighting died down on 12 February. On

15 February it was the turn of the British – in fact, 2nd New Zealand division and 4th Indian division. The latter attacked Monastery Hill during the night, but were driven back to their start line with heavy losses. The New Zealanders got into the town, but were ejected by an armoured counter-attack by 15. *Panzergrenadier* Division.

The British assault was preceded by the destruction of the sixth century Benedictine Abbey on Monastery Hill. Many of the treasures inside this priceless historical site had been removed, but several hundred civilian refugees died when British and American bombers attacked at the request of the commander of 4th Indian Division, General Tuker. German propaganda made a predictable

Thin Green Line
German airborne in Italy

AS ITALY STARTED TO WAVER and then collapsed altogether in the autumn of 1943, Hitler was forced to commit more and more troops and material to protect his southern flank. These reinforcements included the 1st and 4th Parachute Divisions, which fought superbly in defence of Italy and the Italian mainland. Since Crete the parachute elite had been relegated purely to fighting as infantry. In Italy their role would remain unchanged.

But of all the *Fallschirmjäger* actions in WORLD WAR 2 it was the battles to hold the monastery of Monte Cassino and the town below it that have entered military folklore. The men of the 1st Parachute Regiment earned the title 'The Green Devils of Cassino' for their performance in a battle which Hitler characterised as "a battle of the First World War fought with weapons of the Second."

Above: The Fallschirmjäger *were charged with blunting the Allied spearhead in Italy. Paratroops would arrive in a combat area either through conventional parachute drop or by glider. The Gotha 232 glider (above left) could carry up to 23 troops in cramped conditions.*

meal out of this and the controversy would dog Tuker's commander, General Freyberg for years after the war. It took until 1969 for the US government to admit that previous claims to have certain knowledge the abbey was occupied were untrue. However, as David Fraser observed, 'nobody should underestimate the influence of the monastery on the morale of our own troops, none of whom could believe that its brooding presence was of no military significance. And the beliefs of soldiers, even if mistaken, are military realities if the soldiers are to be required to attack and to die.'

DEVILS IN THE ABBEY

The ruins were promptly occupied by 1. *Fallschirmjäger* Division, commanded by 48-year-old Richard 'Arno' Heidrich.

Dubbed 'Green devils' by the Allies, the German paratroops held Cassino against another attack by the New Zealanders on 15 March. The intensive fighting that followed was also distressingly like the Western Front of 1914-18. In the labyrinth of broken masonry, the German positions were protected by interlocking zones of fire. The Allies' advantages in tanks and aircraft availed them little in a war of attrition in which the grenade and machine-gun were the decisive weapons. The 1. *Fallschirmjäger* division held off the New Zealand division, elements of 78th division and at least a brigade of 4th Indian division. General Alexander wrote to Sir Alan Brooke expressing his frank admiration for the German defenders: "I don't think any troops could have stood up to it, except those para boys."

From 11-18 May Monte Cassino was attacked with tremendous dash by the Polish Corps, which suffered 3500 casualties before the 12th Podolski Lancers occupied the top of Monastery Hill and ran up the Polish flag above the ruins of the Abbey. However, French mountain troops had fought their way through the Aurunci mountains, taking Mount Faito and outflanking the position. Already in receipt of orders to withdraw, the 'Green Devils' began to fall back on 17 May, slipping north to fight another day.

THE ROAD TO ROME

Troops had been poured into the Anzio beachhead while the battle raged around Monte Cassino. On 23 May, the US VI Corps broke out of Anzio in overwhelming strength. The German forces in the south might have been cut off

had the American forces obeyed General Alexander's command to strike north-east to Valmontone, but Mark Clark sent them north-west to Rome. He succeeded in his ambition: his US 5th Army was the first Allied formation to capture an enemy capital. He ordered his men to prevent British troops advancing there, authorising the use of force if necessary. His shameless glory-hunting enabled the Germans to extract their 10th Army while Clark's men battered their way through the 'Caesar Line.' US troops entered Rome on 4 June, Clark's publicity triumph being eclipsed within 48 hours by the D-Day landings.

Kesselring ordered his army group to withdraw to the next defensive position, the 'Gothic Line,' covering the approaches to the Po Valley. Above that lay the Alpine passes and the Reich itself.

Above: One veteran of the fighting described a typical day under fire. *"The sun lost its brightness and an uncanny twilight descended. It was like the end of the world. Comrades were wounded, buried alive, dug out again and buried for a second time. Whole platoons and squads were obliterated by direct hits. Others rushed headlong into the enemy to escape from this hell."*

Below: The strains of combat involved in holding Monte Cassino were intense. Here men of the 1st Parachute Division take a few moments rest from the fighting, much of which was at close quarters and often hand-to-hand. Away from the fight living conditions for the defenders, especially in the winter were often difficult.

Above: One of the most fearsome sounds heard on any World War 2 battlefields was the 'tearing linoleum' howl of the rapid-firing German MG42 machine gun.

Below: Generalmajor *Richard Heidrich (standing) with Feldmarschall Albert Kesselring in the Italian theatre, mid-1944. Heidrich assumed command of the Cassino sector on 20 February, with Cassino and Monte Cassino being entrusted to Oberst Heilmann's 3rd Parachute Regiment.*

Below: A Sturmgeschütz *III provides support to the embattled defenders at Cassino. The excellent cover provided by the ruins made it virtually impossible to spot German armour in the town's ruins. Strong points backed by panzers were particularly difficult to dislodge.*

The invasion of Normandy was the greatest seaborne military operation in history. It required nearly 5,000 craft of a hundred different types to land more than five divisions on the first day alone.

D-DAY

Axis catastrophe

The invasion of France was one of the biggest military operations of all time. Three airborne divisions and five infantry divisions stormed 'Fortress Europe' at Normandy under the largest ever protective umbrella of air and sea power.

Although the Allied invasion of Europe had long been expected, it came as something of a surprise when it actually happened. Faced with a storm of fire from an Allied force which commanded sea and sky, German units could do little but take cover and survive.

"**T**HE SIGHT that was indescribable... between the last barge and the shore was a pier formed by piles of dead men. It was impossible to reach the shore without treading on the dead, and the sea around the cove was red with blood."

Thus did a young British officer of World War I describe Winston Churchill's first try at an amphibious landing. The slaughter at Gallipoli – there was so much blood in the water that it could be seen from the air – weighed heavily on the British prime minister's mind when it came to planning the liberation of France. But Hitler's 'Atlantic Wall,' bristling with concrete bunkers and minefields, was far more formidable than the Turkish defences at the Dardanelles. And the political stakes were higher. Gallipoli cost Churchill his job as First Sea Lord in 1915; if the Allied invasion of France was defeated, would a second attempt even be considered?

Hitler could not stop the Allies from landing. By early 1944 the Luftwaffe was losing control of the skies over the Reich itself. *Luftflotte* 3 had 820 aircraft on 6 June, of which 170 were serviceable; the Allies committed over 5,000, flying some 10,000 sorties on that day alone.
The *Kriegsmarine* readied its submarine flotillas at Brest and Lorient for what was recognised as a suicide mission; the bulk of the submarine force had already been withdrawn to Norway. S-boats and a handful of destroyers stood no chance of obstructing an invasion fleet 5,000 vessels strong, manned by over a quarter of a million men. Nine Allied battleships, 23 cruisers and 73 destroyers were assigned to shore bombardment missions alone.

TARGET NORMANDY
So the Allies would have to be beaten ashore. But where? And how? Field Marshal Gerd von Rundstedt, Commander-in-Chief of the German army in the west,

believed the invasion would take place in the Pas de Calais area, where the Channel is at its narrowest. The Germans would have less time to react once the invasion fleet had been detected, and, once a beachhead had been secured, Rundstedt feared the enemy could reach the Rhine in four days. Inland lay good tank country.

Normandy he ruled out because inland it was dominated by the *bocage:* narrow lanes and high hedgerows ideal for defence. And there were no major ports, which were assumed essential. The Allies' 'Mulberry' artificial harbours would come as a disagreeable surprise.

His conclusion was reinforced by German intelligence, which reported a major concentration of Allied troops in the south-east of England. The First US Army Group or FUSAG was commanded by none other than General George S Patton – the one general in the British and American armies that the Germans really feared.

Hitler agreed with his commanders, and the Pas de Calais sector received the bulk of the new fortifications and the strongest concentration of troops.

SWEPT FROM THE SKIES
But it would be difficult to beat the Allies since they would have uncontested control of the air. Although the Luftwaffe could still make devastating local attacks in the East, it could do very little to contribute to the ground battle in France.

Field Marshal Rommel, who had endured similar conditions for more than a year in Africa, believed the Allies had to be destroyed on the beaches. Once a beachhead was established, under that all-powerful air umbrella, he had little confidence that the German army could throw the invaders back into the sea. He wanted panzer divisions positioned near enough to the coast to intervene within hours, not days.

Von Rundstedt disagreed. He planned a conventional defence

Above: A German 88-mm gun battery in action as the understrength Germans attempted to maintain a ring of steel around the invasion beachhead. In spite of their efforts, the Allies quickly built up men and material in preparation for the almost inevitable breakout.

Below: In the run up to D-Day Field Marshal Rommel was tireless in his duties, preparing the defences in France against an Allied invasion. Here he confers with General Meindl, who commanded the 3rd and 5th Parachute Divisions in Brittany.

Below: The overall quality of the German troops along the invasion front was not high, even when braced by experienced SS units as seen here. The invasion front was just too long to be adequately defended by the Reich's depleted armies. This was obvious even to the OKW, where the prevailing strategy was to maintain a large reserve to throw against the Allies once the main invasion site was known.

which accepted that the Allies would probably succeed in landing. Once the Germans had identified the enemy's main thrust, he would counter-attack with a concentrated blow led by the panzer divisions.

He accepted that movement behind the lines by day would be vulnerable to air attack, but most divisions received additional anti-aircraft gun batteries. In May 1944 an officer from 12. *SS Panzerdivision Hitlerjugend* had the idea of mounting the *Flakvierling* quadruple 20 mm anti-aircraft gun system on to a Panzer IV chassis: the resulting *'Wirbelwind'* self-propelled flak unit was rushed into production on Hitler's orders.

Above all, the German high command trusted the training and discipline of their men – particularly their night fighting ability – to smash the invasion before the Allies could bring their superior numbers to bear.

SECOND LINE TROOPS

It bears repeating that the bulk of the German army remained on the Russian Front where the Red Army was poised to launch five operations, each of which was larger than 'Overlord.' Of the 285 divisions available to Hitler, 164 were in the East compared to 60 in the West. And half of the latter were poor quality infantry divisions, filled out with wounded, semi-invalids, older men (a quarter of the German army was aged over 34 by 1944) and foreign troops of dubious loyalty. Many divisions included a battalion of former Soviet troops, 'volunteers' for the anti-Communist army RONA whose reliability was increasingly suspect as the Red Army's westward advance continued.

The infantry divisions had an impossibly long coastline to defend. In north-east France divisional sectors averaged 50 miles; along the Normandy coast they were 120 miles long, rising to more than 200 miles along the shores of the Atlantic and Mediterranean.

German hopes in France

rested on 11 armoured and four airborne divisions, the paratroops functioning as elite ground troops rather than in their intended role. Across the Channel were the equivalent of 50 divisions, including 21 American, 15 British, three Canadian and one each from Poland and France.

As commander of Army Group 'B', Field Marshal Rommel threw himself into the task of making the 'Atlantic Wall' of Goebbels' propaganda a truly effective shield. Slave labour combined 17 million cubic yards of concrete with 1.5 million tons of iron to build a network of bunkers, pillboxes, observation towers and machine gun nests. Anti-tank ditches were dug inland; steel girders were fixed at low water to impale incoming landing craft.

But his disagreement with von Rundstedt over how to fight the battle was never resolved. Hitler assigned some panzer divisions to Rommel, others to Rundstedt's reserve, but decreed that none could move without his personal authorisation.

In the months leading up to D-Day the Allied air forces systematically bombed the French railway system. Bridges, marshalling yards, and key junctions were attacked in a campaign that cost the lives of some 10,000 French civilians. The result was that German reinforcements found it slow going to get to the front. The 9th and 10th SS *Panzergrenadier* divisions took as long to cross France as they did travelling from Russia to the Franco-German border.

ALLIED DECEPTION

Radar installations were knocked out one by one in the final days. Only one survived on 6 June: the station at Calais detected a massive radar contact crossing the sea at an apparent speed of eight knots. The invasion fleet!

But it was another Allied 'spoof.' The Calais station had been spared deliberately. Lancasters of 617 Squadron and Stirlings of 218 Squadron flew

Atlantic Wall

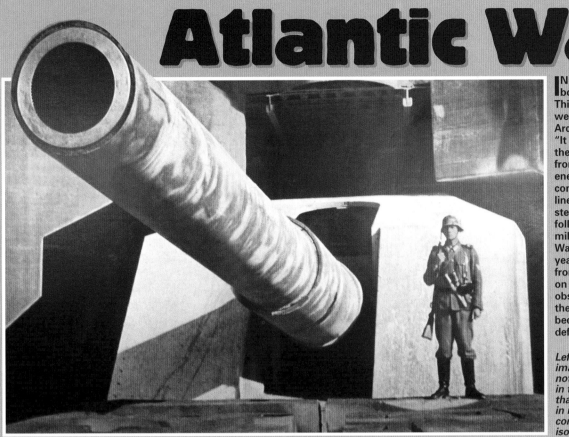

IN DECEMBER 1941, Adolf Hitler boasted to the world that his Third Reich controlled the entire west coast of Europe from the Arctic Ocean to the Bay of Biscay. "It is my unshakable decision," the Fuhrer added, "to make this front impregnable against every enemy." To keep his vow, Hitler conceived of an awesome defence line – a broad band of concrete, steel, guns and troops that would follow the shoreline for 2,400 miles. He called it the Atlantic Wall. In the next two and a half years a quarter of a million men from *Organisation Todt* worked on it night and day. It became an obsessive project for Hitler. For the Allied invasion planners it became the most formidable defensive barrier of the War.

Left: The impressive propaganda images in German magazines did not reflect reality. The commander in the Pas de Calais area admitted that the Wall was, at best, a "thin, in many places fragile, length of cord with a few small knots at isolated points."

By 1943, the pressed labour working on the Wall were pouring up to 800,000 tons of concrete monthly into the giant fortifications. In the period 1942-1944, the Germans used over 17 million cubic metres of concrete and 1.2 million metric tons of steel for the Atlantic Wall. "I am the greatest fortress builder of all time," boasted Adolf Hitler

The foundations for some of the largest German coastal artillery emplacements along the French coast were laid as early as 1940. These gun positions in the Pas de Calais were intended to support a German invasion of Britain. Subsequently, they fired on Allied shipping in the Channel and regularly shelled Dover, Folkestone and elsewhere along the British coast.

Some 15,000 bunkers and other installations protected harbours and points along the French coast where there were important facilities or likely landing spots. In some instances the Germans used elaborate camouflage schemes to avoid detection by Allied reconnaissance aircraft.

Allied Landing

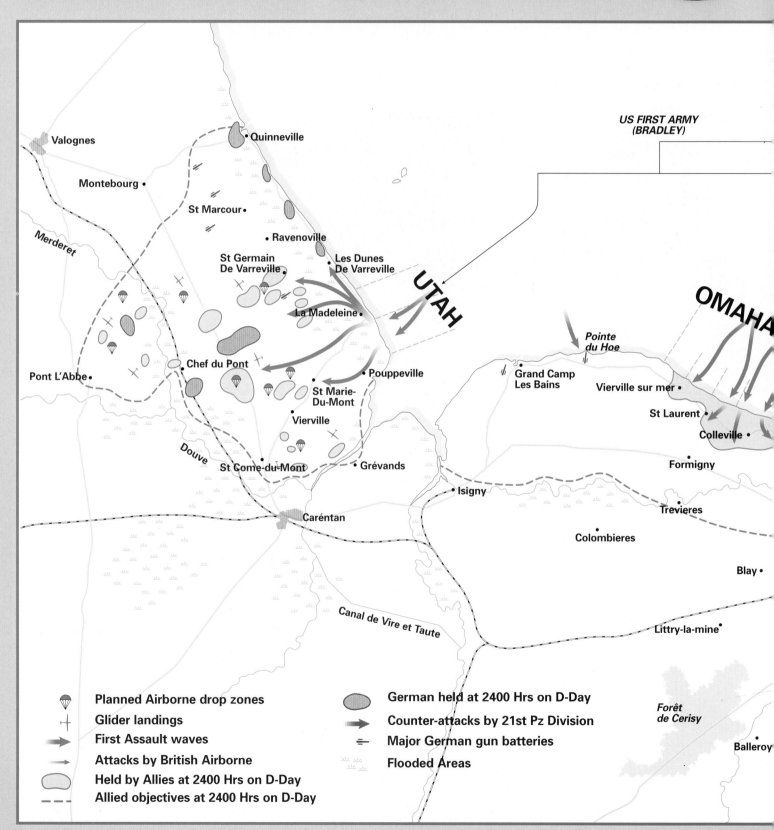

US FIRST ARMY
(BRADLEY)

Valognes

Montebourg •

Merderet

St Marcour •

Quinneville •

Ravenoville •

St Germain
De Varreville

Les Dunes
De Varreville

La Madeleine •

UTAH

Pont L'Abbe •

Chef du Pont •

Pouppeville •

OMAHA

Pointe
du Hoe

Grand Camp
Les Bains

Vierville sur mer •

St Marie-
Du-Mont

St Laurent •

Vierville •

Colleville •

Douve

St Come-du-Mont •

Grévands •

Formigny •

Isigny •

Trevieres •

Caréntan •

Colombieres •

Blay •

Canal de Vire et Taute

Littry-la-mine •

Forêt
de Cerisy

Balleroy •

Planned Airborne drop zones

Glider landings

First Assault waves

Attacks by British Airborne

Held by Allies at 2400 Hrs on D-Day

Allied objectives at 2400 Hrs on D-Day

German held at 2400 Hrs on D-Day

Counter-attacks by 21st Pz Division

Major German gun batteries

Flooded Areas

in Normandy

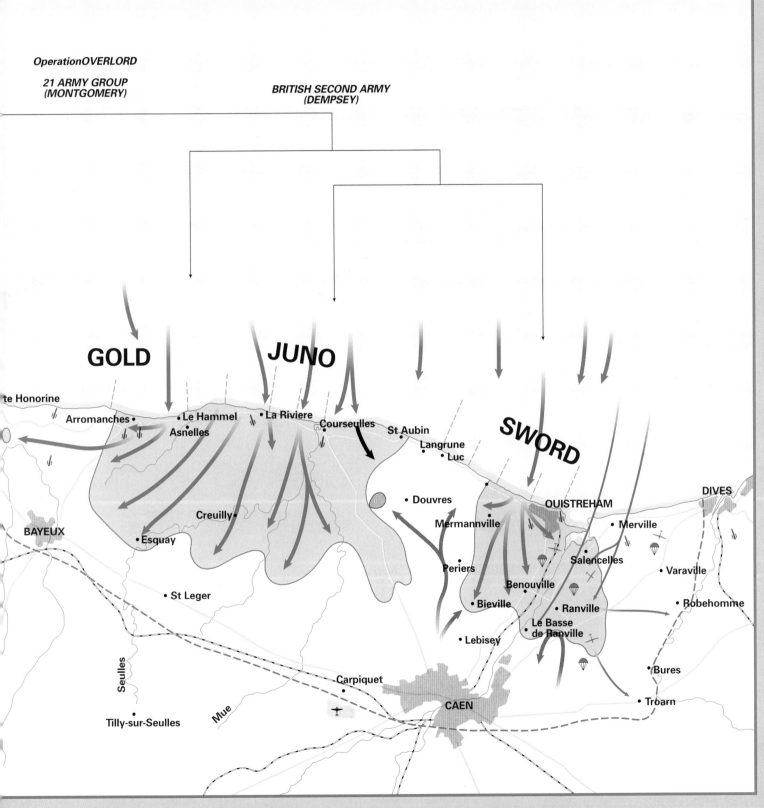

OperationOVERLORD

**21 ARMY GROUP
(MONTGOMERY)**

**BRITISH SECOND ARMY
(DEMPSEY)**

GOLD

JUNO

SWORD

te Honorine

Arromanches •

• Le Hammel
Asnelles

• La Riviere

Courseulles

St Aubin

Langrune
• Luc

Creuilly •

BAYEUX

• Esquay

• Douvres

Mermannville •

OUISTREHAM

DIVES

• Merville

• St Leger

Periers •

Salencelles

• Varaville

Benouville
•

• Bieville

• Ranville

• Robehomme

Seulles

Le Basse
de Ranville

• Lebisey

Carpiquet

• Bures

Mue

CAEN

• Troarn

Tilly-sur-Seulles

Above: By 2400 hours on Decision Day the Allies had taken their first German prisoners. The Allied attack was not expected on the Normandy coast and the troops garrisoned there were not of great quality.

Below: Two first class field commanders, neither of whom had the answer to the conundrum posed by the Allies. Rundstedt (right) wanted to let the Allies land and then concentrate his reserves for a knock-out blow to force them back into the sea. Rommel wanted to destroy the Allies on the beaches. By the end of July Rommel would be lying critically ill and Rundstedt had been replaced for his failure to stop the Allies.

low over the sea, dropping patterns of 'window', strips of foil that appeared as a mass of radar reflections, while a flotilla of small boats fitted with radar reflectors made for France. At 04.00hrs the two 'fleets' lay off the coast, broadcasting the sounds of anchors rattling through hawsepipes from behind a thick smokescreen. Then they turned for home.

Thus in the early hours of 6 June German commanders had reports of landings from Calais and Normandy, while RAF bombers dropped dummy paratroopers to further confuse the issue. They assumed that the real attack would come at Calais, even after they knew the Allies were ashore in strength.. Normandy must be a feint.

NON-EXISTENT ARMY

Not until many days later did OKW realise its mistake. FUSAG had never existed. Patton's tours of his 'command' were widely reported, but his army group consisted of dummy vehicles, empty barracks and some very busy radio operators whose stream of radio traffic was monitored from the other side of the Channel. The *Abwehr* spy network in Britain had been eliminated. Luftwaffe reconnaissance flights were few and far between; the real invasion forces along the south coast were heavily camouflaged while FUSAG units exposed huge dummy supply dumps to aerial observation.

The timing of the attack added to the German surprise, since the weather seemed so hostile. But since German weather ships had been swept from the Atlantic, the Allies had the advantage in forecasting – they knew a break in the weather was on its way.

When the landings began, Rommel was in Germany, visiting his wife, many junior officers were away, ironically on an anti-invasion staff exercise – and Hitler was asleep.

Hitler was still asleep by the middle of the morning, by which time Rommel's staff had

badgered Rundstedt to request the Führer's permission to commit the panzers. No-one dared wake him.

It was not until the late afternoon of 6 June that the nearest armoured unit was given permission to move – which meant that Rommel's defensive strategy had collapsed before the battle had really begun.

ON TO THE BEACH

The landings took place on a 100-km front, with five divisions assaulting from the sea and three by air. The British and Canadian forces landed on the three eastern beaches, code-named Gold, Juno and Sword, while the Orne river crossings were seized in advance by the 6th Airborne division. The German 716th division – a second line formation including an *Ostruppen* battalion – was pounded by naval gunfire, bombed by the RAF, then driven from its defences exactly according to plan. The 'Atlantic Wall' was pierced by a number of ingenious armoured assault vehicles: 'flail' tanks that beat paths through the minefields, bridgelayers and tanks fitted with 'bunker busting' howitzers.

Only the belated intervention of the 21st Panzer Division prevented a complete disaster for the Germans. Once unleashed, the veteran tank unit acted with characteristic aggression and skill. 21st PD counter-attacked the Canadians, and was only stopped short of the beach by naval gunfire. As a result the city of Caen, a key Allied objective for D-Day, was held by the Germans.

HOLDING THE LINE

At the extreme west of the Allied line, Utah beach was seized to facilitate a rapid advance towards the vital port of Cherbourg. Defended by elements of the second-line 709th Infantry Division, it was within reach of several first-line units, notably the 91st Infantry Division and the 6th *Fallschirmjäger* regiment. However, such was the confusion caused by the American airborne assaults – scattered across the battlefield to the bewilderment of both sides – neither German formation reacted in time.

Only at Omaha beach did the Allies face determined resistance. Allied intelligence had not detected the recent arrival of the German 352nd Infantry Division, a battle-hardened formation fresh from the Russian Front. A last minute raid by 480 B-24 heavy bombers looked spectacular, but the bombs fell too far inland. Naval bombardment damaged some positions, but a few newly built machine gun nests were not included in the fire plan.

The first waves of US troops suffered hideous losses. Small groups of men eventually found their way up various gulleys – one of the storming parties was led by Brigadier-General Norman D Cota, deputy commander of the 29th Infantry Division. They outflanked the pillboxes and one by one, the gun positions fell silent. Follow-on waves of troops came ashore in relative safety.

Of the 35,000 US troops landed at Omaha on 6 June, 2,200 became casualties. The German 352nd division retreated grudgingly, contesting every feature without giving way. Of its 6,000 men, some 1,200 were killed, wounded or captured.

ROAD TO BERLIN

Hitler's plan had failed. The Allies had put 170,000 men ashore by the end of the first day, losing fewer than 5,000 in the process. Thanks to the Mulberry harbour system, they were then able to feed troops and supplies into the beachhead almost as quickly as if they had captured a port. By contrast, German units ordered to Normandy found it next to impossible to move by day, due to the incessant Allied air attacks. The Allied armies in Normandy grew faster than the Germans'. A month after D-Day there were a million Allied troops in France. The ghost of Gallipoli had been laid to rest.

The Martin B-26 Marauder provided much of the medium bomber support at Normandy. A tricky aircraft to fly because of its high wing loading, the B-26 nevertheless packed a heavy punch.

RUIN FROM THE AIR

Above: The Hawker Typhoon was the RAF's primary ground-attack aircraft. It was employed in 'taxi rank' attacks – squadrons loitered over the battlefield until called down by the ground troops. It could respond quickly, delivering pinpoint attacks with four 20-mm cannon and bombs or rockets.

Below: Railways were an inviting target, as this Typhoon pilot has found. Large numbers of heavily-armed Allied fighters roamed the battlefield, having a major impact on the German counter-attacks.

Above: The Douglas A-20 Boston/Havoc was an extremely versatile light bomber, also used in large numbers in support of the Normandy invasion. To aid in recognition, all Allied aircraft involved in operations on the Normandy front were painted with prominent black and white 'invasion' stripes.

Below: The Luftwaffe mounted fewer than 300 sorties on 6 June – compared with 14,674 Allied missions. With no air force the Wehrmacht depended for its survival upon flak, guile and the cover of night.

Normandy Breakout

For several weeks in June and July 1944, the Allies feared for the success of Operation Overlord. To east and west the Wehrmacht had put a containing ring of steel around the Normandy beachhead. German survival depended on stopping an Allied break-out.

IDNIGHT ON D-Day saw an Allied lodgement all along the Normandy coast. The counter attack by 21st Panzer Division based near Caen had penetrated the area between Juno and Sword beaches, but had been driven back. The British and Canadians who had landed on Gold, Sword and Juno had penetrated, at places, almost eight kilometres inland. At Omaha the US Vth Corps were ashore albeit

after a bloody battle, and to the west, at Utah, the US VII Corps had crossed the flooded area close to the beach and linked up with the men of the 82nd and 101st Airborne Divisions. By midnight 57,500 American and 75,000 British and Canadian troops were ashore.

Perversely, Hitler welcomed an Allied landing because he was sure that German forces in France would repeat the carnage that the Canadians had suffered in their landing at Dieppe in 1942. But even though the Germans at

Above: American-equipped troops of the French 2nd Armoured Division prepare to move out on 1 August. It was the first stage of an operation that would end in the liberation of Paris in less than a month.

Below: The Germans facing the Allied Armies on the Normandy front fought with enormous professionalism and courage. But the constant threat of air attack, partisan operations behind the lines and longer tours of duty than their opponents inevitably took a toll.

Omaha had inflicted over 3,000 casualties on the US 1st and 29th Infantry Divisions, even here they had not stopped the landing.

Field Marshal Erwin Rommel had predicted that the Allies would have to be stopped on the beaches, and had urged that the defences should be stronger. However, at the landing at Anzio in Italy in January 1944, Field Marshal Kesselring had shown that an amphibious beachhead could be contained and perhaps even eliminated. Hitler was convinced that if the Allies were defeated in this major landing they would not attempt another. This would give the Germans greater strategic flexibility and the opportunity to fight the Soviet Union to a stand-still.

The Allies also feared that the invasion might become stuck in a crowded beachhead, and so their first priority was to link up along the coast. This was achieved on 11 June.

STORM IN THE CHANNEL

But on 19 June disaster struck. A severe storm in the Channel wrecked the prefabricated harbour at Omaha. The Allies only had two of these harbours which were essential to the success of 'Overlord.' The capture of a port now became a major priority. The US VII Corps under Lt General J. Lawton Collins drove up the Cotentin peninsula and pounded the garrison of Cherbourg into submission using naval gunfire from three battleships and four cruisers as well as 1100 tons of bombs. However the harbour and dock facilities had been comprehensively destroyed and it took six weeks before it began to be a viable port.

By the beginning of July the Allies had advanced about 32 km into the interior but bad weather had neutralised the advantage of air power and the Germans were rapidly reinforcing the front. The opposing forces had reached a rough parity with Allied strength in France at a million men and 177,000 vehicles. Stalemate had set in, and some British and American commanders feared that another Anzio was in the offing.

STALEMATE

Conditions favoured the German defenders who were familiar with the terrain. The area known as the *bocage* consisted of small fields divided by earth banks planted with trees or thick hedges. This canalised vehicle movement down narrow lanes, or forced attacking infantry to cross exposed fields where German MG42 crews were dug in to give interlocking fire and the 8-cm mortars would catch infantry in their forming up positions prior to an attack. Faced with complete Allied air superiority the Germans became masters of camouflage using the dense vegetation to conceal men and vehicles.

To the west, the British and Canadians fought to break out and reach Caen. In the D-Day plans the town had optimistically been listed as an objective that would be secured within a day of landing. As long as the Germans held Caen they could prevent the Allies from reaching the plain stretching 30 km to Falaise – good tank country

and ideal for the construction of airfields.

Once again the Germans held good defensive positions and had concentrated the XLVII Panzer Corps, II SS Panzer Corps and 1 SS Panzer Corps opposite the Allied right flank. In the British and Canadian sector 14 divisions including six Panzer faced the Allies. Though the Anglo-Canadian forces of the 21 Army Group under Montgomery launched two major attacks, Operation Epsom on 26 June - 1 July, and Operation Goodwood between the 18 and 20 July, they were unable to break through. At Goodwood Montgomery had used heavy bombers of the RAF and USAAF to blast the German positions but despite this the attack ground to a halt with heavy losses in infantry and armour.

The constant battering against the German right flank was costly to the Anglo-Canadian forces – but it sucked in German reserves, leaving only 11 seriously weakened divisions to the west, facing the Americans. Of these divisions only two were armoured and they faced the powerful US 1st Army under Omar Bradley.

THE BOMB PLOT

On July 20 in the Führer's headquarters in Rastenburg in East Prussia the Bomb Plot reached its explosive climax. Hitler saw his survival as a miraculous confirmation of his place as leader of Germany and her armed forces, a conclusion that would cause him to intervene disastrously at a tactical level in operations in Normandy.

The weather was bad at the end of July, causing problems for General Bradley as he readied six divisions of the 1st Army for Operation Cobra. This was a plan to punch through the German lines west of St Lô. It was due to start on 24 July 1944, after bombers of the USAAF 8th Air Force had carpet bombed the German forward positions.

Bad weather led to a postponement, but not before part of the bomber force had already attacked. Some 'friendly' bombs

dropped short – inflicting 25 dead and 131 wounded in the US 30th Division. They had pulled back from their front line positions, and the German troops of the 901st Panzergrenadiers opposite had shrewdly occupied the vacated American defences.

On 25 July the full weight of Cobra – 15 American divisions – fell on the Panzer Lehr Division. An elite formation, Panzer Lehr had been ground down by constant combat, so that only 2,200 men and 45 operational armoured vehicles faced the Americans.

Before US armour and infantry attacked they were again preceded by a massive preliminary bombardment. At 9.38 am, 500 fighter bombers launched a 20 minute attack, concentrating on the forward defences in a belt 250 metres long. They were followed by 1,800 B-17 heavy and medium bombers.

Yellow panels and smoke markers had been prepared to show the US front line, and the road from St Lô to Lessay provided a clear east-west reference point. However even though the squadrons had been instructed by Bradley to attack on that axis, they approached the target from the north. Under an torrent of high explosives German bunkers were caved in, barbed wire ripped up, ammunition dumps exploded and even tanks were thrown into the air.

FRIENDLY-FIRE

Unfortunately, dust and smoke from the attack obscured the target and the reference points, and again some bomb aimers began to toggle their loads prematurely. By the time the air attack was over, another 111 soldiers from the luckless 30th Division had been killed, with 490 more wounded. It required considerable fortitude for Brigadier-General William Harrison to put the 30th on its feet and send it into the attack.

As artillery fire from 1,000 guns crashed into the 7,000 metre front, M4 Sherman tanks began

Above and below: On 13th June 1944, following a drive from Beauvais under repeated air attack, Michael Wittmann led a company of four Tigers and a Panzer IV to Villers Bocage. His orders were to stop the advance guard of the British 7th Armoured Division. At about 8:00am, Wittmann struck the British who were advancing on a sunken road. He waited until the vehicles were a 100 meters off and then destroyed leading and tail vehicles, blocking the escape route for the rest of the column. In a hectic five-minute engagement, Wittmann's force destroyed some 25 Cromwell and Firefly tanks and another 28 assorted vehicles.

Cobra uncoils

As early as 11 June 1944, Montgomery stated that his objective was to draw the greatest possible weight of enemy strength on to the eastern end of the bridgehead, towards Dempsey's forces aimed at Caen. This would weaken the Germans opposing Bradley, so facilitating a break-out in the West at the appropriate time.

Montgomery's assessment was uncannily accurate. On 24 July, four days after 'Cobra's' launch, the stalemate was over. Bradley's tanks were in open country.

Right: Generals Montgomery, Dempsey and Bradley in conversation. The success of 'Cobra' was partly due to an unusual degree of cooperation between the Allied commanders.

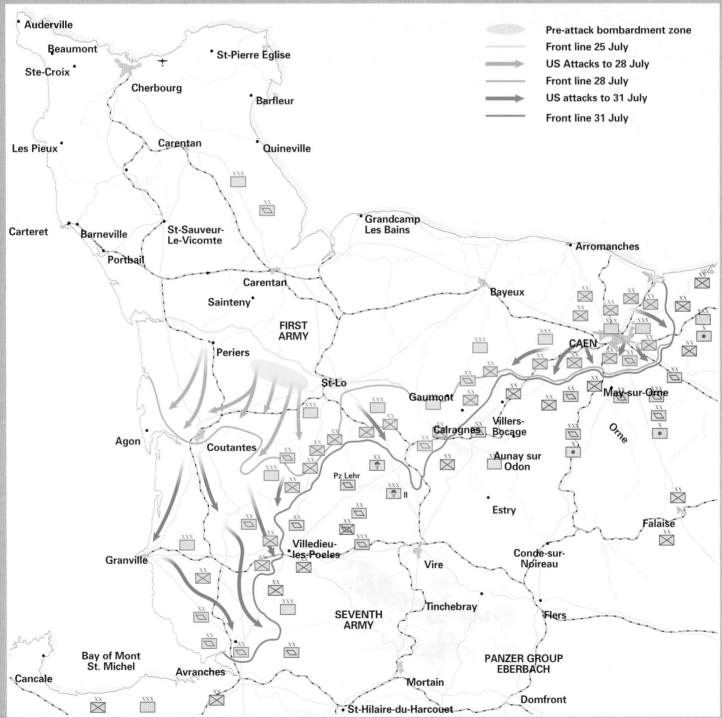

Pre-attack bombardment zone
Front line 25 July
US Attacks to 28 July
Front line 28 July
US attacks to 31 July
Front line 31 July

Auderville
Beaumont
Ste-Croix
St-Pierre Eglise
Cherbourg
Barfleur
Les Pieux
Carentan
Quineville
Carteret
Barneville
St-Sauveur-Le-Vicomte
Grandcamp Les Bains
Arromanches
Portbail
Carentan
Bayeux
Sainteny
FIRST ARMY
Periers
CAEN
St-Lo
Gaumont
May-sur-Orne
Agon
Calragnes
Villers-Bocage
Orne
Coutantes
Aunay sur Odon
Pz Lehr
Estry
Falaise
Villedieu-les-Poeles
Granville
Conde-sur-Noireau
Vire
Tinchebray
Flers
SEVENTH ARMY
Bay of Mont St. Michel
PANZER GROUP EBERBACH
Cancale
Avranches
Mortain
Domfront
St-Hilaire-du-Harcouet

147

to roll forward. Welded to their glacis plates were ploughs made from Czech hedgehog anti-tank obstacles that had been recovered from the Normandy beaches and cut up and welded together. The ploughs cut through the *bocage* hedgerows and the tanks were no longer trapped in the narrow country lanes.

BREAKOUT

Initially, to their amazement, the Americans encountered resistance, but it was only a thin grey line. By 28 July the US VIII Corps under Major-General Troy Middleton and the VII Corps under the dynamic Lt.-General L. J. (Lightning Joe) Collins had pushed the Germans back over 20 kilometres. The *Fallschirmjäger* of General Meindl's II Parachute Corps counter attacked the left flank of the salient, but were brushed aside by the Americans. Crossing the river Sienne near Coutances, Middleton's troops linked up with Collins to trap German troops at Roncey.

By 30 July American troops had reached Avranches and a day later were across the river Sélun

Despite this rupture of their left flank, the German forces in Normandy held on – though in the west Montgomery was hammering away at the Caen front and had even outflanked the bomb-ravaged town.

CHANGES OF COMMAND

Following the July Bomb Plot Hitler replaced the veteran Field Marshal von Rundstedt by Field Marshal Günther von Kluge – who was himself to commit suicide following the revelation of his involvement in the Bomb Plot. Rommel, who had commanded Army Group B in France, was recovering in Germany from severe injuries caused by RAF fighters in Normandy on 17 July.

Von Kluge was finally given leave by Hitler to release the armoured divisions from the Pas de Calais area for a counter attack on the deep narrow spearhead of the US advance, which stretched from Avranches to Mortain. The exchange of signals between

Above: He who wins the logistics race wins the battle. Allied success at Normandy depended upon the continual functioning of the Mulberry harbours. One of these was knocked out by a severe storm on 19 June.

Left: The Allies resupply task was aided by the early fall of the important port of Cherbourg. Here, General von Schliemann surrenders to Bradley's US First Army.

Below: Lack of fuel often paralysed the German panzer armies. The Allies, by contrast, had laid a cross-channel pipeline to feed their advance.

BOCAGE Death in the Ditches

Arguably the best 'tank-killer' of the war, the German Jagdpanther could destroy any Allied tank ranged against it in Normandy. But neither Allied nor German armour could operate effectively in the bocage.

Above: Normandy was to be no 'cake-walk' for the confident GIs, and death lurked behind every hedge. The average life expectancy of a front-line infantryman in the Normandy fighting was 14 days.

Above right: The German defenders were experts in the use of camouflage. Their stubbornness frustrated Allied plans for a quick break-out from Normandy. As June gave way to July Eisenhower and his subordinates feared that Normandy might turn into another Anzio.

Right: A German paratrooper in the bocage awaits another US attack. Applying lessons learned in Russia, German troops did not form continuous lines of defence, preferring to rely on mutually-supporting strongpoints which channelled attackers into kill zones.

Above: Saturation bombing by 2,000 Allied planes preceded the final Allied assault on Caen. Captured German defenders, deafened by the attack, could not be interrogated for 24 hours.

Left: A stricken Sturmgeschütz III in Normandy. The German assault gun was, by this stage of the war, serving as a frontline tank as well as in its intended role as an infantry-support gun.

Below: British Cromwell tanks east of the Orne river in July 1944. The Cromwell, which first saw action in Normandy, was the last and best in the line of British cruiser tank designs.

Hitler and von Kluge was intercepted by the ULTRA teams at Bletchley Park and General Hodges, who had taken command of the US 1st Army, was alerted well in advance.

The Mortain counter attack was launched on 6 August and made some progress against the 1st Army and those corps of Patton's 3rd Army not fighting in Brittany. The attacks were finally stopped and broken up by artillery fire and devastating fighter-bomber strikes.

While the Germans were preoccupied, an attack by the Canadian 1st Army threatened Falaise. More bad news came with the success of Operation Anvil/Dragoon, the Allied landing in southern France. Field Marshal Walther Model, the 'Führer's Fireman', had arrived to replace

Kluge. He was ordered to pull back from the attack at Mortain. The tough monocled general had earned the reputation of being able to save crises on the Eastern Front, but the Anglo-American forces in Normandy were just too strong for him to make a difference.

TURKEY-SHOOT
As the Allies ranged into France, they threatened to trap the bulk of the German forces in a huge pocket at Falaise. By 10 August, the US XX Corps had reached Nantes and a day later Angers. Patton's 3rd Army liberated Le Mans on 8 August and then swung north to Argentan on 13 August. The Canadians drove through to Falaise on 16 August.

US and Anglo-Canadian forces pressed forward from Normandy.

The 5th *Panzer Armee* and the composite force *Panzergruppe Eberbach*, were caught in a trap with a narrow exit to the east.

With the return of good weather, Allied fighter-bombers ranged over the pocket with brutal efficiency. Machine guns, cannon, bombs and rockets pulverised vehicles that clogged the roads and river crossings. Most of the German troops in Normandy were now in a pocket 65 km long and 20 to 25 km wide. By the night of 18 August this had reduced to 9 km by 11 km, and the Falaise gap had shrunk to between 5 and 8 km.

SPRINGING THE TRAP
By 19 August, the tough Polish tank crews of the 2nd Armoured Regiment serving with the British 4th Armoured Division had

fought through to hold an isolated position at the village of St Lambert. Both sides knew the Polish position was the cork in the bottle of the shrinking Falaise Pocket, and they had to hold it against desperate German attacks from both east and west. When on the same day the Canadians, Poles and Americans linked up at the town of Chambois, the trap was sealed shut.

Some Germans did manage to slip through the Allied lines at night, but up to 50,000 were taken prisoner. Between 5,000 and 10,000 died in the Falaise pocket. In total, the Normandy campaign had cost the Germans 200,000 men (including 91,000 POWs), 1,500 tanks, 3,500 guns and 20,000 vehicles. With them went any hope of stemming the Allied advance.

Having failed in their counter-offensive directed at Avranches, the German 5th and 7th Panzer Armies found themselves surrounded after the Americans and British linked up South of Caen. In the ensuing carnage, the Allies wiped out German armour in Normandy. The way to Paris was now open.

Falaise – Killing Ground

Right: The Hawker Tempest, although not a success as an air-superiority fighter, found its niche as probably the most effective ground-attack aircraft of the war. It is shown here with 20-mm cannon and rocket projectiles. Aircraft of No. 193 squadron were responsible for shooting-up Rommel's staff car on 17 July 1944.

Below: The rail network had long since been destroyed, and Allied air superiority meant that any German vehicle moving by day would be an easy victim. German units had to escape the Falaise pocket by whatever means they had left to them. Most had to make their way back to friendly lines on foot, under the cover of darkness.

ARNHEM
Monty's Gamble

Field Marshal Bernard Montgomery had a plan to end the war by Christmas 1944. British armour was to drive into the heart of the Reich, spearheaded by an airborne army.

HITLER INSISTED that the German army cling to its positions in Normandy until it was too late for an orderly withdrawal. The result was catastrophe. Instead of the fighting retreat across France, envisaged by his generals, the German army collapsed in rout. US armoured columns fanned out in pursuit, Allied aircraft strafing and bombing every road east.

Between D-Day, 6 June and the end of August 1944 the German army lost 221,000 men killed, missing or captured in France. Another 67,000 were wounded. The *Westheer* began the campaign with 50 infantry divisions and 12 panzer divisions. By the time Field Marshal Model gathered up the wreckage, there were only 24 infantry divisions, all reduced to a fraction of their authorized strength. Eleven panzer divisions remained, but none was larger than a regimental Kampfgruppe and their average number of operational tanks was between five and ten.

The Germans were driven back to the borders of the Reich. The British army crossed into Belgium. Antwerp was liberated on 4 September. *Generaloberst* Kurt Student was ordered to establish a defensive line to hold the Low Countries, although his grandly titled 1st *Fallschirmjager* army consisted of rear echelon troops, returned wounded and

Left: On 17 September 1944, three airborne divisions under Lieutenant-General 'Boy' Browning were landed in Holland by 2,800 aircraft and 1,600 gliders.

Right: The British Airborne forces were landed right on top of the 9th and 10th SS Panzer divisions. The battle for Arnhem had been lost before it began.

Bottom: The lynchpin of Market Garden was the seizure of the road bridge at Arnhem, which General Browning famously dubbed "A bridge too far".

raw recruits. But the headlong Allied rush following the Normandy invasion was at its zenith. Tenacious resistance by German garrisons in French ports restricted the Allies supplies. The Allied armies were short of frontline infantry replacements. Men were exhausted, vehicles in desperate need of fuel and an overhaul. The helter-skelter advance slowed, then stopped.

VAULTING AMBITION

The British commander, Field Marshal Sir Bernard Montgomery, planned to break open the German defences in the north before they had the chance to solidify. He planned 'Operation Comet', an airborne assault by the British 1st Airborne brigade and the Polish Parachute Brigade. The idea was to land near the Dutch town of Arnhem, behind the German forces opposing his leading formation, XXX Corps. The attack was planned for 6-7 September, but cancelled when fierce German resistance slowed the advance of the British ground troops. However, after a meeting with the Allied Supreme Commander, General Dwight Eisenhower, the British plan was expanded into a far more ambitious plan.

'Operation Market Garden', as it became, called for the US 82nd and 101st Airborne divisions to drop too. They would seize the bridges from Eindhoven to Arnhem, ahead of an armoured drive by the British XXX corps. If the bridges fell intact into Allied hands, tanks could be through Holland and

Above: Following the capture of the complete Allied plans for the operation, German Flak and other ground units were ideally placed to intercept subsequent parachute drops.

Below: The remains of a British Horsa glider. Gliders offered the advantage of putting down a platoon of men in one spot. Paratroops could be more scattered and take longer to prove an effective force.

into Germany's industrial heartland before winter. Given the collapse of German forces on the eastern front, the operation held out the prospect of ending the war in 1944.

OVER BY CHRISTMAS

The German defence rested on a line of rivers running parallel to the front line. The first obstacles faced by the Allies were the Meuse-Escaut and Zuid-Willems canals. Some 25 km northeast lay the river Maas, with a bridge at Grave. A major bridge lay over the river Waal at Nijmegen, 15 km northeast of Grave. A further 15 km north of Nijmegen was the biggest obstacle of all: the lower Rhine. There was a modern road bridge at Arnhem plus a railway bridge and a ferry crossing just upstream.

Field Marshal Model anticipated an Allied airborne assault, but expected the blow to fall further to the east. Although he gave orders to prepare the target bridges for demolition, permission for their destruction was withheld. Whether under Hitler's direct instructions or not, Model seems to have intended some sort of operational level counter-stroke for which he would need the bridges intact. Some of his subordinate commanders criticized this after the war, arguing quite correctly, that if all these great bridges had been dynamited without delay, the 'Arnhem campaign' need never have happened.

POTENT OPPOSITION

Allied intelligence believed that the only opposition to their elite airborne forces would be German units of old men, teenage conscripts and Dutch SS men who could not wait to change sides. However, the Germans had received timely reinforcements. The veteran 9th and 10th SS panzer divisions had been sent to the area to refit and re-organize. For reasons still unclear today, British intelligence lost track of both divisions, and their presence so near to the airborne landing

zones upset the Allied plan from the very beginning.

On Sunday 17 September, an airborne armada droned over England, the noise bringing schoolchildren out of class to watch an apparently endless line of transports and gliders heading south. The formation was 16 km across and 150 km deep. Fewer than 50 Luftwaffe interceptors were available to attack, and they made no impression. Flak caught some as they neared the landing zones, but within 80 minutes there were 20,000 paratroopers on the ground. Model himself had to flee his headquarters as US paratroops formed up nearby. At the same time, the British XXX Corps attacked along the road to Eindhoven, the advance of the tanks preceded by a rolling artillery barrage that knocked out many of the anti-tank guns that lay in wait in nearby woods.

ARNHEM BRIDGEHEAD

The US 101st Airborne division captured the bridge over the canal at Veghel. The US 82nd Airborne took the bridge at Grave. But the bridge at Nijmegen was held by the SS and although 2 Para, commanded by 34-year-old Major John Frost, seized one end of the bridge at Arnhem, the battalion was isolated. The rest of the British 1st Airborne division was outside the city, blocked by German forces more numerous and better trained than they had been led to expect. It did not help that this, the division with the toughest mission, had to be landed in two waves as there were not enough aircraft to carry them in one lift.

Equally crucial was the German reaction. As a post-war British Army study commented, "2nd SS Corps reaction to the crisis reads like a staff command and control exercise". General Bittrich's II SS corps may have been in urgent need of rest and replenishment, but its veterans reacted with blistering speed.

By the afternoon of 18 September, tanks from the British Guards Armoured

HELL'S HIGHWAY

MONTGOMERY'S PLAN was simple: three-and-a-half airborne divisions would land along a 100 km corridor and the ground forces would charge along it to link up with them within three days. The road from Eindhoven to Arnhem was christened 'Hell's Highway' by the Americans, who had to hold it against repeated German counter-attacks. The problem was that the road, while a good one, was elevated on a bank for much of the way. The surrounding terrain was waterlogged and largely unsuitable for armoured vehicles.

Above: Horrocks's armour raced along the raised main road which linked up the target bridges. The high silhouette of the advancing vehicles presented an irresistible target for well-camouflaged German anti-tank crews.

Below: The massive creeping barrage that preceeded the Allied armour failed to take out every German defended position. The 30,000 vehicles of the XXX Corps took serious losses.

Above: The ground on both sides of the road was marshy and could not support tracked vehicles. The Germans were well aware of this: their 1940 invasion plans had taken the terrain into account and had been rerouted.

Below: Model refused to demolish the Nijmegen bridge, as he considered it vital for any German counter-attack. The SS defenders nevertheless prepared charges, which in the event failed to go off.

Bottom right: Two thousand three hundred trucks and 9,000 engineers accompanied XXX Corps, ready to build Bailey bridges for the armour just in case any of the crossings in their path had been blown by the Germans.

Above: Determined German resistance to Market Garden was conducted by (from left to right) Feldmarschal Model, General Student, SS-Obergruppenführer Willi Bittrich, Major Knaust and General Harmel.

Above: Ordered to hold Arnhem for up to four days, the British clung to their positions for nine. They hoped in vain for the breakthrough of General Horrocks's XXX Corps, lying just a few kms outside the town.

Below: As German pressure increased it became obvious that the British forces had to be evacuated. On 25 September General Horrocks ordered General Urquhart's men to fall back.

Division had linked up with the 101st at Eindhoven. By the 19th the ground troops were at Nijmegen: an advance of nearly 80 km in 48 hours. But the same day saw the British Airborne admit defeat: 4 Para brigade tried but failed to reach 2 Para. The British formed a defensive perimeter at Oosterbeek while 2 Para endured a series of increasingly heavy assaults that could only end one way unless help arrived soon. A 10th SS Panzer Division *Kampfgruppe* experienced the same thing at Nijmegen, clinging to the bridge in the teeth of intense artillery barrages and tanks firing across the river.

SUICIDE MISSION

Nijmegen was taken by a desperate gamble. The 3/504 Parachute Infantry paddled over the Waal in assault boats at 1530 on the 20th. They crossed downstream where the German defenders were thinly stretched, but within a few minutes alert German observers directed artillery and mortar fire on to the river. The bridge itself was taken by a suicidal British tank platoon: four Shermans charged it through a smokescreen thickened by nearby buildings burning down. German engineers were among the bridge girders, secured by harnesses, checking the demolition charges. The tanks shot them down with their machine guns as their drivers worked up to top speed. British artillery silenced the 88 mm guns guarding the bridge exit. When a frantic German officer pressed the plunger to detonate the charges, nothing happened. The road to Arnhem lay open.

DEATHRIDE

The SS had attempted to rush 2 Para on Arnhem bridge the previous day. Viktor Graebner, commander of 9th SS Panzer Division's reconnaissance battalion led the charge, straight over the bridge. It was the sort of bold manoeuvre that worked on the Russian front and for which Graebner had just received the *Ritterkreuz*. But the Paras greeted the armoured cavalcade with PIAT bombs and 6-pdr anti-tank guns. Graebner was killed and the wreckage of his battalion lay on the bridge for the rest of the battle. As one paratroop officer-turned historian wrote, "it was a typical armoured commander's approach to an infantry problem"

ABSOLUTE HELL.

The Germans had captured an intact set of operational orders from a crashed glider, so they had full details of where the 101st were deployed and what they were trying to achieve. German airborne commander Kurt Student wrote, "I knew more than anybody else that an airborne landing is at its weakest in the first few hours, and must be sorted out quickly and determinedly". However, Student began the fight with very few units he could rely on, whereas the Americans were veteran airborne troops, the best in the US Army.

2 Para's last stand ended in surrender on 21 September. Officers and men of 2 SS Panzer Corps were united in praise for Frost's men — and the rest of the division now pinned against the Rhine. As one German NCO remembered, "This was a harder battle than any I fought in Russia. It was constant close range hand-to-hand fighting. The English were everywhere…it was absolute Hell". Another commented, "The only way to get the British out of the houses was feet first". The Germans dubbed the Arnhem sector, the 'witches cauldron'. The paras refused to stay in their perimeter and launched frequent counter-attacks. The SS resorted to their usual tricks, on one occasion an ambulance drew up to rescue the wounded, but out came a section of stormtroops, sub-machine guns blazing. There were atrocities on both sides.

'Operation Market Garden' was defeated along 'Hell's Highway'. The British landed the Polish Parachute Brigade late on 21 September, dropping

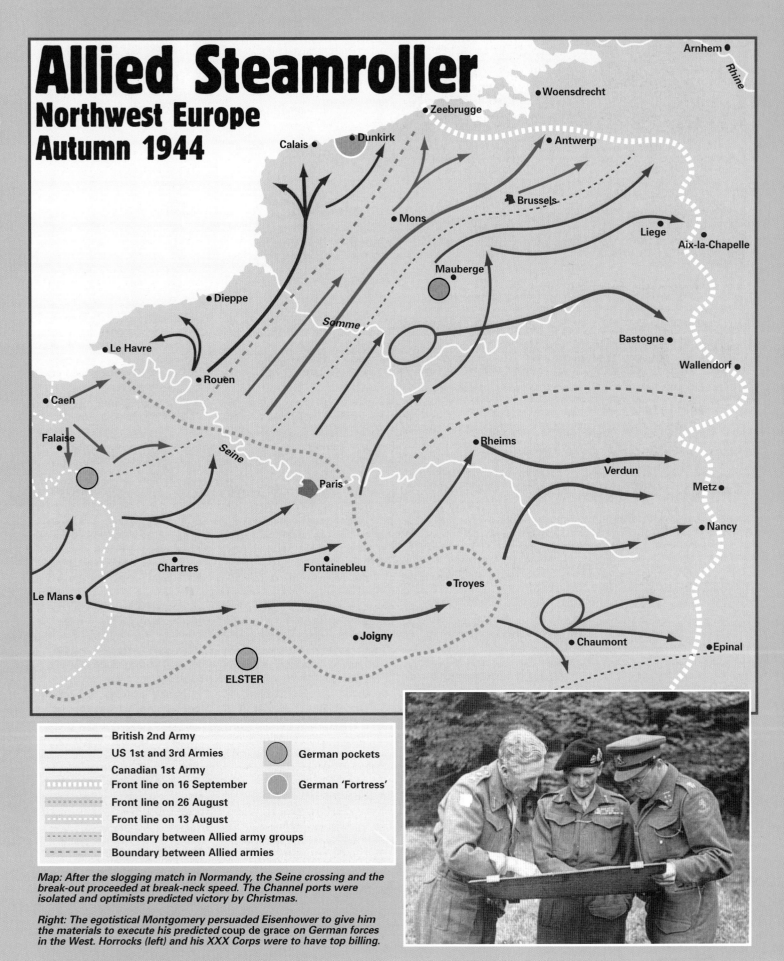

Allied Steamroller
Northwest Europe
Autumn 1944

Arnhem

Rhine

Woensdrecht

Zeebrugge

Calais

Dunkirk

Antwerp

Brussels

Mons

Liege

Aix-la-Chapelle

Mauberge

Dieppe

Somme

Le Havre

Bastogne

Rouen

Wallendorf

Caen

Falaise

Seine

Rheims

Verdun

Metz

Paris

Nancy

Chartres

Fontainebleu

Le Mans

Troyes

Joigny

Chaumont

Epinal

ELSTER

	British 2nd Army		
	US 1st and 3rd Armies		German pockets
	Canadian 1st Army		German 'Fortress'
	Front line on 16 September		
	Front line on 26 August		
	Front line on 13 August		
	Boundary between Allied army groups		
	Boundary between Allied armies		

Map: After the slogging match in Normandy, the Seine crossing and the break-out proceeded at break-neck speed. The Channel ports were isolated and optimists predicted victory by Christmas.

Right: The egotistical Montgomery persuaded Eisenhower to give him the materials to execute his predicted coup de grace on German forces in the West. Horrocks (left) and his XXX Corps were to have top billing.

Above: Initial resistance by the local Dutch SS battalions was light, but German opposition was soon stiffened by the experienced veterans of the 9th and 10th SS panzer divisions.

Right: The fatal delay. Between four and six hours elapsed before British troops could arrive at Arnhem bridge. Progress was slowed by enthusiastic Dutch civilians welcoming their liberators.

Below: 2 Para reached the bridge, but were then cut of from further support. A German assault on the bridge was beaten off, but the lightly armed British troops soon ran short of ammunition.

them south of the Rhine, the other side of the river from 1st Airborne division. But the Germans prevented them from breaking through to Arnhem. The next day at Veghel, two *Kampfgruppen* counter-attacked, with German *Fallschirmjager* and a panzer brigade spearheading the assaults. The advancing British XXX Corps was obliged to pull back one of its armoured brigades to keep the road open. On 24 September the road was cut south of Veghel by *Bataillon Jungwirth*. The German battle groups suffered grievous losses, but they slowed the northward progress of XXX corps while a new defensive line was established north of Nijmegen.

BRITISH EVACUATION

The ground between Nijmegen and Arnhem is a low-lying 'island' ringed by rivers and too swampy for armoured vehicles to manoeuvre off-road. The British pushed forward an infantry division, the 43rd Wessex, which managed to reach the beleaguered paratroops on 22 September. But it was a token effort, achieved with boats. Unless a bridge could be secured, the airborne division was doomed. On 25 September the survivors were withdrawn over the Rhine. It was a difficult and dangerous operation, attempting to pull out

from a small perimeter surrounded by a vigilant enemy determined to overrun the position before it could be reinforced. Just over 2,000 men got away. The Germans captured 6,000 men from 1st Airborne — more than half of them wounded.

A BRIDGE TOO FAR

Within 24 hours of the withdrawal and surrender of 1st Airborne division, Montgomery signalled London that the failure to secure a bridgehead over the Lower Rhine would not affect operations "eastwards against the Ruhr". This was nonsense. Between them, Model and Student had denied the

Allies a strategic victory that could have dramatically foreshortened the war.

The battle did not end with the loss of the Allied bridgehead. The forces north of Nijmegen were involved in heavy fighting into October and their records are incomplete. Total Allied casualties amounted to 13,000 men. Total German losses are estimated at 6-8,000.

Montgomery's gamble had failed. The blood of his elite troops had been spilt merely to gain a salient in the German line. From this point a new Allied offensive would be launched in time. But this would not come until 1945.

Market Garden

Map: Operation Market Garden perfectly illustrated both the strengths and weaknesses of airborne operations. Montgomery's failure ensured that Allied campaigning would be limited to the West of the Rhine until 1945.

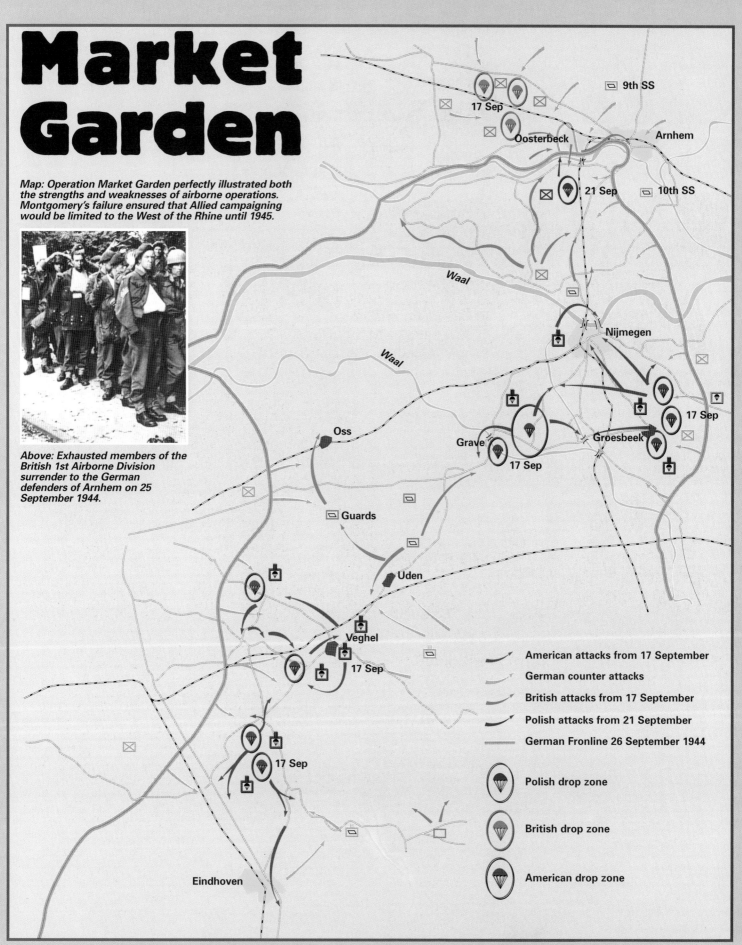

Above: Exhausted members of the British 1st Airborne Division surrender to the German defenders of Arnhem on 25 September 1944.

9th SS

17 Sep

Oosterbeck

Arnhem

21 Sep

10th SS

Waal

Nijmegen

Waal

17 Sep

Oss

Grave

Groesbeek

17 Sep

Guards

Uden

Veghel

17 Sep

17 Sep

American attacks from 17 September

German counter attacks

British attacks from 17 September

Polish attacks from 21 September

German Fronline 26 September 1944

Polish drop zone

British drop zone

American drop zone

Eindhoven

159

Ardennes Offensive
Going down fighting

In December 1944, in the deep snow of the Ardennes Hitler gambled everything on one final roll of the dice.

AT 5.30 AM on the misty morning of 16 December 1944, in the snow covered hills of the Belgian Ardennes, 200,000 men of German Army Group B launched an attack against the VIII Corps of the US 1st Army. The 113 km front stretched from Monschau in the north to Echternach in Luxembourg in the south. Although with the benefit of ULTRA the Allies were able to decode German radio traffic, the attack was unexpected, and caught both the British and American commanders by surprise.

Part of the reason for this was that the Germans were attacking out of home territory and were therefore using domestic or military telephone lines rather than radio. For added security they were sending messages by despatch rider. The other reason for the surprise was that to the Allies it seemed insane to commit carefully husbanded reserves on one all-out attack.

GHOST FRONT

From north to south the German armies committed to the offensive were the 6th *SS-Panzer Armee* under *Generaloberst der Waffen-SS* "Sepp" Dietrich, the 5th *Panzer Armee* under the energetic General Hasso-Eccard von Manteuffel and the 7th Army under General Erich Brandenburger. The force comprised twenty-five divisions of which eleven were armoured. The three armies were designated as Army Group 'B' under the overall command of the hard driving Field Marshal Walther Model.

In preparation for the offensive Hitler had moved his headquarters from the *Wolfsschanze* – the Wolf's Lair in East Prussia – and occupied the HQ at Ziegenberg. This headquarters bunker complex had been built in 1939 near Bad Nauheim, Hesse under the direction of Albert Speer. During the invasion of France in 1940 Hitler had deemed it too luxurious, but it now found a new use.

Bad weather had grounded the Allied air forces, and the German assault initially enjoyed considerable success against the six US divisions in the area. Three of these were new to Europe, and three were resting in what was regarded as a quiet area that had therefore been nicknamed the 'Ghost Front'. Under the shock of the attack, some 9,000 men from the 106th Division were captured on the Schnee Eifel on 19 December.

Above: German losses in the offensive amounted to 82,000 men killed, wounded and captured, together with 750 tanks and 600 aircraft. Although Allied losses were comparable, they had the resources to lose. The Germans did not, and had now exhausted their final reserves.

Left: In their last major offensive on the Western Front, the Germans used up the last few remaining first class troops that they still possessed.

Despite superior equipment, including over 100 Tiger II heavy tanks, and with a reputation as hard fighters, the men of the 6th *SS-Panzer Armee* made only halting progress. They hit the one concentrated American force in the Ardennes. The men of the 2nd Infantry Division had been conducting a local attack through the lines of the 99th Infantry Division. These two divisions held a feature known as the Elsenborn ridge for two days before they withdrew, having imposed a critical delay.

To the south of the ridge, a *Kampfgruppe* made up from units of the *Leibstandarte-SS Adolf Hitler* enjoyed the only real success, pushing as far as Stoumont on the Amblève river. It was men from this formation, commanded by 29-year-old *Standartenführer* Joachim 'Jochen' Peiper, who would be held responsible for the killing of 71 US PoWs at the town of Malmédy in Belgium on 17 December.

EARLY SUCCESS

Considerable gains were made following attacks by elements of the 5th *Panzerarmee*. This formation had only two Panzer divisions, and included a high proportion of lowly *Volksgrenadier* divisions. The timetable of the 5th *Panzer Armee* was delayed by the determined defence at St Vith where the 7th Armoured Division, a combat command of the 9th Armoured and a surviving regiment of the 106th Division formed a horseshoe-shaped defence around the town. The town should have fallen by the second day, according to German plans. General von Manteuffel finally seized it on December 21.

Above: Once again, the Germans underestimated the fighting abilities of American forces. Apart from the surrender on the Schnee Eifel, the GIs defended stubbornly against Hitler's massed panzer divisions.

Below: The penalty for failure: men of Obersturmbannführer Otto Skorzeny's special sabotage commando, captured behind the lines wearing American uniforms, are prepared for the firing squad.

Below: At 5:30 A.M. on 6 December 1944, eight German armoured divisions and 13 German infantry divisions lauched an all-out attack on five divisions of the United States 1st Army. At least 657 light, medium, and heavy guns and howitzers and 340 multiple-rocket launchers were used in the opening artillery barrage on unprepared American positions.

The thrust by the 2nd Panzer and *Panzer Lehr* Divisions took them a to point less than 10 kilometres from the Meuse at Dinant. Here, on 24 and 25 December they encountered the British 29th Armoured Brigade, part of the British XXX Corps that had been moved south to provide defence in depth.

To the south the 7th Army, with only the 5th *Fallschirmjäger* Division as elite troops, enjoyed limited success. By 24 December the paratroops had advanced over 50 kilometres and cut the road south from Bastogne to Arlon.

Wacht am Rhein was marked by some unusual improvisations. For lack of artillery the Fieseler FZG 76 *Kirschkern* – Cherry Stone, better known as the V1 flying bomb, was employed. However, though it had a 1 tonne HE warhead it was an inaccurate delivery system and was therefore employed against targets like the major logistics centre at Antwerp.

IN ENEMY UNIFORMS

A unique force, designated Panzer Brigade 156, was committed to *Unternehmen Greif* – Operation Griffin. They were tasked with the capture of bridges across the Meuse and with spreading confusion in the rear areas of the US Army. The unit was composed of about 2,000 English speaking German soldiers dressed in US uniforms, driving US vehicles. They were commanded by *Obersturmbann-führer* Otto Skorzeny. However only 150 could speak convincing "American", and they were organised into nine four man teams in Jeeps commanded by *Hauptsturmführer* Steilau. One group penetrated as far as the Meuse on 17 December but they were killed by an anti-tank mine. Eighteen of those who were caught were subsequently shot. Their presence behind American lines did however cause considerable confusion, and led to a rumour that they were an assassination squad that had targeted General Eisenhower.

On the night of 15 December, a reinforced battalion of 1,200 paratroops from FJR 6, commanded by the veteran *Oberst* Freiherr August von der Heydte, parachuted behind American lines near Malmédy. They were to block the movement of reinforcements south from the US V Corps.

PARA DISASTER

Dropped by inexperienced Ju 52 pilots, the battalion was badly scattered. Once on the ground von der Heydte had about 200 men, only a fraction of his force, under command. With no communications with the main German ground forces, the commander of what had become *Kampfgruppe von der Heydte* thought that the best move was to break through to German lines.

Most were captured, including von der Heydte, though about 100 did link up with the ground forces. They achieved nothing, but the very presence of paratroops and the deception plans initially convinced American intelligence officers that a large scale airborne operation had been launched. It was the last German airborne operation of the war.

German fuel reserves at the beginning of the campaign were critically low. Continued success of the operation was dependent upon the capture of enemy fuel dumps. Although it was a close-run thing, 6th *SS Panzer Armee* failed to capture the huge fuel depot at Stavelot, and two further stockpiles were denied the Germans by furious local defence.

AIR POWER

On 23 December the weather cleared and the Allied air forces came out in strength. Fighter bombers attacked German vehicles and artillery positions, while medium bombers hit the crowded road and rail network in Germany. The good visibility also allowed supplies to be air-dropped by C-47s to the 101st Airborne Division in Bastogne.

By Christmas Eve, the OKW realised that *Wacht am Rhein* had

Wacht am Rhein

The plan

IN DECEMBER 1944 the Germans had been pushed back to the borders of the Reich, but Hitler had no intention of going over to the defensive. With new powers, following the failure of the July Plot, *Reichsministers* Goebbels and Speer had increased production of weapons and equipment, as well as finding men to make up new formations for the Waffen-SS and new – and largely ineffective – *Volksgrenadier* divisions for the army.

With these men and weapons, Hitler proposed that an operation code named *Wacht am Rhein* – Watch on the Rhine – be launched through the Ardennes, across Belgium to the port of Antwerp. This would cut off the Allied forces in north west Europe.

It was a fantastic plan, which showed little grasp of reality. "If we succeed" enthused Hitler "we will have knocked out half the enemy front. Then let's see what happens!" The more clear-headed planning staff at OKW had looked at a 'small solution', a pincer attack that would cut off US forces, but Hitler wanted a re-run of May 1940.

Below: Hitler's plan appalled his generals. To ensure obedience, the attack was led by the 6th SS Panzer Army; the first time so large a unit was designated SS.

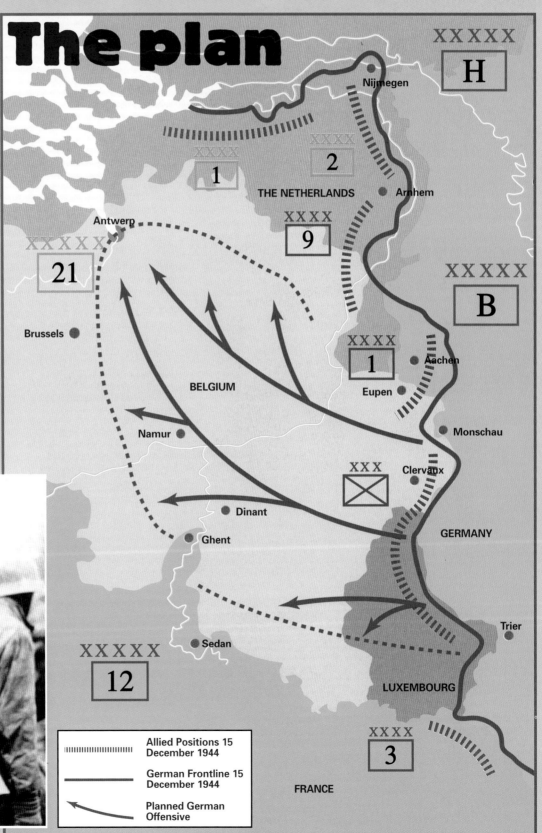

Allied Positions 15 December 1944

German Frontline 15 December 1944

Planned German Offensive

"NUTS"

IN THE RUGGED Ardennes, the road junctions at Bastogne made that town a critical objective. By 20 December it had been surrounded and came under heavy artillery armoured and infantry attacks. A battle of epic proportions soon developed. Eisenhower refused to be panicked by the German assault. In a meeting with Bradley, Patton and Devers he stated: "the present situation is to be regarded as one of opportunity for us and not disaster". He ordered up the veteran 'Screaming Eagles' of the 101st Airborne Division to assist in the defence of Bastogne. It reached the town by road just seven hours ahead of the Germans after a 200 km overnight drive from Rheims. Some German units bypassed the objective, but in the hard going across country the tanks soon ran out of fuel. The siege of the town was finally broken when tanks of the 4th Armored Division from General George S. Patton's 3rd Army broke through from the south on 26 December. They linked up with the 'Battered Bastards of Bastogne' as the 101st had prosaically dubbed themselves.

Right: On 22 December German officers under the flag of truce delivered a message from General der Panzertruppe von Luttwitz, demanding the surrender of Bastogne. After receiving the message Brigadier General Mcauliffe, commander of the 101st exclaimed "Aw, nuts" – which was his official reply to the request for surrender.

Above: Because the Americans were surrounded they could only be re-supplied by air drop. However, the weather conditions were the worst in living memory and Allied planes were grounded.

Above: In Bastogne's neighbouring villages and in the surrounding woods hand-to-hand fighting of enormous savagery took place.

Left: Bastogne was a strategic position which both the Germans and Americans wanted to occupy. This lead to a race between the American 101st Airborne division and the Germans. The Americans managed to get there first and occupied the town. The Germans were not far behind and quickly surrounded and besieged the American defenders.

run its course. It would not be until 8 January that Hitler finally authorised a withdrawal. The 2nd Panzer Division and *Panzer Lehr* had been halted, and by 4 January the US 1st and 3rd Armies were beginning to counter attack along the salient that had become known as 'The Bulge' by Allied commanders and their staffs.

In just twelve days the Germans had been pushed back to their start lines on the border.

LUFTWAFFE'S LAST GASP

It was typical of German planning in 1944/45 that *Unternehmen Bodenplatte,* which was meant to support *Wacht am Rhein*, took place on 1 January 1945, too late

to affect the outcome. 'Operation Baseplate' was another last-gasp attack, this time by the Luftwaffe. Eight hundred fighters struck at Allied airfields in Belgium and Holland. Like *Wacht am Rhein,* it was a final spectacular gesture that cost the Allies about 500 aircraft, including General Montgomery's personal C47.

However, Allied strength was such that losses could be replaced in a fortnight. Few Allied aircrew were lost, while the Luftwaffe lost 170 pilots killed and 67 taken prisoner.

The *Wacht am Rhein* delayed the end of the war by about six weeks and destroyed the bulk of the German armoured reserve.

Malmedy Imfamy

ON THE SECOND day of the offensive, a truck convoy of the American 285th Field Artillery Observation Battalion was intercepted southeast of Malmedy by a regiment of the 1st SS Panzer Division of the Leibstandarte-SS, under the command of 29-year-old SS Lt. Col. Jochen Peiper. His troops had earned the nickname 'Blowtorch Battalion' after burning their way across Russia, and had also been responsible for slaughtering civilians in two separate villages.

Upon sighting the trucks, the Panzer tanks opened fire and destroyed the lead vehicles. This brought the convoy to a halt while the deadly accurate tank fire continued. The outgunned Americans abandoned their vehicles and surrendered.

The captors then opened fire on the prisoners. Survivors were killed by a pistol shot to the head, in some cases by English speaking SS who walked among the victims asking if anyone was injured or needed help. Those who responded were shot. A otal of 81 Americans were killed in the single worst atrocity against U.S. troops during World War II in Europe.

Top: Following the defeat of Nazi Germany, 74 former SS men, including Jochen Peiper and SS Gen. Sepp Dietrich, were tried by a U.S. Military Tribunal for War Crimes concerning the massacre. 43 were initially sentenced to hang.

Above: A unit from Kampfgruppe Peiper in a posed photo . The atrocity at Malmedy was counter-productive. Two survivors escaped and reached the Allied lines, where their story roused intense fury. News of the massacre strengthened the resistance of even the greenest units.

Left: The captured U.S. soldiers were herded into a field. An SS tank commander then ordered an SS private to shoot into the prisoners, setting off a wild killing spree as the SS opened fire with machine guns and pistols on the unarmed, terrified POWs.

Battle of the Bulge

The commanders in charge of the offensive were Field Marshal Gerd von Runstedt, Commander in the West, Field Marshal Walther Model who was in tactical command, with panzer armies led by Josef 'Sepp' Dietrich and Hasso von Manteuffel. All were skeptical about Hitler's plan. They felt that taking Antwerp was something that just could not be accomplished by the German army at the time. Model was quoted as saying: "This plan hasn't got a damned leg to stand on". Hitler was presented with a new, smaller plan which changed the objective to only launching a small attack to weaken the Allied forces in the area, rather than launching an all out attack to retake Antwerp. The generals pleaded with Hitler to change the plans, but he refused.

The resulting land battle was one of the largest of World War II. There were more than a million participants, including some 600,000 Germans, 500,000 Americans, and 55,000 British. The German military force consisted of two Armies with ten corps (equal to 29 divisions), while the main American opposition included a total of three armies with six corps(equal to 31 divisions).

Above: The turning of the tide. A Tiger II heavy tank, abandoned by its crew after it ran out of fuel, is examined by an American unit. German failure to secure Allied supply depots doomed the offensive.

Below: Even though the German Offensive achieved total surprise, nowhere did the American troops give ground without a fight. Within three days, a determined American stand at St Vith and the arrival of powerful reinforcements ensured the ultimate failure of German ambitions, and signalled the end of Hitler's last great gamble.

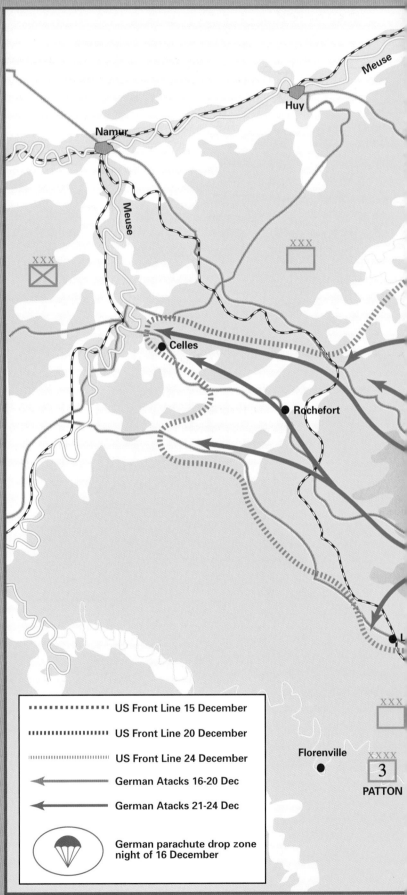

.... US Front Line 15 December

▪▪▪▪▪▪▪▪▪▪▪▪▪▪▪ US Front Line 20 December

▬▬▬▬▬▬▬▬▬▬ US Front Line 24 December

⟵ German Atacks 16-20 Dec

⟵ German Atacks 21-24 Dec

🪂 German parachute drop zone
night of 16 December

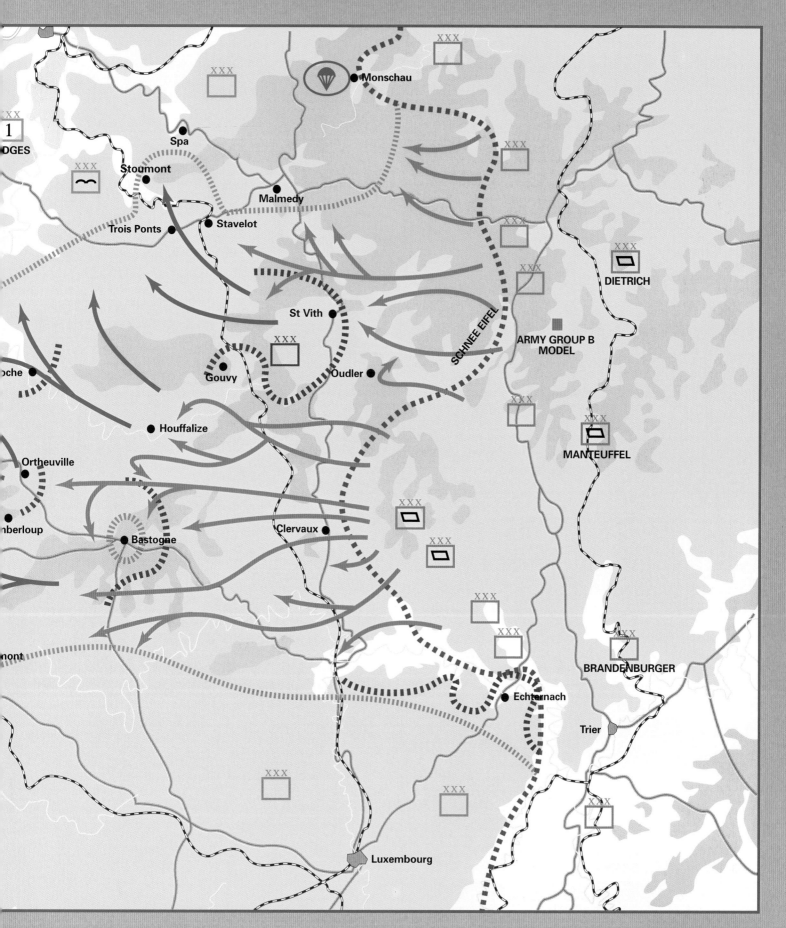

DGES

Spa

Stoumont

Trois Ponts

Stavelot

Malmedy

Monschau

St Vith

Gouvy

Oudler

SCHNEE EIFEL

DIETRICH

ARMY GROUP B
MODEL

oche

Houffalize

MANTEUFFEL

Ortheuville

nberloup

Bastogne

Clervaux

nont

BRANDENBURGER

Echternach

Trier

Luxembourg

Race for the Reich

American troops from Patton's Third US Army drive out of France and Belgium, heading for the crossings of the Moselle and towards the Rhine. Allied armies advanced along a broad front towards western Germany's main river artery, and in spite of some hard fighting were poised to cross by March 1945.

The failure of the Ardennes Offensive squandered the Wehrmacht's last major reserves in the West – reserves which would desperately be needed as Allied armies drove into the German heartland.

Above: Although the Wehrmacht had been decisively defeated in the Battle of the Bulge, there were still plenty of experienced, well-trained German soldiers available to slow down Allied advances.

B Y JANUARY 1945, the defence of Nazi Germany was in the hands of the fanatical, the very young, or the very old. In the east, they fought to prevent Soviet forces wreaking revenge for the death and suffering that had been cause to the Ukraine and Belarussia by German occupation. In the west they hoped that the longer they could delay the Allies, the greater was the chance that there would be a split between them and the Soviet Union. This was a delusion sustained by Nazi propaganda.

Waffen-SS troops and *Fallschirmjäger* often found themselves fighting alongside the *Volkssturm* - the Peoples' Storm, the German civilian home defence force. Many of the SS men were foreign volunteers who knew they were unlikely to receive a welcome at home after the war.

The *Volkssturm* had been established in September 1944 and was composed of civilian males aged between 16 and 60 who were capable of bearing arms. It was trained and organised on military lines, but a shortage of weapons restricted both training and operational deployment. In January 1945

Hitler ordered that the *Volkssturm* should be amalgamated with *das Heer* – the Regular Army – which accounted for the number of schoolboys in baggy ill fitting uniforms and older men taken prisoner by the Allies at the end of the war.

The less well equipped and trained soldiers were sometimes placed in forward positions to take the initial impact of an attack. This would allow the veterans time to react and counter-attack to stabilise the front. Incredibly, right up to the last weeks of the war in Europe, the Germans were capable of assembling ad hoc *Kampfgruppen* - battle groups – that could launch local counter attacks capable of stalling the Allied advance.

BULGE ELIMINATED

As 1945 dawned, the Allies had almost flattened out the Ardennes Salient. By now, the front line ran from the Scheldte Estuary past Nijmegen on the Waal, across a narrow land bridge to the Maas. It followed the river south as far as Roermond, then followed the Roer itself as far as the dams. These were key objectives in any Allied offensive: still in German hands the dams could turn the

Above: British infantrymen in winter gear patrol eastwards from Belgium into Holland. The end of 1944 saw most of the German gains in the Ardennes retaken, and Allied armies were now aimed at the Rhine.

Below: Further south, American armies were already in Germany: the US 1st Army had crossed the border north of Trier in September, Aachen had been taken in November, and now they were on the Upper Rhine.

Above: Hitler ordered the formation of the Volkssturm *in September 1944. By the turn of the year this rag-bag collection of the very young and very old were in the field against the Allies both east and west.*

Below: The British XXX Corps fought through the flooded Reichswald in February 1944. It was a tough campaign, but it drew what German strength there was away from the American attack to the south.

Below: Astonishingly, the Germans failed to blow the Ludendorff Bridge across the Rhine at Remagen. Captured by units of the US 1st Army on 7 March, it enabled the Allies to establish a firm bridgehead on the east bank two weeks ahead of schedule.

Roer from a narrow river to a raging flood. From the Roer the line followed the old Westwall fortifications down to the Black Forest.

The task for the Canadian and British armies to the north, the four US armies stretching down to Strasbourg, and the French army in the Vosges, was to cross the Roer and reach the Rhine. In addition to the resistance they could expect from the German army, always difficult to winkle out of defensive positions, the Allies faced problems with the weather. Repeated frosts and thaws turned the ground to glutinous mud or uncertain slush. Until March, soldiers all along the front lived in miserable conditions.

The race for the Rhine began on 15 January 1945. The British XII Corps – one armoured and two infantry divisions assisted by specialised armour and massed artillery – attacked along the whole of their front into what was called the Roermond Triangle. Two German divisions waited for them behind concrete, wire and mines.

MINES IN THE MUD

The battle was never going to be anything but a dreadful slogging-match. Mines lay buried everywhere, heavy ground hampered the mine-clearing Flail tanks, vast flooded craters needed bridging, and the all-important engineer vehicles floundered in mud. Strongpoints required the attention of the Crocodile flame-throwing tanks, but wooded ravines hid German anti-tank guns which all-too often turned the incendiary vehicles into flaming coffins.

But superior Allied resources eventually told, though at terrible cost. It took until 25 January for the Germans to succumb to the war of attrition.

The US First Army moved to seize the Roer dams, There were seven of them, holding back more than one hundred million cubic metres of water. The levels were particularly high as a result of the thaw, and when on

10 February the Americans took the last one they found that the Germans had efficiently sabotaged the overflow valves. This meant that any crossing of the river would have to wait until the water had all drained down into the North Sea.

ON TO THE RHINE

The main Allied offensive was ready to go in the first week of February. On 8 February RAF Lancasters bombed Cleve and Goch, as a preparation for the Battle of the Reichswald. An artillery bombardment then blanketed the approach area as the four infantry divisions of XXX Corps rolled forward.

It was one of the bitterest and most depressing battles fought on the Western Front. Canadians had to use amphibious DUKWs just to move from village to village. The most appalling traffic congestion wrecked every plan 10 minutes after it was launched. Broken roads and sodden tracks saw massive armoured columns jammed solid within the ranks of plodding, miserable infantry.

Once again, the Allies bulled through. By 21 February, Goch, Cleve and Calcar were in British and Canadian hands, and to the south the US Ninth Army was now free to launch Operation Grenade. This started by flinging bridges across the Roer opposite Mönchen Gladbach, which the Americans took on 1 March. Five days later Cologne was in American hands, and on 7 March, to the astonishment of the Allies and to Hitler's fury, the Remagen Bridge over the Rhine had been taken, apparently undamaged, and was in use by US First Army.

BRIDGEHEAD

One bridge was not enough, however, so auxiliary bridges were thrown across, both up- and down-stream from Remagen. This was fortunate, since on 17 March the Remagen Bridge collapsed. It had been weakened by bombing, by the attempted German demolitions,

Approach to the Rhine

THE APPROACH of the Western Allies to the Rhine was carried out on a broad front. The British and Canadians attacked in the north after completing the liberation of Belgium. The Americans provided the muscle in the centre and the south, while the revitalised French army attacked across the border in the extreme south.

Even though the Allies were far better equipped and supplied than the Germans, the defenders resisted fiercely in many places. It was an often grim and desperate business, for Hitler had decreed that the age-old barrier protecting the Teutons from the Latins was to be defended to the last. Army units, SS men, elderly *Volkssturm* volunteers and Hitler Youth fanatics heeded his word.

Hitler ordered that any German soldier retreating across the Rhine in the face of the enemy would be subject to immediate death by firing squad – and large numbers were shot by roving bands of SD and Gestapo men.

Though encouraging to the most fanatical, this kind of ultimatum did not appeal to many ordinary troops. As a result, by 24 March over 150,000 German soldiers had surrendered and were in Allied PoW camps.

Below: Canadians from Montgomery's 21st Army Group take on a nazi strong-point during the battle for the Reichswald in February 1945.

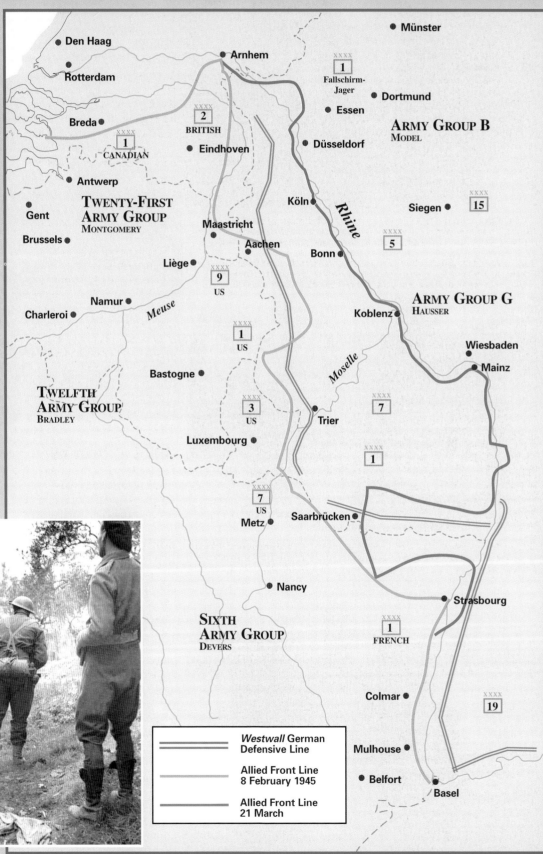

Map labels:

Den Haag
Rotterdam
Breda
Antwerp
Gent
Brussels
Liège
Namur
Charleroi
Arnhem
Eindhoven
Maastricht
Aachen
Bastogne
Luxembourg
Metz
Nancy
Münster
Dortmund
Essen
Düsseldorf
Köln
Bonn
Siegen
Koblenz
Wiesbaden
Mainz
Trier
Saarbrücken
Strasbourg
Colmar
Mulhouse
Belfort
Basel

Rhine
Meuse
Moselle

1 Fallschirm-Jager
2 BRITISH
1 CANADIAN
9 US
1 US
3 US
7 US
15
5
7
1
1 FRENCH
19

ARMY GROUP B
MODEL

ARMY GROUP G
HAUSSER

TWENTY-FIRST ARMY GROUP
MONTGOMERY

TWELFTH ARMY GROUP
BRADLEY

SIXTH ARMY GROUP
DEVERS

Legend:
Westwall German Defensive Line
Allied Front Line 8 February 1945
Allied Front Line 21 March

Above: The defenders of the Reich's borders could still call on one of the most powerful tanks in the world. Unfortunately, fewer than 500 King Tigers were built – compared to 2,250 Stalin tanks, and 40,000 T-34s!

Below: Stalin called artillery the "Red God of War", and the Soviets were the world's most enthusiastic user of guns and howitzers. No Red Army offensive was complete without a massive opening barrage.

Above: Designed as a 'Cavalry Breakthough' machine, the T-34 was one of history's few genuine war-winning weapons. Advanced in design, if crude in manufacture, the T-34 was the workhorse of Red tank armies.

by the drumming of thousands of infantry feet and by the heavy lurches of overladen vehicles. Though the whole bridge fell sideways into the Rhine, taking 28 US engineers to their deaths, at least the disaster did not cut off the bridgehead on the east bank from all supplies.

By that time the US and French armies to the south had all crossed their own river barriers, breaking through or outflanking the Siegfried Line. Now they were fighting their way to the Rhine.

EAST AND WEST

By the end of the month the west bank of the Rhine from the Channel to the Swiss border was in Allied hands. The British and Americans were now only 300 miles from Berlin.

The Soviets were even closer. Stalin's armies were only 50 miles from the German capital.

At the turn of the year only a few pockets of German resistance remained on Soviet territory. The front line ran from Memel on the Baltic Sea, around the eastern quarter of the East Prussia border, down and across the Narew towards Warsaw to reach the Vistula just south of the Polish capital. From there it continued down the line of the river as far as Sandomir, where it bulged westwards in a significant bridgehead, across eastern Czechoslovakia to the Danube. There was another salient above Budapest, from where the battle area continued along Lake Balaton and the river Drava into the area controlled by Marshal Tito and his Partisans.

There were a lot of Soviet soldiers in that line. Eleven guards armies, five shock armies, six tank armies, and 46 infantry or cavalry armies, all fully equipped and supported by

13 air armies, gave the Red Army commanders absolute superiority over the 200 German and Hungarian divisions facing them. The only palpable advantage the Wehrmacht commanders might have had was the fear and hatred of the 'Mongol Hordes' so firmly implanted in the hearts of every Axis soldier.

The three Fronts at the northern end of the Red Army line – 1st Baltic under Bagramyan, 3rd Belorussian under Chernyakhovsky and 2nd Belorussian under Rokossovsky – were to concern themselves with Baltic matters.

GERMAN RESISTANCE

As was fully expected, the onslaught which began on 13 January was fiercely resisted, and within hours it was clear to Chernyakhovsky that his road to Königsberg would be won only

by hard fighting. German engineers had built defence lines every few miles, and after six days his five armies had only driven 15 of them. Even with an extra Guards army fed through, it was not until 20 January that Insterburg – a third of the way to the objective – was reached.

Rokossovsky, who had attacked across the Narew on the same day, sent two armies through the Masurian Lakes with orders to link up with Chernyakhovsky at Königsberg. Five more armies on the left were pushed in the direction of Danzig and Bromberg.

They all experienced two to three days of bitter fighting, but once the hard shell of the defences was broken, tank armies were fed in and raced ahead. By 19 January they had reached Mlawa, then broke through east of Tannenberg. A week later they had reached the

Battle for Budapest

O KH PLANNED TO defend the line of the Oder river against the coming Soviet onslaught, but Hitler disagreed with Heinz Guderian, the Chief of Staff. The Führer decided that preserving Germany's last surviving oil fields in Hungary was more important than blocking the Red Army's route to Berlin. Accordingly, he ordered Sepp Dietrich's 6th Panzer Army to relieve Budapest, which had been under siege since the end of 1944.

The Soviets had captured the city by 12 February, so the position was already hopeless by the time the SS Army launched its attack. Dietrich seems to have assumed that he could retake the city in a week or so, and then his troops would be moved north to bolster the Oder defences. It was an impossible task, and Dietrich's men failed.

Hitler was enraged: rather than calling the 6th SS Panzer Army back to defend Berlin, he rebuked these, the most loyal of all of his followers. In any case, it was a panzer army in name only: by the time the Soviets captured the Hungarian oilfields on 2 April, the formation had the grand total of six operational tanks. Dietrich eventually ordered his men to head west to surrender to the Americans.

Above and right: 'Sepp' Dietrich had little strategic skill, but he was a hard fighter, who looked after and brought the best out in his men. However, by the time his Panzer Army with its small force of King Tigers was deployed to relieve Budapest, there was nothing he could do to overcome the massive Soviet advantage in manpower and momentum.

Below: Budapest had been surrounded at the end of 1944. The only hope for its defenders was that the SS-led relief column could get through – a hope which was never to be fulfilled.

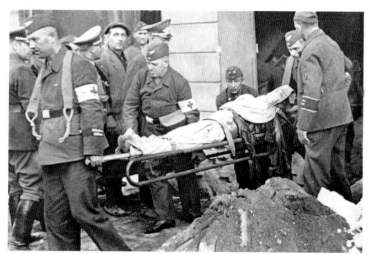

Above: Every member of the various Nazi uniformed organisations was conscripted into the final struggle, in either a fighting, combat support or non-combat civil defence role.

Above: Germany's last defenders were a mixed bag. Some were poorly trained volunteers or conscripts, while others, like these SS men, had been hardened by over three years of constant combat in the East.

Below: No matter how motivated the Germans were, it was not enough to overcome the sheer power of the Red Army. By now it was the most powerful military organisation the world had ever seen.

Baltic at Elbing, cutting off the huge German garrison at Königsberg, which was isolated.

But it was further south that the greatest advances were made. Marshal Zhukov's 1st Belorussian Front attacked Army Group A along the direct Warsaw – Berlin Axis. After a hurricane bombardment from 16,000 guns – packed 400 per mile, and backed up by rocket batteries – the Front was 10 miles into the German defences in the first 24 hours.

ZHUKOV'S OFFENSIVE

To the south Zhukov's infantry had ripped open so wide a gap that he fed in two tank armies, and by evening of 15 January they were marauding nearly 30 miles ahead. Meanwhile, two of his armies had met west of Warsaw, and on the evening of 17 January the First Polish Army (serving with the Red Army since before Stalingrad) entered the ruined capital to succour the unfortunate survivors of the ill-fated revolt of the previous year.

By this time, the breach torn in the German defences by Zhukov's armies was 180 miles wide. There was nothing to stop the tank armies racing ahead the rest of the way across Poland and into Germany itself. They brushed aside several German formations hastily thrown in their way, and on the last day of the month they reached the River Oder just north of Kustrin, where they crossed to form a bridgehead on the western bank.

By the end of the first week in February, the east bank of the Oder from Zehden down to Fürstenberg was in Zhukov's hands. The thunder of his guns could be heard in Berlin's Unter dem Linden. But Marshal Ivan S. Konev's 1st Ukrainian Front had done at least as well.

KONEV'S ATTACK

This was the biggest front of all, with two tank armies numbered among Konev's total force of 14 armies. The bulk of them broke out of the Sandomir bridgehead on 12 January under yet another massive artillery bombardment. This so stunned the unsuspecting defenders of the important town of Kielce that most of them were still deafened and half blind when Russian infantry occupied the town two days later.

RED ARMY RAMPAGE

Then the armies fanned out, one driving down the west bank of the Vistula towards Krakow, with another driving for Czestochowa. Within a week the 1st Ukrainian Front was advancing on a 170 mile-wide sweep. At one point Russian tanks had penetrated nearly 100 miles, smashing two German armies on the way.

Konev's forces raced up past Beuthen and Oppeln towards Breslau, and then along the line of the Oder until it closed up to the demarcation line with Zhukov's 1st Belorussian Front. By the end of January the river was in Red Army hands from where its headwaters left the Carpathians up to just north west of Berlin.

Further south, in Hungary, fierce battles were fought by 2nd and 3rd Ukrainian Fronts when German and Hungarian armies tried hard to relieve the forces trapped in Budapest. During March the Sixth SS Panzer Army put in an attack around Lake Balaton.

SS DEFEAT IN HUNGARY

In many ways this resembled the fury and last-minute desperation of the battle in the Ardennes, but it suffered the same fate, beaten back in the end by greater numbers supplied by greater sources of weapons, ammunition and manpower. By 19 March, the SS were fleeing back over the Austrian border towards Vienna, and by that time, too, the armies of the Belarussian Fronts had fought their way across the Oder and closed up to the line of the River Neisse.

It was time to take stock of the whole situation, and prepare for the last battle – for Berlin.

Collapse in the East

THE FINAL Soviet Winter Offensive of the war opened in January 1945. While General Konstantin Rokossovsky's Second Belorussian Front smashed into East Prussia and drove for the Baltic, the main punch was provided by Marshal Georgi Zhukov's First Belorussian Front and by Marshal Ivan Konev's First Ukrainian Front. Between them, the two rival marshals had two and a quarter million men in 163 divisions under command. They had 6,460 tanks, assault guns and self-propelled guns, together with more than 32,000 artillery pieces. They were supported by 4,772 aircraft. To the north, First and Second Belarussian Fronts under Rokossovsky and General Chernyakhov had a further 1,600,000 men.

OUTNUMBERED AND OUTGUNNED

Outnumbered five-to-one, his tanks almost immobile due to lack of fuel, and with less than 300 front-line aircraft available, Army Chief-of-Staff Heinz Guderian warned Hitler that the entire Eastern Front was a "House of cards". However, the Führer refused to believe his military advisers. "Russian Tank Armies," he said, "have no tanks".

Guderian begged for Army Group Courland, isolated north of Königsberg, to be brought back to defend the Oder. Hitler refused until it was too late to make a difference. Civilian evacuation began in the middle of January, and between January and May some two million people had been rescued from Courland, Pomerania and East Prussia.

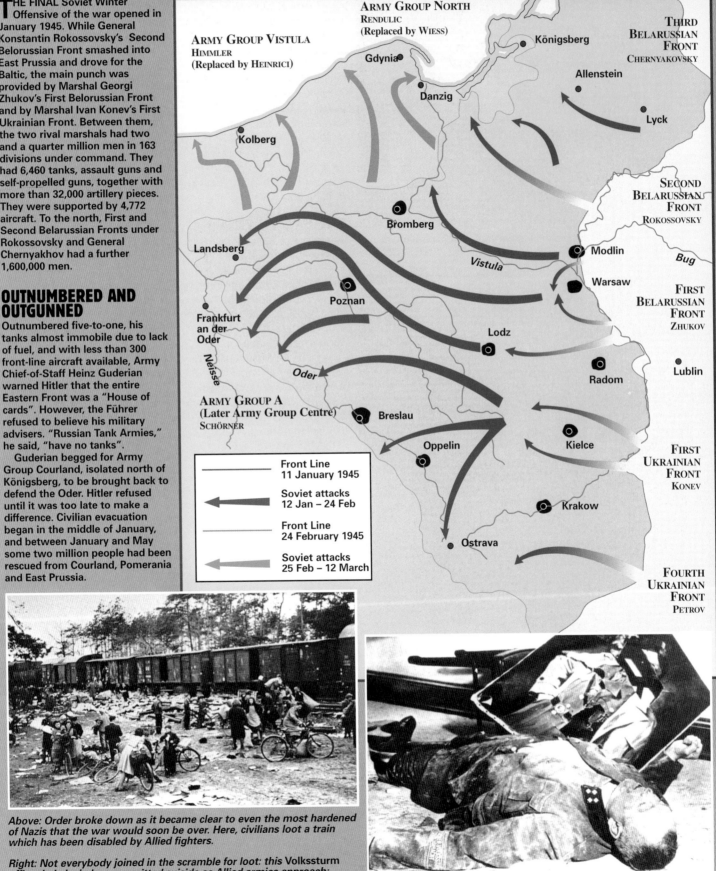

ARMY GROUP VISTULA
HIMMLER
(Replaced by HEINRICI)

ARMY GROUP NORTH
RENDULIC
(Replaced by WIESS)

THIRD BELARUSSIAN FRONT
CHERNYAKOVSKY

SECOND BELARUSSIAN FRONT
ROKOSSOVSKY

FIRST BELARUSSIAN FRONT
ZHUKOV

ARMY GROUP A
(Later Army Group Centre)
SCHÖRNER

FIRST UKRAINIAN FRONT
KONEV

FOURTH UKRAINIAN FRONT
PETROV

Königsberg · Allenstein · Lyck · Gdynia · Danzig · Kolberg · Landsberg · Bromberg · Modlin · Warsaw · Poznan · Frankfurt an der Oder · Lodz · Radom · Lublin · Breslau · Kielce · Oppelin · Krakow · Ostrava

Vistula · *Bug* · *Neisse* · *Oder*

—	Front Line 11 January 1945
←	Soviet attacks 12 Jan – 24 Feb
—	Front Line 24 February 1945
←	Soviet attacks 25 Feb – 12 March

Above: Order broke down as it became clear to even the most hardened of Nazis that the war would soon be over. Here, civilians loot a train which has been disabled by Allied fighters.

Right: Not everybody joined in the scramble for loot: this Volkssturm officer in Leipzig has committed suicide as Allied armies approach; Americans from the west and Soviets from the east.

175

Across the Rhine and the Oder

Closing the Jaws on the Reich

Large rivers are major barriers to fast-moving mechanised armies. In 1945, the German heartland was protected by two; the Rhine and the Oder.

PLANNING FOR the Rhine crossings had started even before the previous year had ended. By the time the Allies had occupied the entire west bank of the river, most preparations were completed. It was not simply a matter of piling up men and supplies for the crossing, as a great deal of preparatory training was necessary.

One of the largest programmes concerned the conversion of several tank regiments to the use of LVTs (Landing Vehicles, Tracked), or Buffaloes as they were known to the British. These were to be used to carry the first waves of men across and they were to be followed up by a second wave travelling in assault boats.

The crossings would also require a considerable engineer involvement, especially in the huge operation to be mounted by Montgomery's 21st Army Group. The bridging equipment necessary to cross the Rhine had to be assembled, and the approach roads and other transport facilities had to be made ready. In the end this was managed only by the allocation of several US Army engineer regiments to help out. Ultimately, engineer units used up over a quarter of all supplies and equipment involved in the Rhine crossings.

To add to the planners' problems, the Rhine had its own say in the matter. The area where the crossings were to be made is flat and prone to flooding. There had been a lot of rain and snow the previous winter. By March, the flood plains were still very wet. This might have been ideal terrain for the Buffaloes, but it was not so easy for the other vehicles. Nevertheless, it was a risk that had to be accepted.

On the night of 23 March 1945 the crossings began, under a massive artillery barrage. The first troops went across in Buffaloes, assisted by amphibious DD Shermans and

Above: Tank transporters move Buffaloes – the British name for American-built LVT amphibious assault vehicles – towards the Rhine. Designed for beach landing, the vehicles were ideal for river crossings.

Left: British and American expertise in amphibious operations was used to the full on the Rhine. Here, members of Patton's Third Army are ferried eastwards in landing craft developed for the Normandy invasion.

Right: Airborne forces were the spearhead of the massive operation by Montgomery's 21st Army Group. An entire airborne army attacked German positions at the same time as the main amphibious assault.

other special vehicles. Air support was so intense that Wesel itself was confidently bombed by RAF Bomber Command when Allied troops were only a few hundred yards away. This not only cleared Wesel of the enemy but prevented the Germans from moving through the town to mount a counterattack.

The Allies did not have it all their own way, though opposition to the landings was patchy. In some areas the defenders fought fiercely, while in others the preliminary bombardment had been so effective that organised defence was slight. However, the mud was so bad in places that not even the Buffaloes could make much forward progress, with the result that some of the second assault waves, crossing in boats, came under intense fire and took heavy casualties.

The sheer weight of the onslaught was such that in most locations the Allies were soon able to wade ashore and establish sizeable bridgeheads. However, the main strength of the attack was yet to come – from the air.

This arrived at about midday when the first of the Allied airborne forces came into sight. What became known as the 'armada of the air' flew over the Rhine to disgorge two divisions of parachute troops, who seemed at times to make the sky dark with their numbers. They were soon followed by glider tugs. These unleashed their charges to land in two main zones; in the Diersfordter Wald and at Mehr-Hamminkeln.

HIGH COST OF SUCCESS

The gliders did not all land unscathed. Despite all efforts of Allied air forces to neutralise flak near the landing zones, some guns survived. Their fire power meant that about one quarter of all glider pilots involved became casualties in this operation.

Even so, most landed safely, ensuring that the airborne forces and the troops that had made the river crossings were able to join up, often well in advance of the anticipated times. By nightfall the Rhine bridgeheads were secure. Despite some local counterattacks, the British were across the river to stay.

The major Allied effort was made in the British sector, since it had always been realised that the crossing of the Rhine here would be most strongly resisted. In part, this was because of the close proximity of Germany's vital Ruhr industries, but it was also because the German high command knew full well that the gap between the Ruhr and the Dutch border led directly to the north German plain – the main route to Berlin.

AMERICANS ACROSS

Crossing operations by the American armies along the more southern stretches of the Rhine, although allocated smaller resources and mounted by fewer men, were just as successful.

One, by an assault regiment of the US 5th Division, had occurred the day before Montgomery's Army Group launched the main crossing. The 5th Division was part of XII

Corps of Patton's Third Army.

Major-General Leroy Irwin was told to throw his division across the Rhine south of Mainz, between Nierstein and Oppenheim. Irwin complained about the short time he was given for preparation. However, in the face of Patton's urgency he sent the first wave of assault boats across the 1,000-feet wide river just before midnight, under a brilliant moon. The assult had heavy artillery support, but the gun group later complained that it could find little in the way of worthwhile targets.

The first Americans to land captured seven German soldiers, who promptly volunteered to paddle their assault boat back for them. Although later waves ran into sporadic machine-gun fire, the regiment was across before midnight and moving towards the villages on the east bank, with support regiments flooding across behind them. By the evening of 23 March the entire 5th Division was across the river; a bridgehead had been formed and was awaiting the arrival of an armoured division already on the west bank.

MORE CROSSINGS

During the next few days, crossings were made at Boppard, St Goar, Worms and Mainz, and by the end of the month Darmstadt and Wiesbaden were in US hands. Armoured columns were driving for Frankfurt-am-Main and Aschaffenburg beyond; further south, the French had put an Algerian division across, near Germersheim. Now a huge Allied bridgehead could be formed from Bonn down to Mannheim, from which would be launched the last Western offensive designed to meet the Russians on the Elbe and split Germany in two.

INTO GERMANY

The main objective for the US Twelfth Army Group would be the industrial region of Leipzig and Dresden. To the north, Montgomery's Twenty-first

Army Group was to drive north towards Hamburg, its Canadian left flank clearing Holland of the enemy and then driving along the coast through Emden and Wilhelmshaven.

The US Ninth Army on the right was to curve around the Ruhr to meet Hodges' First Army at Lippstadt, encircling Field Marshal Walther Model's Army Group B in the Ruhr. After Hamburg, the British would drive up to the Baltic and Schleswig-Holstein, at the same time pushing east to the Elbe down as far as Magdeburg.

RUHR ENCIRCLED

The Ruhr, Germany's industrial heartland, was surrounded by the US 1st and 9th Armies on 4 April. The huge pocket contained the remnants of German Army Group B together with elements of Army Group A's Parachute Army. It finally fell on 18 April, yielding 325,000 prisoners. The last few German units surrendered on 21 April. Model, the 'Führer's Fireman', committed suicide.

On 13 April the Allies liberated Belsen and Buchenwald concentration camps and Vienna fell to the Red Army. Nuremberg, the spiritual home of the Nazis, fell to the US 7th Army on 20 April, while Dachau was liberated by the US Army on the 25th. To the north, elements of the German 11th Army were trapped in a pocket in the Harz Mountains, but fought hard before surrendering.

RED RIVER CROSSINGS

In the East, the Red Army swung northwards to clear Pomerania and Silesia, where the grandiosely named Army Group Vistula was under the inept command of the *Reichsführer-SS* Heinrich Himmler. Marshal Konstantin Rokossovsky's 3rd Guards Tank Corps spearheaded the push to the Baltic coast and reached it on 1 March. This cut off the German garrisons and depots at Danzig (Gdansk) and Gotenhaven (Gdynia), while

Above: British forces enter Bremen in April 1945. Montgomery's 21st Army Group had been tasked with seizing Germany's main North Sea ports, simultaneously driving eastwards towards the Baltic.

Above: A Sherman engages a German strongpoint while infantrymen watch carefully from cover. Their caution was justified; there was often heavy sniper activity as the Allies pushed through German cities.

Below: German resistance could be fierce. Sometimes, elite units like these Fallschirmjäger fought back hard. At other times, the resistance came from die-hard Nazi fanatics or brainwashed Hitler Youth members.

Assault on a River

The Western Allies were taking no chances with crossing the Rhine. Allied air forces were tasked with neutralizing the rump of the Luftwaffe – what remained of it after the heavy losses sustained during the Ardennes offensive. Patrols were flown over all Luftwaffe airfields likely to become involved in the crossings, mainly to prevent the Luftwaffe seeing the vast build-up of men and matériel close to the crossing points.

New railheads had to be established in the British sector to enable 662 tanks of all kinds, 4,000 tank transporters and 32,000 vehicles of every variety to be brought up. Moreover, there were 3,500 field and medium guns to be assembled, together with a quantity of super- heavy artillery that would cover the main crossings.

Above: Developed primarily for use by the US Marines in the Pacific, the Landing Vehicle Tracked gave Allied armies significant river-crossing ability, as well as providing mobility in flooded terrain.

Left: Amphibious 'Duplex Drive' or DD Sherman tanks were designed to accompany the first wave of assault troops going ashore at Normandy. They were invaluable in providing real firepower to the assault troops.

Above: Once the assault troops had secured a bridgehead on the east bank of the Rhine, Allied engineers could bring up pontoons and landing craft to ferry across fuel, ammunition, supplies, and reinforcements.

Below: The final stage in the river crossing was to build bridges. There was little threat of air attack since the Luftwaffe had no fuel. Even so, a constant watch was needed – against sabotage as much as aircraft.

Above: Waffen SS troops move past a knocked-out IS-2 'Josef Stalin' Tank. The best German troops were still capable of fierce resistance, but the Red Army simply had too many men, tanks and guns to be stopped.

Below: German industry still managed to provide advanced weapons right up to the last months of the war. This infantryman, fighting at Grandenz in February 1945, is armed with a self-loading Gewehr 43.

Below: By February 1945, German resistance to the Russians was largely an infantry affair, since fuel for vehicles was in short supply. The only answer many Wehrmacht units had to the hordes of Soviet tanks was the one-shot Panzerfaust anti-armour weapon.

supporting Zhukov's drive that reached the coast at Kolberg. This Baltic port held out against the besiegers until 18 March.

Four days later, the 1st Belarussian Front launched a flanking attack on Küstrin which fell on 30 March. To the south, in Silesia, Marshal Ivan Konev's 1st Ukrainian and Colonel-General Petrov's 4th Ukrainian Fronts drove towards Grottkau and Moravska Ostrava. In Breslau, the main city in Silesia, the population had been evacuated to Dresden and the city was declared a fortress. Defended by 35,000 troops, reinforced with paratroops through an improvised airstrip, it held out until 8 May 1945.

HELL FROM THE AIR

As the land offensive closed in on the Reich, the Allied air attacks continued with unabated fury. Nearly a quarter of a million tons of bombs had been dropped since the final offensives began, and British and American heavy bombers were almost out of worthwhile targets. Dresden had no strategic value, but that did not stop RAF Bomber Command and the US 8th Air Force from destroying it. In a series of raids from 13–15 February, a firestorm was kindled which burned out the old city. The city's population, swollen by some 100,000 refugees, suffered horribly. The casualty toll will never be known, but the lowest estimate of those killed is 35,000 and the highest as much as 135,000.

ESCAPE FROM REALITY

On 12 April, Hitler learnt of the death of US President Franklin Roosevelt. The Führer and his few followers, buried in the Berlin bunker, were now so far removed from reality that they were consulting astrologers.

Even the highly-educated Joseph Goebbels was not immune – he wrote a note to Hitler claiming ecstatically:

"My Führer, I congratulate you! Roosevelt is dead! It is written in the stars that the

second half of April will be the turning point for us." Unfortunately for Hitler and his followers, the Allies were not reading the same stars.

ON TO BERLIN?

There had already been some argument, mostly by Montgomery, that his Army Group should race across the North German plain for Berlin.

Eisenhower was more cautious: he was casting a wary eye on the mythical 'Bavarian redoubt' to the south, where the Nazis were reputed to be preparing a (non-existent) last stand. In any case the supreme commander, solidly supported by Roosevelt, felt that it would be easier for the Russians to take the German capital. The ailing president was sure that if he let the Red Army have the capital, Stalin would prove both co-operative and amenable in regard to post-war European responsibilities.

Stalin would have been amused had he learned of the arguments. But he was taking steps to ensure that the Red Army captured the prize.

THE END IN SIGHT

The real life Götterdamerung of the Third Reich reached its violent conclusion as the Red Army closed in on Berlin. The final Soviet offensive began on 16 April, with a huge pincer movement. On the Baltic, the 2nd Belarussian Front pushed across the Oder at Stettin. To its left the 1st Belarussian Front had already crossed the river Oder and established a jumping off point at Küstrin. To the south the 1st Ukrainian Front hooked east and north across the rivers Oder and Neisse.

The Soviets three offensives employed 2.5 million troops, 6,250 armoured vehicles, 10,400 guns and mortars and 7,500 aircraft between them. This red tide, moving irresistibly westwards, swept away all opposition. The life expectancy of Hitler's Thousand Year Reich could now be counted in weeks.

Red Juggernaut

THE SOVIET ARMY poised on Germany's eastern borders at the beginning of 1945 was the most powerful military force ever assembled. The front was much shorter than it had been two years earlier, stretching 2,000 kilometres from Memel on the Baltic down to Yugoslavia. Massed along that line were over six million Soviet soldiers, deployed in nine 'Fronts' or Army Groups.

The Soviet strategy was simple: the southern Fronts would attack into Hungary, threatening Germany's last remaining oil supplies and drawing the Wehrmacht reserves away from Army Group Centre. The northern Fronts would reduce the German forces on the Baltic, pushing into East Prussia and driving westwards.

The main push would be in the centre, where the fronts commanded by Rokossovsky, Zhukov and Koniev would smash their way into the heart of Germany. The largest and most powerful group of forces was intended to destroy the *Ostheer* once and for all.

Top: The Red Army of 1945 was a very different beast from the one which had suffered such catastrophic losses in 1941 and 1942. Veteran soldiers in huge numbers operated powerful weapons and equipment which had stood the test of battle. Spearheading that force was the IS2 heavy tank, with its powerful 122mm gun.

Above: Stalin's army was led by determined, skillful commanders. These are the Marshals who directed the final attacks on Germany: (Front row, from left) I. Konev, A. Vasilievsky, G. Zhukov, K. Rokossovsky, K. Meretskov; (Back row, from left) F. Tolbukhin, R. Malinovsky, L. Govorov, A. Yeremenko, and I. Bagramyan.

Third Reich Dismembered

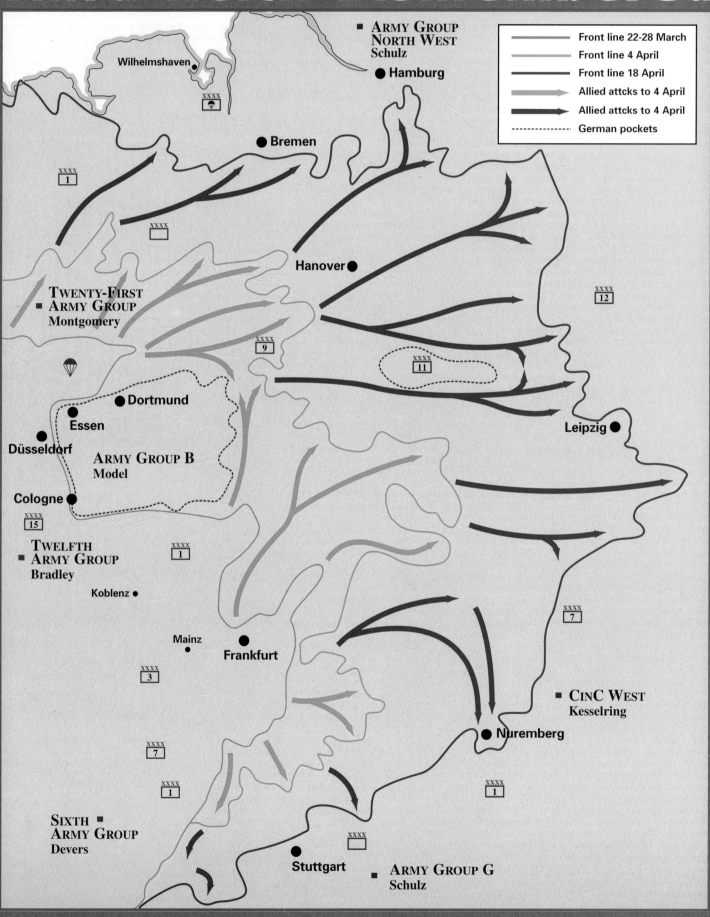

ARMY GROUP
NORTH WEST
Schulz

Wilhelmshaven

● Hamburg

| Front line 22-28 March |
| Front line 4 April |
| Front line 18 April |
| Allied attcks to 4 April |
| Allied attcks to 4 April |
| German pockets |

● Bremen

XXXX
1

XXXX

XXXX
12

Hanover ●

TWENTY-FIRST
ARMY GROUP
Montgomery

XXXX
9

XXXX
11

● Dortmund

Essen

Düsseldorf

ARMY GROUP B
Model

Leipzig ●

Cologne

XXXX
15

TWELFTH
ARMY GROUP
Bradley

XXXX
1

Koblenz ●

XXXX
7

Mainz ●

Frankfurt ●

XXXX
3

CinC WEST
Kesselring

XXXX
7

● Nuremberg

XXXX
1

XXXX
1

SIXTH
ARMY GROUP
Devers

XXXX

Stuttgart ●

ARMY GROUP G
Schulz

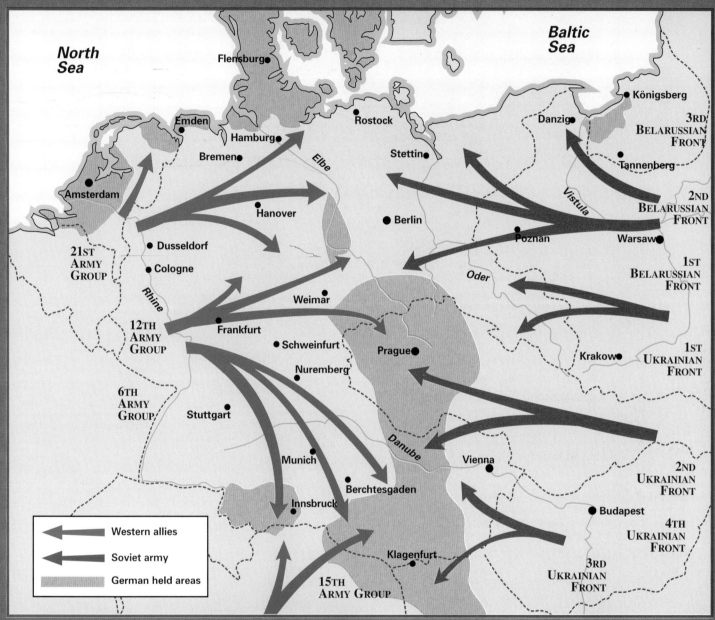

North
Sea

Baltic
Sea

Flensburg

Emden

Hamburg

Bremen

Rostock

Elbe

Stettin

Königsberg

Danzig

3RD
BELARUSSIAN
FRONT

Tannenberg

2ND
BELARUSSIAN
FRONT

Amsterdam

Hanover

Berlin

Vistula

Poznan

Warsaw

21ST
ARMY
GROUP

Dusseldorf

Cologne

Oder

1ST
BELARUSSIAN
FRONT

Rhine

Weimar

12TH
ARMY
GROUP

Frankfurt

Schweinfurt

Prague

Krakow

1ST
UKRAINIAN
FRONT

Nuremberg

6TH
ARMY
GROUP

Stuttgart

Danube

Munich

Vienna

2ND
UKRAINIAN
FRONT

Berchtesgaden

Innsbruck

Budapest

4TH
UKRAINIAN
FRONT

Klagenfurt

15TH
ARMY GROUP

3RD
UKRAINIAN
FRONT

Western allies

Soviet army

German held areas

At the beginning of 1945, the German army was on the defensive, having failed in its last attempt at taking the initiative. Allied armies stood poised on the borders of Germany itself, but had barely penetrated the home territory of the Reich. Senior commanders, notably Heinz Guderian, knew that this was the calm before the storm. Germany would be destroyed within a matter of months, dependant on just when the Allies chose to attack.

The first hammer blow came with the start of the main Russian offensive in January. Pouring through Poland and into East Prussia, the Red armies were hammering on the borders of the Reich within days. In the west, the British and the Americans were on the Rhine by the end of February, and in March their armies were struck out into Germany. Within a month, they had driven across the country, and on 25 April the American 1st Army had linked up with units of Konev's First Ukrainian Front at Torgau on the Elbe. With Montgomery's forces meeting Rokossovsky's further north, Berlin was cut off, and what remained of the Wehrmacht was squeezed into Bohemia, Bavaria and the Alps, with isolated commands in Norway, Denmark, Holland, and on the Baltic Coast. There was nowhere left to run.

Right: At 4.40 in the afternoon of 25 April 1945, a patrol of the American 69th Infantry Division met the forward elements of the Red Army's 58th Guards Division at Torgau on the Elbe. Russians who had marched all the way from Stalingrad met Allies who had raced eastwards from Normandy, and in that meeting Adolf Hitler's Third Reich was cut in half.

Final Battle
The Fall of Berlin

In April 1945, the awesome power of the Red Army was deployed to the full as it battered its way into the German capital – against an army of old men, boys, and desperate SS fanatics.

Above: For two days the German defences on the Seelöwe heights east of Berlin held out against the overwhelming might of Zhukov's 1st Belorussian Front. But there were simply too many Russians to stop.

Left: The Red banner is waved from the roof of the Reichstag, symbolising the utter defeat of Adolf Hitler's 'Thousand-Year Reich'. Berlin had exchanged one dictator for another.

I N BERLIN, in April 1945, that city's inhabitants hardly registered the sound of artillery fire which was an ever-present reality in what passed for normal life in that doomed city. Amid the smoking debris of what had once been one of Europe's major urban and cultural centres, life somehow managed to continue. Civilians were outnumbered by the military, who ranged from the last of the old regular German army to a rabble of 'foreign legions', party organisations and virtually untrained conscripts, many of whom were as young as 14 years. By day and night the Allied and Red air forces flew over the city adding to the piles of rubble below and stoking the ever-burning fires on almost every street.

Remaining in the city, when much of the party and civil administration had already left for the southern hinterland of Germany, Hitler used his last reserves of power to condemn thousands more to death at a time when all was already lost. His party henchmen competed to add to the death total. All through the early days of April 1945, squads of party fanatics roamed the debris of Berlin seeking out ' deserters' and hanging them on the spot from nearby lamp posts. Any restraints to the excesses of the Party had been loosed. Berlin was being turned into to a carnal pit.

VENGEFUL REDS

Away across the Oder, the Soviets had encountered similar testimony to nazi rule. In their advances across Poland and East Prussia they had uncovered many examples of concentration and extermination camps and mass burial pits, where the nazis had attempted to hide their crimes. Within the Soviet Union itself the brutal rule of the *Gauleiters* had condemned millions of Soviet citizens to death by local forced labour or deportation to the labour camps of the Reich. The Red Army was in no mood to be generous to a vanquished enemy.

On 1 April, Marshals Zhukov and Konev had arrived in Moscow for a briefing on the subject of the Battle for Berlin. Stalin informed them that the devious and conniving Western Allies were planning a swift Berlin operation with the sole object of capturing the city before the Red Army could arrive – an announcement which, not surprisingly in view of the recent achievements of the Red Army, incensed both of the tough commanders.

They had expected to mount the attack on Berlin in early May, but in these special circumstances they would accelerate all preparations and be ready to move well before the Anglo-Americans could get themselves solidly inside German territory.

WHO TAKES THE PRIZE?

Which of the two fronts – Zhukov's 1st Belorussian or Konev's 1st Ukrainian – should have the task, and the honour, of

Above: The last defenders of the Reich could only sit and wait as the armies commanded by Zhukov and Konev prepared to launch the final Russian offensive of the war. Only the deluded dared think of victory.

Below: Although Germany had nominally been fighting a 'Total War' since 1943, it was not until the end of 1944 that the last reserves – those formerly considered too old to fight – were called up as the Volkssturm.

Below: Berlin was swollen with refugees from the east, fleeing the advancing Red Army. These people brought stories of mass rape and pillage, as the out of control Soviets rampaged through Prussia.

driving straight for Berlin? It was a question to which the wily Georgian left an ambiguous answer, by drawing on the map a demarcation line between their commands. It ended short of Berlin, at Lübben, 20 miles to the south east of the capital.

When the last offensive of the Red Army was launched its aims were to advance to the Elbe and to annihilate all organised German resistance before them – which would entail the capture of Berlin and the reduction of its garrison. For this purpose, Marshals Zhukov and Konev had some 1,640,000 men under their command, with 41,600 guns and mortars, 6,300 tanks, and the support of three air armies and 8,400 aircraft.

IMPROVISED DEFENCE

Opposite them were 7 panzer and 65 infantry divisions in some sort of order. There were also around a hundred independent battalions, either remnants of obliterated divisions or formed from old men, children, the sick, criminals or the simple-minded.

They had been collected together by SS teams sent out from the Chancellery bunkers, in which Hitler and his demented entourage were living out their last fantasies. Their orders were to conjure yet another army from the wreckage of the Thousand Year Reich.

Unorganised and half-trained though they might have been, most of the German formations defending Berlin against the Red Army nevertheless fought at first with a blind ferocity and a blistering efficiency. They demonstrated yet again that the epitome of high morale in combat is that of the cornered rat – which is the reason he so often escapes.

But there would be no escape for the Germans now.

THUNDER OF THE GUNS

At dawn on 16 April, a tremendous artillery and air bombardment opened all along the Oder and Neisse Rivers, and out of the Soviet bridgeheads stormed the first waves of shock troops. There was no finesse in these massed attacks. The Russian artillery was arranged wheel-to-wheel in rows, and thundered away for hours in a massive preliminary barrage.

TANKS TO THE FORE

When the bombardment lifted the tanks moved forward. The T-34/85s and the IS-2s lumbered from their hides. They carried with them the 'descent' infantry squads riding on their hulls with their submachine guns and grenades ready to fall upon any infantry positions that were left in a state to defend themselves.

It took Zhukov's northern thrust two days to smash through some four miles to reach the Seelöwe Heights. His southern thrust had not done much better, advancing only eight miles. At that point they had seen no sign of a crack in the German defences despite the casualties on both sides.

Konev's shock troops were not so strongly opposed, and they advanced eight miles the first day. On 18 April Konev fed in two tank armies and ordered them to fight their way to the north west, into the Berlin suburbs. His right flank brushed Lübben, but only just.

BREAKTHROUGH

Perhaps inspired by competition, Zhukov now drove his infantry and tank armies forward with ruthless vigour. By 19 April both his thrusts had advanced 20 miles on a front almost 40 miles in width, destroying as they did so the bulk of the German Ninth Army, immobilised in the path of the attack by lack of fuel. On 21 April General Chuikov reported that his Eighth Guards Army, which he had led all the way from Stalingrad, was into Berlin's southeastern suburbs.

Within the city Hitler inhabited a world of dreams. Already unhinged by the attempt on his life the previous July, the Führer's mind withdrew into a realm where the German army

"Who will take Berlin?"

STALIN KNEW that he needed successful generals to win the war with Hitler's Germany, but was also aware of the danger to his own power that they represented. In November 1944 he had decreed that Marshal Zhukov's 1st Belorussian Front would be given the honour of taking Berlin. By the end of March 1945 it was clear that allowing Zhukov, who was already a national hero, to take sole credit for capturing Berlin would give him far too much status in the post-war Soviet Union.

Stalin encouraged Ivan Konev, who had his own ambition to take the city, to detach two tank armies from his primary drive on Dresden and a meeting with the Western Allies on the Elbe. While Zhukov's front was still assigned to take the city, the Soviet dictator had in effect set up a race between his two most successful generals. A third Front – Rokossovsky's 2nd Belorussian – would attack north of Berlin to provide flank security for the entire operation.

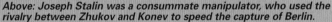

Above: Joseph Stalin was a consummate manipulator, who used the rivalry between Zhukov and Konev to speed the capture of Berlin.

Left: Ivan Stepanovich Konev was one of Russia's toughest, most courageous generals. He overcame disgrace in 1941 to command Fronts at Kursk, in the Ukraine, and in the final drive into Germany.

Below: Georgi Konstantinovich Zhukov was the pre-eminent Soviet commander of World War II. While he respected Konev professionally, there was no love lost between the two outstanding generals – a fact that Stalin was quite happy to use to his own advantage.

187

and party divisions of 1939 still existed. He ordered nonexistent armies about his large-scale maps as though he was still in command of a mighty force.

The reality was otherwise. Outside the bunkers, what remained of the German army and the party machine shattered into a myriad of individuals who took the precautions for the future that they thought fit. This ranged from murdering old rivals or suspected political opponents to burying home movies and looted treasures from all over Europe. In a final frantic orgy of destruction, the party anti-deserter squads carried out their last 'executions' and then ran to the west.

DRIVE TO THE WEST
Konev, having thrown his own counter into the battle for the capital, now devoted the bulk of his endeavour due westwards towards the Elbe. By 20 April two of his tank armies had reached Luckenwald – thus splitting the German Army Group Centre from Berlin and the defences in the north. He then drove two more armies

Right: The defensive line on Zhukov's front consisted mainly of mines, dug-in artillery and anti-tank guns. Konev, on the other hand, encountered fierce resistance from the 21st Panzer Division, and intelligence reported that two more German tank divisions were being moved up into the defences. Both Russian commanders countered German moves by attacking in great strength, by day and night.

given him by STAVKA up towards Potsdam where on 25 April they linked up with one of Zhukov's Guards tank armies which had come around the north of Berlin. The city, its inhabitants and its 200,000-man garrison were surrounded.

GERMANY DIVIDED
On the same day, units of Fifth Guards Army reached the Elbe at Torgau and within minutes were exchanging drinks, hats, buttons and photographs with Americans of the US First Army. The scenes of triumphant comradeship and co-operation which followed were repeated up and down the central axis of Germany, as soldiers who had fought westwards from Stalingrad met those who had fought eastwards from Normandy. During the brief period in which they were allowed to fraternise, they learned to recognise each others' qualities. It is a tragedy that friendships made then were not allowed to continue.

By 27 April, Red Army tanks were in the Potsdamer Platz and through the

sound of artillery fire the chatter of small arms could be heard, even in the Chancellery bunker where Hitler still held court with an entourage of the party faithful.

Finally, in the afternoon of 30 April, Hitler took the inevitable step. Escaping responsibility and retribution, he took his own life along with that of the loyal Eva Braun. Their bodies were burned in the garden outside the bunker and the flames added their small glimmer to the holocaust about them.

THE STREETS OF BERLIN
Around the bunker the Red Army moved into a desolate wilderness of ruined buildings

where isolated pockets of resistance still lingered. Many of the remaining strongpoints were manned by various units of Waffen-SS 'foreign legions'– men who knew only too well what to expect once they fell into Red Army hands, and so preferred to go down fighting.

With such pockets of resistance the Red Army commanders wasted no time. They quickly called forward a number of 152-mm howitzers and sited them close to the source of the resistance. Then the howitzers simply blasted them away. Red Army cameramen recorded the scene to show workers back in the USSR what their labours had

Street fighting

Above: It was appropriate that General Vasily Ivanovich Chuikov was the first General approached by the Germans with surrender terms: the tough peasant from Tula had commanded his Army all the way from one hell in Stalingrad to another in Berlin.

HITLER ORDERED that the defenders of Berlin fight "to the last man and the last bullet". However, three of Zhukov's armies were in the outer suburbs of the city by 21 April, with General Ivan Chuikov's 8th Guards Army and the 1st Guards Tank Army in the lead. At the same time, Konev's 3rd and 4th Guards Tank Armies were approaching the southern suburbs, having taken the General Staff headquarters at Zossen. But fighting into the city was a nightmare: the German defenders blew up buildings to block the advance, and die-hard groups had to be winkled out of cellars and ruins by direct artillery fire and flamethrowers. By 27 April, the Germans held a strip about ten miles by three, and the Russian tanks were moving in for the kill. There was no hope for the Germans, and on 30 April Hitler committed suicide.

Top left and above: Street fighting is amongst the most brutal of all forms of warfare, and in the struggle for Berlin the fighting reached a ferocity which has seldom been matched in history. Although some officers and men found it difficult to shoot down schoolboys in uniform, many did not. The Red Army had taken immense casualties, and the soldiers, inflamed by front-line propaganda decrying the German soldier as a beast, needed little provocation to commit bestial acts themselves.

Left: The last attack on the Reichstag was launched at 13.00 on 30 April. Sergeants Yegerov and Kantriya managed to wave the Red Banner from the second floor in the middle of the afternoon. Hitler was in his bunker only a couple of hundred yards away: an hour later the German Führer was dead. At 22.50 the Russian flag was finally atop the Reichstag, surveying the grave of the Reich.

made possible.

On 1 May, General Chuikov, now well inside the Berlin city centre, was approached by General Krebs, the Chief of the German General Staff, with three other officers bearing white flags desirous of negotiating a surrender. With almost unbelievable effrontery, the German general opened the conversation with the remark: "Today is the First of May, a great holiday for our two nations."

"A GREAT HOLIDAY"

Considering the outrages carried out in his country by the nationals of the man addressing him, Chuikov's reply was a model of restraint.

"We have a great holiday today. How things are with you over there, it is less easy to say!"

But the first moves towards an official end to hostilities in Europe had been made.

Berlin surrendered unconditionally on 2 May. On 4 May Field Marshal Montgomery took the surrender of all German forces in the north. On 7 May the 'Unconditional surrender of Germany to the Western Allies and to Russia' was agreed, the instrument itself signed by General Jodl for the defeated, and Generals Bedell Smith and Suslaparov for the victors, General Sevez also signing for France.

Stalin was outraged: he wanted the final surrender to be signed in Berlin, which his army had captured. The next day, Field Marshal Keitel, Marshal Georgi Zhukov and British Air Marshal Tedder signed a second unconditional surrender. The war in Europe was at an end.

GÖTTERDAMERUNG

Before committing suicide the Führer had made a will leaving the leadership of his country to Admiral Dönitz. A man of enormous but demonic gifts, Hitler had lifted his country from a position of weakness to unparalleled power, and then dropped her back into chaos again – in just 12 years.

Above: The German army had given Hitler three years of triumph, but it was not enough. Professional skill and sheer fighting ability were not enough to win against half the world. The final defeat in Berlin was the inevitable outcome of the world's greatest ever conflict.

Below: Field Marshal Montgomery joins Marshals Zhukov and Rokossovsky through the streets of Berlin after the final German surrender.

Battle of Berlin

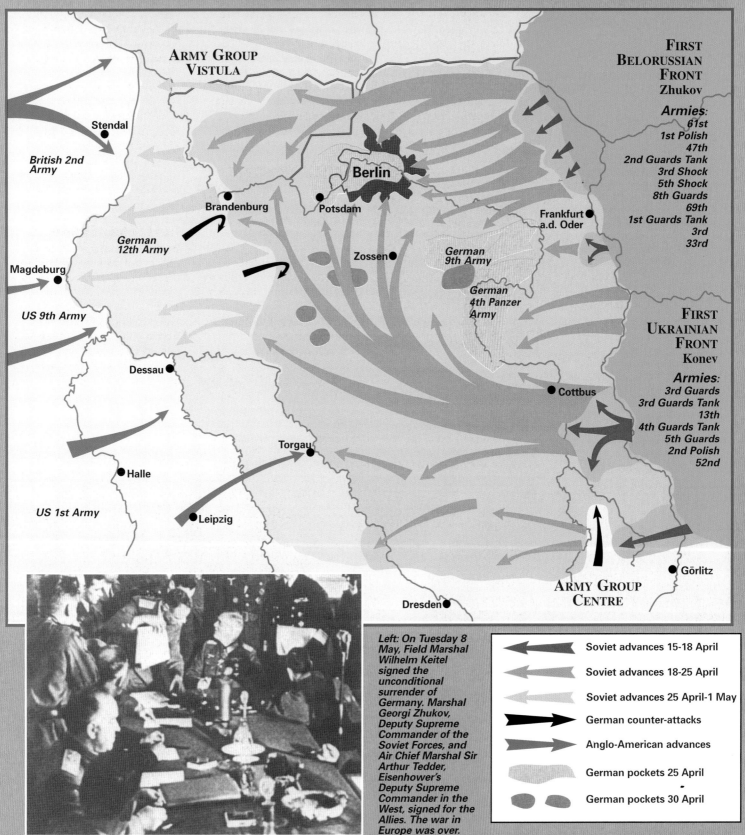

ARMY GROUP
VISTULA

Stendal

British 2nd
Army

Berlin

Brandenburg

Potsdam

German 12th Army

Magdeburg

Zossen

US 9th Army

German
9th Army

German
4th Panzer
Army

Dessau

Cottbus

Torgau

Halle

US 1st Army

Leipzig

FIRST
BELORUSSIAN
FRONT
Zhukov

Armies:
61st
1st Polish
47th
2nd Guards Tank
3rd Shock
5th Shock
8th Guards
69th
1st Guards Tank
3rd
33rd

Frankfurt
a.d. Oder

FIRST
UKRAINIAN
FRONT
Konev

Armies:
3rd Guards
3rd Guards Tank
13th
4th Guards Tank
5th Guards
2nd Polish
52nd

Görlitz

ARMY GROUP
CENTRE

Dresden

*Left: On Tuesday 8
May, Field Marshal
Wilhelm Keitel
signed the
unconditional
surrender of
Germany. Marshal
Georgi Zhukov,
Deputy Supreme
Commander of the
Soviet Forces, and
Air Chief Marshal Sir
Arthur Tedder,
Eisenhower's
Deputy Supreme
Commander in the
West, signed for the
Allies. The war in
Europe was over.*

⬅	Soviet advances 15-18 April
⬅	Soviet advances 18-25 April
⬅	Soviet advances 25 April-1 May
→	German counter-attacks
→	Anglo-American advances
▬	German pockets 25 April
▬	German pockets 30 April

Index